Contents

Figures and Tables

The Election of 2000
Reports and Interpretations

Gerald M. Pomper
Anthony Corrado
E. J. Dionne Jr.
Kathleen A. Frankovic
Paul S. Herrnson
Marjorie Randon Hershey
William G. Mayer
Monika L. McDermott
Wilson Carey McWilliams

CHATHAM HOUSE PUBLISHERS
SEVEN BRIDGES PRESS, LLC

NEW YORK · LONDON

To Edward A. Artinian
publisher, colleague, friend

Seven Bridges Press
135 Fifth Avenue
New York, NY 10010-7101

Publisher: Ted Bolen
Managing Editor: Katharine Miller
Composition: ediType
Cover Design: Judith Hudson
Printing and Binding: Victor Graphics, Inc.

Library of Congress Cataloging-in-Publication Data
The election of 2000 : reports and interpretations / Gerald M.
Pomper ... [et al.].
    p. cm.
  Includes bibliographical references and index.
  ISBN 1-889119-46-6 (pbk.)
    1. Presidents – United States – Election – 2000. 2. United States.
Congress – Elections, 2000. I. Pomper, Gerald M.
JK526 2000d
324.973'0929 – dc21

                                      2001000342

Manufactured in the United States of America
10 9 8 7 6 5 4 3 2 1

A Personal Preface

The end crowns all,
and that old common arbitrator, Time,
will one day end it.
— Troilus and Cressida (IV, 5)

TWENTY-FIVE YEARS AGO, I began this series with an extravagant comparison of the 1976 election to Faust's search for the perfect moment, when he could say, "Tarry a while, you are so beautiful." After a quarter of a century, I now know — as Goethe taught — that the glories of our lives come from the quest for growth, not in any final achievement.

This volume completes a series of studies over seven national elections, among which the election of 2000 certainly stands out. We have begun the new millennium with both the most rapid communication technology and the slowest counting of votes. We have witnessed both extravagant campaigning and cramped balloting. We have elected a president and Congress after votes were cast by 105 million citizens, 538 electors, and nine justices.

The dramatic events of this election offer a remarkable culmination of the volumes in this series. It was essentially a tied vote, its outcome uncertain for five weeks. Over 50 million Americans voted for both Al Gore and George Bush. In the official but controversial count of the electoral college, 271 electors chose Bush and 267 favored Gore. In the ultimate forums, the courts, Gore won a 4–3 victory in the Florida Supreme Court, and Bush won a final 5–4 victory in the U.S. Supreme Court. This even division of votes was mirrored in the congressional elections, which resulted in a 50–50 split in the Senate and a mere five-seat Republican majority in the House. The election of 2000 became so complicated and its materials so profuse that we must rely on the new technology of the Internet to tell the story fully. Additional data can be found at this website: www.chathamhouse.com/pomper2000

Over the last quarter of the twentieth century, American politics has provided many disappointments, a fair measure of missed opportunities, and a considerable number of personal foibles and failures. The tainted vote of Florida in 2000 and its ultimate resolution by a tainted Supreme Court decision exemplify those flaws.

But these years also have conferred many inspirations and successes, such as the end of the Cold War, the opening of political opportunities to women and ethnic minorities, and the transformation of the national economy. An exemplar of these beneficent changes was the nomination of Senator Joseph Lieberman — the first national candidacy of an American Jew — which was most remarkable in fact because it generated so little controversy. The American republic stands, better if still imperfect.

To me individually, the years have been kind. I have learned a lot, gained the love and friendship of many good people, and worked productively in a stimulating and supportive environment. I take this opportunity to thank those who helped.

My professional gratitude begins with those colleagues who have collaborated on these volumes. Wilson Carey McWilliams, the only author to share in each book, has consistently been a personal support and an intellectual guide. I am indebted to the gifted analysts who have contributed to these studies in the past: Chris Arterton, Walter Dean Burnham, Barbara Farah, Marion R. Just, Scott Keeter, and Ethel Klein.

I owe a particular debt to previous collaborators who were also colleagues at Rutgers University: Ross K. Baker, Charles Jacob, and Henry Plotkin. And, for both past and present contributions of mind and spirit, I fully thank the authors of 2000: Anthony Corrado, E.J. Dionne, Kathleen A. Frankovic, Marjorie Randon Hershey, William G. Mayer, and Monika L. McDermott.

This volume was particularly challenging. With the rest of the nation, we had to endure weeks of spectacles, uncertainties, and reversals of fortune — Shakespearean events without Shakespearean heroes. But we also faced the special difficulty of authors delayed in writing a story that had no apparent conclusion.

In meeting this unique problem, we gained much from the discussions and manuscript critiques of friends and colleagues, including Ron Cowan, Milton Finegold, Irving Louis Horowitz, Elizabeth Hull, Milton Heumann, Stanley Kelley, and Beth Leech. For hospitality at the national conventions, I thank Kerry Haynie, Ronnee Schreiber, and Mina Silverberg. In the actual process of publication, we had exceptional help from Joanne Pfeiffer of the Eagleton Institute of Politics, and from the new leadership of Chatham House: Ted Bolen, publisher, Katharine Miller, our editor, and John Eagleson, our compositor.

My personal gratitude extends much further. Marlene Michels Pomper helped with scholarly insights and careful reading of manuscripts. More important, she provided encouragement, exemplary dedication, and pure love. My sons Marc, David, and Miles, and my daughters-in-law Rayna and Erika, inspire pride in their intellect, commitment, and zest for life. My grandsons — Aidan, Jacob, Zachary, and Daniel — convince me that America will be yet better when their generation builds on our work.

Three persons who inspired these volumes did not reach the twenty-first century. My aunt, Lorraine Cohen, combined an immigrant's love of America with an intellectual's probing of its problems. My father-in-law, Emanuel Michels, exemplified the promise of American politics in his personal enthusiasm and optimism. Because politics inevitably involves compromise, it could not match his goodness, but his life remains as an ideal of citizenship. By this book, I personally memorialize their contributions to the nation they served.

Collectively, we dedicate this book to Edward Artinian. Ed originally inspired this series, personally supervised every detail of publication from contracts to page proofs, and treated the contributors as both prized authors and valued friends. Through his efforts, Chatham House encouraged new talent, strengthened the discipline of political science, and developed a list of original, teachable, and insightful books. With news and gossip, with words and wine, Ed transformed work into fun and research into achievement.

If still with us, Ed surely would be laughing uproariously at the antics of the election of 2000, even as he would be planning to make this book the best possible analysis. We hope we have met his high expectations. In his memory, a portion of the royalties from this book will be donated to the Edward Artinian Fund of the American Political Science Association, for the support of young scholars. They will carry on his dedicated work.

—Gerald M. Pomper

CHAPTER 1

The Clinton Enigma:
Seeking Consensus, Breeding Discord

E.J. Dionne Jr.

> *So quick bright things come to confusion.*
> —A Midsummer Night's Dream (I, i)

THE BITTER RECOUNT FIGHT at the end of the 2000 election seemed, sadly, the perfect coda to the Clinton presidency.

When Bill Clinton was elected in 1992, his hope was to establish a new consensus — moderately liberal, pragmatic in its use of government, socially open but respectful of traditional values. He hoped to create a new Democratic majority by holding the party's base, bringing home socially conservative Reagan Democrats in the South and the blue-collar suburbs of the Northeast and Midwest, and adding suburban moderates who grew more prosperous during his presidency.

In one sense, he succeeded. He won two presidential elections. Many would argue further that absent ballot snafus in Florida and a much contested U.S Supreme Court decision, his vice president, Al Gore, would have won the right to succeed him. (Many Democrats will always insist that Gore actually did win.) As a measure of how the country as a whole felt about matters, it's worth noting that Gore won the popular vote with the most ballots ever cast for a Democratic presidential candidate. Whatever the result of 2000 meant, it could not be interpreted as a repudiation of Bill Clinton.

But Clinton also failed. The man who actually took the oath of office on 20 January 2001 was a Republican named George W. Bush. Largely because of the sex scandal that scarred his second term and the impeachment that followed, Clinton laid the groundwork for deep divisions in the country. His Republican opponents, sensing Clinton's weakness, threw their all into an effort to discredit him. They failed to remove him from office but succeeded in creating a substantial constituency that disapproved of him personally and disliked all who were associated with him — notably including Al Gore.

Gore and his strategists sensed the power of the anti-Clinton feeling, and the central difficulty of Gore's campaign was sorting out how he should position himself toward the president. The ambiguity of the Clinton legacy left Gore's campaign in strategic gridlock.

On the one hand, it was clear that the country felt good about itself and the prosperity that had accompanied Clinton's years in office. On most issues of practical concern, a substantial majority of Americans saw Clinton as a good president. As a result, many Democrats denounced Gore for not embracing Clinton fully and for not running on the Clinton record. Why, pro-Clinton Democrats asked after the votes were tallied, couldn't Gore have done better than he did at a moment when two-thirds of the electorate believed the country was on the right track?

Yet Clinton's pollster Stan Greenberg sensed that there was also an anti-Clinton mood in the nation, especially among non-college-educated white voters and in rural areas. Greenberg saw the "trust and values issues" hurting Gore because "of the culture war to bring down Clinton that has been waged since 1992."[1] Most of the Gore apparatus sensed that too close an embrace of Clinton would aggravate Gore's problems among the very swing voters Gore most needed to win.

In the end, it can be argued that Clinton failed Gore by handing him the difficulties of the scandals, and that Gore failed Clinton by not making full and effective use of the president's record and achievements. The fact that both assertions are fair highlights the contradictions of the Clinton term and the continuing resonance of the impeachment campaign against him. That battle sewed seeds of partisan discord and mistrust that germinated after 7 November into the most bitterly contested presidential election in 124 years.

The bitterness was strange. On so many issues that had divided the parties from the 1960s to the 1980s, Clinton succeeded in reducing Democratic disadvantages and soothing partisan divisions. At that level, Clinton truly was the protean politician.

As a result, almost everything that is said about Clinton can be true — and so can its opposite. Did his failures in the first two years lead to the 1994 Republican sweep that weakened the Democrats at every level? Yes. Did Clinton beat back Newt Gingrich's revolution and push American politics so far away from the right that George W. Bush was forced to defend government? Yes.

Did Clinton preside over a golden age of capitalist growth and create a climate in which the public imagination is dominated by stock ownership and high-tech millionaires? Yes. Did he make taxes far more progressive? Yes. Did he sign a Republican-sponsored welfare bill that ended public assistance as an entitlement? Yes. Did he preside over unprecedented increases in public spending for the working poor (expanding the Earned Income Tax Credit, Medicaid, and child care for the low paid)? Yes.

Did he push hard for free trade? Yes. Did he argue that the global economy needed to recognize labor rights and environmental concerns? Yes.

In sum, did he move the United States to the right? Yes. Did he move it to the left? Yes. Welcome to the Clinton paradox.

The paradox also means that a politician of extraordinary talent missed the opportunity to be an extraordinary president. A Republican opponent who knows him well has said that Clinton was "Roosevelt without the steel" — the most talented American politician since FDR, but without the discipline and the toughness.[2] And, in fairness, without a war and a depression to create opportunities for heroism, the steel this Republican had in mind never had a chance to show. In his own battles for survival, it must be said, Clinton surely showed he was made of rather tough stuff.

The paradoxes of Clintonism have a parallel: the paradoxes of interpreting Clinton. Where people stand now often depends on where they stood in 1992. Those who believe that the Democrats needed to make strategic corrections — on crime, welfare, family policy, defense, and fiscal prudence — are inclined to be sympathetic to what Clinton tried to do. Those who thought New Democrats were always and everywhere sellouts are much more suspicious of and much tougher on this president. A small but significant number of them voted for Ralph Nader, depriving Gore of the national majority he would probably have won absent Nader's candidacy. And of course there are Republicans who never forgave Clinton for winning, upending the Republican Revolution, and then winning again.

In truth, Clinton never governed entirely as either a New Democrat or an old one. He understood that a Democratic president needed to blend the two. So he went for a balanced budget, but courtesy of progressive taxation; he sought to establish national health insurance, but with a plan that tried to balance state and market; he spoke more respectfully of religion and tradition than most liberals, but favored gay rights.

In the most colossal policy failure of his presidency, he lost his battle for national health insurance. Yet, as many liberals forgot but conservatives always remembered, he was the first president since Truman to make a serious effort to close the largest gap in America's social insurance state by proposing his health care plan in the first place. On the health care fiasco, Clinton is assailed from the left (he made too many concessions to the market), from the right (his plan involved too much government), and from the center (he bungled his dealings with Congress).

Clinton's other large failure was rooted in his decision to agree with leaders of the 1993 Democratic Congress and back away from political reform. Not Bill Clinton but Republican John McCain came to be identified as the leading foe of big money in American politics. And the campaign finance abuses during Clinton's reelection effort hardly made it easy for Democrats (such as Al Gore) to stand as the paladins of clean government, despite the party's embrace of the reform plans put forward by McCain and his Democratic Senate partner, Russ Feingold.

Another paradox: Clinton ran as the candidate who would create a new set of Democratic constituencies, yet his staunchest supporters were African Americans, that most loyal of all Democratic constituencies. They sensed that in a deep and fundamental way, he stood with them. No group was more faithful to Clinton during the impeachment battle and no group was more suspicious of Ken Starr, Bob Barr, and the rest of the anti-Clinton crowd. The loyalty of African Americans to the Democratic Party, and their suspicion of Republicans, was reaffirmed during the Clinton presidency and produced the 9-to-1 margins that Al Gore won on Election Day. Gore, in fact, ran better among African Americans than Clinton had in 1996. And the disenfranchisement of African Americans in Florida — because of shoddy voting equipment in poor areas and the failure to recount votes — only reinforced these loyalties.

For all of Clinton's successes, his presidency will be seen historically as a moment of lost opportunities because it is impossible not to contemplate what Clinton might have accomplished absent the scandal that wasted most of 1998. The sense of a lost chance is heightened by the other fact about his term in office: the Clinton years will be seen as a time when American politics changed fundamentally. If Bill Clinton did not achieve as much change as he might have, his presidency fundamentally altered the contours of the American political debate.

The surface changes are obvious enough. When Clinton assumed office, the budget deficit was a central and debilitating fact of public life. Facing a sea of red ink, government could not consider new projects — a reality that helped doom Clinton's own health care proposal. With the deficit eliminated, it is possible again to have that most fundamental of political arguments: whether the government should do more, or just cut taxes.

Shrewd conservatives understood that the end of the deficit meant liberals would be bolder in proposing new programs because they could do so without also proposing new taxes. Paul Gigot of the *Wall Street Journal* warned early on that the era of "balanced budget liberalism" would be dangerous to conservatives who had become accustomed to swatting new programs away with arguments that they were unaffordable in light of the deficit. Had not government grown in the early 1960s and 1970s, Gigot asked, when deficits did not figure so prominently in the political debate?[3]

The ambitious plans offered by Bill Bradley and Al Gore during the Democratic primaries on health coverage, preschool and after-school programs, and child poverty ratified Gigot's prediction. (On the other hand, the failure of Bush's big tax cut to hurt him greatly in the election suggests that the big surpluses may have expanded policy openings on the Republican side, too.)

Perhaps the most significant Clinton contribution was to end old battles over the role of government. Ronald Reagan's cry was "The government is not the solution. The government is the problem." George W. Bush put his case much more modestly: "Government if necessary," he said, "but not necessarily government."

The difference between the two statements is profound, and Bush, at times, went out of his way to underscore just how big the difference was. In the fall of 1999, he criticized "the destructive mind-set" holding "that if government would only get out of the way, all our problems would be solved." Today's "destructive mind-set" was, just yesterday, a principled conservative argument. "Too often," Bush said for good measure, "my party has confused the need for limited government with a disdain for government itself."

The significant shift in our politics was caught shrewdly by a writer from that bastion of American conservatism, the *National Review.* "Whatever they may say, conservatives know in their bones that their position is weak," Ramesh Ponnuru wrote in the late fall of 1999. "What these conservatives sense is that, at a level of politics deeper than the fortunes of the political parties, the ground is shifting away from them. What they have not noticed is that the 2000 election is shaping up to be a ratification not of conservatism but of Clintonism — and will be so even if the Republicans win."[4]

Whether this was rethinking or merely repositioning will await the verdict on the Bush presidency. The cabinet Bush chose — ethnically and racially diverse but firmly conservative — suggested that he was putting a new face on doctrines that Reagan and Gingrich alike might find congenial. In the postelection period, after all, he stuck with his large tax cut, signaled a more prodevelopment attitude toward the use of public lands, chose a labor secretary who had been critical of the minimum wage, and named an attorney general who was anathema to almost all of the Democratic Party's core constituencies.

Yet Bush's awareness of a need at least to reposition the Republican message reflected a central fact of the Clinton presidency: the defeat of the genuinely ambitious antigovernment program the Republicans offered after their triumph in the 1994 elections. Even those who disagree with what the Republicans tried to do owe them a debt for clarifying the issues. In the wake of the budget fights of 1995–96, it was no longer possible to assume that the country is antigovernment, especially if that means cuts — you can still hear the Clinton speeches — in "Medicare, Medicaid, education, and the environment."

That congressional Republicans proposed nearly as much federal education spending as Clinton did in 1999 (albeit in a different form) suggests how well they understood where public attitudes were drifting. Bush was as shrewd about this issue as anyone. He made education a cornerstone of his campaign and successfully challenged the Democrats' traditional advantages on the issue.

That Republicans felt such a strong need to respond to Democratic initiatives in support of prescription drugs for the elderly and a patients' bill of rights suggested how far the political pendulum had moved away from the Republican Revolution. "They're campaigning on our message or imitating our message," Congressman Mike Doyle, a Democrat who represents the Pittsburgh suburbs, said shortly before Election Day.[5] Conservative activists accepted the change in mood as a fact that needed to be acknowledged. "Conservative grass roots organizations have been giving George Bush a pass, and a lot of congressional Republicans a pass," Doyle said, "by letting them run as moderates." Even Republicans, sometimes, wanted to look like New Democrats. That, too, was part of the Clinton legacy.

The most significant policy victory of the post-1994 Republicans was the welfare reform bill of 1996. But the abolition of welfare has had the effect of strengthening the claims of the poor in the public debate. If the poor go to work and still find themselves poor, the moral presumptions of mainstream morality are on their side. And the shift of public spending to programs for the working poor (the Earned Income Tax Credit is the most notable and successful) has made it extremely difficult for opponents of economic redistribution to argue that government was intervening on the side of "dependency" or "laziness."

There is, finally, the simple and very large fact of the prosperity of the 1990s. Debate will go on for years over what precisely created the boom times, when they started — many conservatives still see these good years as part of "the Reagan Economy" — and what combination of policies, economic factors, and accidents brought us back to both low inflation and low unemployment. After the stagflation of the late 1970s and the massive joblessness of the early 1980s, many economists had assumed (reasonably enough) that this Nirvana was impossible.

But if the sources of 1990s prosperity will be debated, what cannot be argued is that all the dire warnings Republicans offered during the 1993 budget debate were proven wrong. The supporters of supply-side economics insisted that the significant tax increases on the wealthy proposed by Clinton would lead to economic doom. They did not. The wealthy may have paid higher taxes, but their incomes rose and so, through most of the Clinton term, did their capital assets.

Here again, shrewd conservatives understood that their side had suffered a significant—and, in this case, self-inflicted—defeat. The Republicans' mistake, wrote the *National Review*'s Ponnuru, "was to overstate the case against Clinton's tax increases."

> Instead of predicting that his bill would reduce growth... they said it would plunge the economy into recession. When this didn't happen, and the economy after a few years of subpar growth started chugging along, Republicans were embarrassed (as much as politicians get, anyway), and, more important, left with nothing to say.[6]

It will take time for him to get credit for this, but Clinton's years also ratified a core argument that American progressives have made for half a century. From

Harry Truman forward, they insisted that near-full employment was the key to dealing with all manner of social problems. Our experiment with sustained low unemployment suggests that is true.

As Thomas B. Edsall wrote in the *Washington Post* shortly before Election Day:

> From 1993 to 1998, income for those in the bottom 20 percent has grown at the fastest annual rate, 2.7 percent, compared with 2.4 percent for the top quintile. The rate of income growth for those in the middle 60 percent is just behind the top. And overall, the pattern of income gains is much more evenly balanced than during the prior 20 years.[7]

"The most recent poverty figures are even more favorable," Edsall continued. The U.S. Census findings on income and poverty released in September 2000 showed that "the poverty rate fell for 1999 to its lowest level since 1979, 11.8 percent. In 1993 the rate had been 15.1 percent. Child poverty, which is at 16.9 percent, is the lowest since 1979." Near-full employment meant that every other problem became a little easier to solve, and gave workers in the middle and bottom of the economy more bargaining power.

To argue all these things defies a certain popular assumption: that Clinton, far from moving the political debate away from the right, capitulated to the Republicans, notably by signing the welfare bill and by declaring that "the era of big government is over." Both were significant concessions, the first in policy, the second in rhetoric. Both enraged liberals and the Democratic left.

It is also true that the Clinton years saw the culmination of a political realignment in the South that guarantees Republicans will be competitive in congressional elections for the foreseeable future. It's hard now to imagine a Democratic lock on the House of Representatives comparable to its dominance in the years 1954 to 1994. That era is over, too.

But in the end, Clinton's tactical shifts toward the right moved the debate away from the right. The fundamental fact of politics in 2000 was new mood. Politics was less ideological, and specifically less ideologically conservative, than it was in the late 1970s and 1980s. Attitudes toward government itself are still far less positive than they were in the early 1960s, before the cultural revolution, Vietnam, and Watergate. But philosophical hostility toward government has ebbed, replaced by a pragmatic inclination sympathetic to the expansion of public goods and in search of public action in spheres such as education, child care, health care, and the effort to right the balance between work and family life.

This paradox of the Clinton moment was obvious in the campaign. On the one hand, Bush, who tried to make himself less antigovernment in the early stages of the campaign, used the old Republican antigovernment mantra toward its end. He cast himself as the man who trusts "the people," and denounced Gore as the candidate who "trusts Washington." On the other hand, as Doyle, the

Democratic congressman, pointed out, Republican congressional candidates won election after election by campaigning on the Democrats' agenda.

The ambivalence suggests that the big government vs. small government argument, though still alive, is not what it used to be, and that is an achievement of the Clinton years. The discussion of work and family issues is no longer cast as a war between the family and feminism. Most Americans accept both the legitimacy of women's quest for genuine equality and the importance of protecting family life. The argument now focuses on how to balance work and family and how to protect the family within a highly competitive labor market.

As Theda Skocpol argues in her book, *The Missing Middle,* a central — perhaps *the* central — purpose of progressive social policy should be "how we as Americans can continue to care for our grandparents, while doing a much better job than we now do of supporting all working parents as they do the hard and vital work of raising our nation's children."[8] So much for any side in the political debate claiming a monopoly on the family or "family values." That — ironically, in light of the Clinton scandal — is an achievement of the Clinton years.

Americans of all races have tired of racial polarization. Arguments about affirmative action still go on, and they may become more fierce during the Bush term. Events such as the O.J. Simpson trial show that large attitudinal gaps between blacks and whites persist. But in the 1990s, at least, much of the discussion about race now focused on expanding opportunities. African Americans found, for the first time in history, that a broad economic recovery was especially beneficial to their community and their families — another reason why the ties between African Americans and the Democrats have grown stronger, and why Al Gore carried so many of their votes.

The recount battle after the 2000 election created new divisions, but also the possibility of new coalitions. African Americans were furious that antiquated voting equipment, concentrated in poorer areas, robbed many in those precincts of their ballots. Reports of intimidation and voters improperly dropped from the rolls added to the outrage. But the outrage was not confined to the black community. In the postelection period, the prospects for a broad, biracial coalition in support of political reform and a new Voting Rights Act seemed as promising as at any time in the past thirty-five years.

Although the welfare bill passed by Congress was deeply flawed, there is little argument that the purpose of social policy should be to promote work and to expand the rewards to those who join the workforce. Here again, Bush's responses are revealing. He chose to take loud public issue with the Republican Congress when it proposed to slow payments of the Earned Income Tax Credit. When he declared it wrong to "balance the budget on the backs of the poor," he was talking about the EITC. The Republican leadership quickly dropped the plan.

The crime issue, so potent in every campaign between 1968 and 1988, has ebbed with falling crime rates. It's hard to accuse anyone on any side of being "soft" on crime. And the gun-control issue, once of enormous benefit to political conservatives, has become something close to a fair fight as suburban voters make their preference for gun regulation known. In 2000 Bush seemed to benefit from opposition to gun control in rural areas, especially in southern and border states, while Gore seemed to benefit from his support for gun regulation in suburban areas, especially in Pennsylvania, Michigan, Illinois, and California.

The discussion of the role of religion in public life has also been transformed. The political influence of the religious right has declined, in part because it is no longer easy to cast political progressives as hostile to the views and interests of religious people. Gore's endorsement of government assistance, within limits, to the work of religious charities reflects a sea change in Democratic attitudes.

And although homosexuality is still a difficult issue for many Americans, as Alan Wolfe reported in *One Nation, After All,* it is less divisive than it once was.[9] Gays and lesbians enjoy an acceptance undreamed-of three decades ago and can find defenders of their rights in both political parties. It is significant that in the 2000 campaign, Bush and his running-mate Dick Cheney endorsed the military's "don't ask, don't tell" policy and opposed a rollback to the antihomosexual rules that existed before Clinton took office. While their position did not go as far as Gore's call for an outright ban on discrimination against gays and lesbians, the fact that the Republican candidates resisted a return to the pre-Clinton status quo suggested how much opinion had moved in favor of gay rights in just eight years.

The rise of a moderate social liberalism under Clinton explains why the transformation of America into a suburban nation did not make it a Republican nation. Speaking before he retired in September 2000, Representative John Edward Porter, a moderate Republican from a suburban area north of Chicago, argued that the "three litmus tests" in his district were abortion, gun control, and the environment. On all three, he said, the more liberal position was also the popular position.[10]

All these changes might be summarized as the decline of the old "wedge" issues that divided the electorate by race, culture, and religion and the rise of what might be called "bridge" issues that assemble new coalitions by reaching across old divides.

Bush's use of the adjective *compassionate* in front of *conservative* is an example of such bridging at the rhetorical level. The groping toward a new consensus on education policy — combining reform and tougher standards with more money — is a substantive example, and it was visible in the plans offered during the campaign by both Bush and Gore. Taken together, their plans suggested a road map to reform.

The education issue is another example of what Bill Clinton achieved. After years of deeply ideological politics, the country seemed of a mind in 2000 to return to problem-solving and to see government not as an automatic enemy but as a potential ally. Clinton balso presided over an unprecedented boom that restored his party's credibility in economic management and weakened the arguments of conservatives that only their policies of low taxes and opposition to regulation could guarantee prosperity.

At the very same time, Clinton became the focal point for the revival of an ideological politics on the right rooted not in the optimism of the Reagan years but in anger over perceived moral decay and fury at the man thought to embody it.

These contradictory legacies help explain the final paradox. The 2000 election, held at a moment of national consensus that Clinton himself helped achieve, resulted in an electorate divided almost exactly evenly into two camps.

It is impossible not to see the bitterness over the Florida recount apart from the impeachment traumas. Republican hatred of Clinton was transformed into harsh attacks on Gore for seeking a Florida recount. In retrospect, it's remarkable that Gore was accused of improper activity simply because he did what every other candidate in an excruciatingly close election had done: he sought to have the votes counted again — exactly what Bush's supporters demanded in New Mexico when final returns showed Gore with a narrow lead there. The GOP seemed not to worry about the contradiction: in the Florida case, Republicans saw *recount* as a synonym for *robbery*. House Republican Whip Tom DeLay had led the charge to impeach Clinton, and he was happy to join the charge against Gore. "A theft is in progress," DeLay thundered. Nothing would stop the Republicans from taking the White House back from a man and a party they had come to loathe — and nothing did.

If the Florida battle is seen as the final engagement of the Clinton presidency, it can also be seen as the first engagement of the Bush years. And this may be the very last of Clinton's legacies: that the partisan anger that hurt Clinton so badly has, as a result of the recount battle, created a furious counterreaction among Democrats that could make it very hard for Bush to govern. If Republicans declined to accept the legitimacy of Clinton's presidency after Clinton had won clear and unambiguous victories, many Democrats wondered why they should accept Bush's legitimacy after an election many of them felt he hadn't won at all.

Bush, like Clinton, ran against partisanship in Washington, and he pledged to be "a uniter, not a divider." Yet the emotions unleashed by the anti-Clinton wars have made unity ever more elusive. And so it is that the very tides Bush rode to power may let loose forces that will be very difficult for him to navigate or control.

NOTES

1. Stan Greenberg, as quoted in Thomas B. Edsall, "Fissures Widening among Democrats after Gore's Loss," *Washington Post*, 16 December 2000, A20.
2. Background interview with author.
3. Paul Gigot, "As Deficit Retires, Liberalism Bids for a Comeback," *Wall Street Journal*, 9 January 1998.
4. Ramesh Ponnuru, "State of the Conservatives," *National Review*, 22 November 1999, 37.
5. Interview with author; see E.J. Dionne, "The GOP's Stealth Agenda," *Washington Post*, 27 October 1999, A35.
6. Ramesh Ponnuru, "We Are All Clueless Now," *National Review*, 8 November 1999, 42.
7. Thomas B. Edsall, "Where Nader Has It Wrong," *Washington Post*, 4 November 2000, A23.
8. Theda Skocpol, *The Missing Middle: Working Families and the Future of American Social Policy* (New York: Norton, 2000).
9. Alan Wolfe, *One Nation, After All: How Middle-class Americans Really Think About: God, Country, Family, Racism, Welfare, Immigration, Homosexuality, Work, the Right, the Left, and Each Other* (New York: Viking, 1998).
10. Interview with author; see E.J. Dionne, "Suburban Prize," *Washington Post*, 29 September 2000, A33.

Chapter 2

The Presidential Nominations

William G. Mayer

> *Oft expectation fails, and most oft there*
> *Where most it promises; and oft it hits*
> *Where hope is coldest, and despair most fits.*
> —All's Well That Ends Well (II, 1)

IF YOU LIKE STORIES about how little guys take on the system and win, then you probably hated the 2000 presidential nomination races. In both the Democratic and Republican Parties, the basic plot line was the antithesis of David and Goliath: one candidate emerged as the clear early favorite, amassed an overwhelming advantage in money, organization, and elite endorsements, suffered just enough setbacks to give some glimmer of hope to his chief rival, and then obliterated the competition when the contest finally got serious.

Thirty years after a series of reforms that were supposed to "open up the parties" and "level the playing field," the American presidential nomination process has become, if anything, even more hostile toward outsiders and insurgents than the system that preceded it. If the 1996 nomination contests went a considerable distance toward establishing this proposition, the 2000 races should remove any lingering doubt. The most productive questions that can be asked about the 2000 nomination contests are all ones that presume this basic framework: Why did Al Gore and (especially) George W. Bush become the early front-runners? How seriously did Bill Bradley and John McCain ever really threaten their hold on the top spots? And absent a major change in the rules, can any non-front-runner reasonably hope to win a presidential nomination?

THE RULES: FRONT-LOADING REDUX

Our story begins with the rules. Well before the candidates actually start to solicit money or hold town meetings in Iowa and New Hampshire, a loose collection of campaign strategists, party leaders, and political reporters are already thinking about the rules that will govern the selection process this time around, how they differ from those that held sway in previous election cycles, and how those differences might affect what the candidates must do to win a major-party presidential nomination. As the 2000 election cycle got underway, the biggest concern for these rules junkies was the same one that had worried them in 1996: the ongoing march of front-loading.

Front-loading is the name given to an important contemporary trend in the presidential nomination system, in which more and more states schedule their primaries and caucuses at a relatively early point in the delegate selection calendar.[1] The basic dimensions of this movement are shown in table 2.1 (p. 14). As recently as 1976, the process of selecting delegates to the Republican and Democratic national conventions began rather slowly. But as the basic dynamics of the contemporary presidential nomination process became clearer, the delegate selection calendar soon took on a very different cast. On the one hand, it quickly became apparent that events held early in the delegate selection season — in particular, the Iowa caucuses and the New Hampshire primary — received a great deal more attention from both the candidates and the media than did events held later in the year, even when those later primaries and caucuses were held in states that were far more diverse and had many more delegates at stake. Partly as a result, candidates who showed poorly in Iowa and New Hampshire tended to withdraw from the race much earlier than they had in the nomination contests of the 1950s and 1960s. States selecting their delegates in May and June thus increasingly found that both parties' nomination races had been effectively settled by then and that their own primaries and caucuses were an empty formality.

States responded to these challenges in an entirely predictable way: they moved their primaries and caucuses to earlier positions in the delegate selection calendar. As the figures in table 2.1 indicate, the front-loading trend was, at first, a rather gradual one — but it accelerated dramatically in the late 1980s and then, after ebbing somewhat in the 1992 election cycle, soared to new heights in 1996.

Concerns about front-loading were sufficiently widespread in 1996 that the Republicans sought to reverse the trend toward front-loading by creating a system of "bonus delegates" for states scheduling their primaries later in the season.[2] The plan was an interesting experiment, but it didn't work: by late 1998, all indications were that lots of states would be moving their primaries forward and very few would be going in the other direction. A final scorecard on the Republican reforms of 1996 is as follows: Of the forty states holding Republican presidential primaries in both 1996 and 2000, twenty-eight had the same position in the calendar both years, eight had moved to an earlier date, and just four had moved to a later date.[3]

Of all the state scheduling decisions announced in the leadup to the 2000 nomination contests, one attracted particular attention. Frustrated by the radical disjunction between the size of its population and its almost complete lack of influence on recent presidential nominations, California moved its primary to

Table 2.1 Trends in Front-Loading, 1976–2000 (cumulative percentage of delegates chosen by end of each week in primary season)

A. Republican Party

	1976	1980	1984	1988	1992	1996	2000
Week 1	1	1	2	1	1	1	1
Week 2	4	4	2	3	2	7	2
Week 3	9	14	18	3	10	22	2
Week 4	15	20	24	49	36	51	9
Week 5	19	30	26	54	44	65	13
Week 6	19	35	37	54	46	77	45
Week 7	30	37	43	56	46	77	68
Week 8	30	37	43	59	56	77	72
Week 9	30	42	43	59	56	77	72
Week 10	35	42	47	65	56	81	78
Week 11	52	57	72	70	60	81	78
Week 12	55	61	75	78	66	88	78
Week 13	64	68	77	80	67	89	78
Week 14	75	72	77	82	71	91	84
Week 15	78	100	99	83	75	93	86
Week 16	100		100	83	99	100	87
Week 17				99	100		92
Week 18				100			92
Week 19							100

B. Democratic Party

	1976	1980	1984	1988	1992	1996	2000
Week 1	1	1	1	1	1	1	1
Week 2	5	6	1	1	1	1	1
Week 3	9	14	18	1	8	15	1
Week 4	17	22	27	42	31	44	1
Week 5	19	36	29	49	41	59	1
Week 6	19	41	41	49	43	73	43
Week 7	35	43	49	51	43	73	65
Week 8	35	43	49	54	56	73	71
Week 9	35	51	49	54	56	73	71
Week 10	43	51	53	63	56	80	79
Week 11	54	61	74	70	62	80	79
Week 12	57	64	77	79	68	86	79
Week 13	65	66	77	81	70	88	79
Week 14	73	70	77	83	72	90	86
Week 15	76	100	100	83	75	92	88
Week 16	100			83	100	100	89
Week 17				100			92
Week 18							92
Week 19							100

Note: Figures include all delegates selected or bound by primary vote.

7 March, the earliest date permitted under Democratic Party rules.[4] Since New York, Ohio, and seven other states were already scheduled to vote on the same day, the California decision seemed to put in place a system that was just one small step away from a national primary. While the Iowa caucuses and the New Hampshire primary would each still have a week to itself, any candidate who made it through those first two events would suddenly be compelled to run a full-fledged national campaign.

Most commentators believed that front-loading aided the fortunes of the early front-runner and further increased the odds against lesser-known and insurgent candidates. When the system was less front-loaded, a candidate without a national reputation or a large war chest might still hope to win the presidential nomination by relying on a gradual, momentum-based campaign. As the calendar became more front-loaded, however, it became more and more difficult — maybe impossible — to "start small." A lesser-known candidate who scored unusually well in Iowa and New Hampshire was almost immediately required to wage an intensive campaign in fifteen or twenty states at once. And unless the candidate already had such an operation in place *before* Iowa, it simply was not possible to create one in such a limited time period.

Indeed, according to a widespread consensus of reporters and political strategists, anyone who hoped to have a realistic shot at winning his or her party's nomination had to raise an enormous war chest — generally estimated at between $20 and $25 million — before the primaries started (see chapter 5 for details on campaign financing strategies).[5]

The 2000 primary and caucus calendar, in both parties, was undeniably a highly front-loaded one. But one last-minute decision substantially opened up the schedule and made it, by some measures, actually less front-loaded than the 1996 schedule had been. When California moved its primary to 7 March, most observers assumed that the New Hampshire primary would take place in the final week or two of February. (In 1996, for example, it had been held on 20 February.) But after a bit of preliminary maneuvering, in late September 1999 New Hampshire finally announced that it would hold its first-in-the-nation primary on 1 February. Though its significance was not immediately appreciated, New Hampshire's decision imparted a somewhat different dynamic to the beginning of the 2000 delegate selection season. Instead of a situation in which, as the *New York Times* put it, "candidates coming out of the New Hampshire race in February will *immediately* be forced into a massive, bicoastal campaign," now, suddenly, five weeks separated the New Hampshire primary and the California-New York extravaganza.[6]

The parties filled these five weeks in very different ways. Since Democratic Party rules forbid any states except Iowa and New Hampshire from holding a delegate selection event before the first Tuesday in March, the five-week gap remained just that: not a single Democratic primary or caucus took place during this period.[7] Republican national rules are more permissive, so a handful of states jumped into the void, ultimately creating a calendar that had at least some pretensions to a gradual beginning. In the end, there was only one Republican primary in each of the two weeks immediately following New Hampshire, and two each in the two weeks after that. And with one exception, none of these six primaries took place in a particularly large state.

By comparison to the calendars of 1976 and 1980, the 2000 primary and caucus schedule was clearly a front-loaded one, but, as the figures in table 2.1 indicate, the situation was not quite as bad as some had feared. A non-front-running candidate who pulled off an upset victory in Iowa or New Hampshire would not face an entirely hopeless undertaking. He now had at least five weeks to nurture and exploit his initial breakthrough.

DEFINING THE FIELD: THE DEMOCRATS

There is no great mystery as to how and why Al Gore became the early front-runner for the 2000 Democratic nomination. Whatever its other shortcomings, the vice presidency of the United States has clearly emerged over the past fifty years as the single best vantage point for seeking a major-party presidential nomination.[8] An incumbent vice president may not learn very much about governing;[9] but he indisputably does acquire a wonderful collection of campaign resources: more national media exposure than almost anybody except the president; unrivaled access to his party's top financial contributors; endless opportunities to curry favor with party activists, candidates for elective office, and allied interest groups; close association with the administration's major successes and (usually) at least some distance from its most glaring failures. And once the campaigning gets serious, the vice president has few real governing responsibilities that might tie him down in Washington, D.C., when he would rather be out on the hustings.[10]

To these formidable institutional advantages, Gore added two of a more personal nature. First, he was generally perceived as having done a creditable job as vice president. Whether Gore was "the greatest vice president in American history," as his supporters sometimes described him, is disputable; but few would contest that he had been an able and effective adviser to the president and that whenever he was given more substantial responsibilities, as in the "Reinventing Government" initiative, he had acquitted himself well. If there were also a few black marks next to his name, such as his fund-raising activities during the 1996 campaign and his perhaps overly exuberant defense of the president during the Monica Lewinsky scandal, these were of a sort unlikely to hurt his standing with the Democratic faithful.

Second, Gore's quest for the White House enjoyed the enthusiastic support of the president.[11] Bill Clinton's support for Gore was testimony both to the good personal relationship between the two men[12] and to the president's conclusion that one of the surest ways to deepen his "legacy" was to make sure that Gore succeeded him. By handing off the presidency to Gore, Clinton could reasonably claim that his tenure in the Oval Office had marked a decisive turning point in the history of the Democratic Party — that he had helped redefine the party's basic philosophy of government and, in the process, had shown the Democrats how to break the Republican stranglehold on the White House.

As the Democrats began to gear up for the 2000 nomination race, then, at least one point was clear: Al Gore would be the early front-runner, and a strong one. In one of the first major polls that assessed public attitudes about the 2000 nomination races, a Gallup poll found in May 1998 that Gore was the first choice of 51 percent of the country's Democrats and Democratic-leaning Independents (see table 2.2, p. 18). His closest competitor was Jesse Jackson, who was preferred by just 12 percent, while none of the other five Democrats whose names Gallup read to its sample even broke into double digits. According to another series of questions in the poll, Gore was viewed favorably by 73 percent of all Democrats, while none of the other potential candidates had a favorability rating above 50 percent.[13]

During the last half of 1998 and the first few months of 1999, media reports on the presidential sweepstakes almost always mentioned six potential challengers to Gore: U.S. Senators Bob Kerrey of Nebraska, John Kerry of Massachusetts, and Paul Wellstone of Minnesota; former Senator Bill Bradley of New Jersey; House Minority Leader Richard Gephardt of Missouri; and civil rights leader and former presidential candidate Jesse Jackson. Several of these men talked openly about their interest in the race; Wellstone went so far as to create a presidential "exploratory committee" in April 1998; Kerrey established his own political action committee, a vehicle often used to lay the groundwork for a presidential bid. Yet, in the end, five of the six decided not to make the race.[14]

Congressman Gephardt was generally seen as Gore's strongest potential opponent: he had already run for president once before; he had used his leadership position to ingratiate himself with party activists and to set up a national network of supporters and financial contributors; and he had strong ties to many of the groups that were most suspicious of Gore, particularly organized labor. But the Democrats' unexpected gain of five House seats in the midterm elections of 1998 headed off Gephardt's challenge. Besides helping to reassure Democrats who were worried about Gore's strength as a general election candidate by suggesting that his close ties to Bill Clinton would not be a major liability, the 1998 outcome also changed the stakes for the 2000 congressional elections. Gephardt and his advisers realized that if the Democrats could pick up just six more seats in the upcoming elections, the Missouri congressman would become Speaker of the House. And, it was widely argued, the Democrats' chances of achieving that goal would be considerably better if Gephardt himself were heading up the campaign, for no other House Democrat had such a national reputation and following.

Table 2.2 **Presidential Nomination Preferences of National Democratic Identifiers (in percentages)**

Sampling Dates	Gore	Bradley	Gephardt	Jackson
All Democrats				
8–10 May 1998	51	8	7	12
23–25 October	41	15	14	11
8–10 January 1999	47	12	13	11
12–14 March	58	21	–	15
13–14 April	54	34	–	–
30 April–2 May	66	23	–	–
23–24 May	59	30	–	–
4–5 June	63	28	–	–
25–27 June	64	28	–	–
16–18 August	58	31	–	–
10–14 September	63	30	–	–
8–10 October	51	39	–	–
21–24 October	57	32	–	–
4–7 November	58	33	–	–
18–21 November	54	35	–	–
Registered Voters				
18–21 November 1999	56	34	–	–
9–12 December	52	38	–	–
7–10 January 2000	59	30	–	–
13–16 January	59	30	–	–
17–19 January	60	27	–	–
25–26 January	67	21	–	–
4–6 February	65	24	–	–

Source: Gallup polls, various dates.

Note: Candidates are dropped from the survey question when they announce that they are not running for president.

Though friends described him as "wistful about forgoing a run for president," in early February 1999 Gephardt made his intentions public: he would not be seeking the 2000 Democratic presidential nomination.[15]

Idiosyncratic and personal factors may have entered into a number of other non-candidacy decisions,[16] but two considerations seem to have carried particular weight with almost all of Gore's adversaries. The first was the simple perception that Gore was so far ahead as to make everybody else — even Gephardt — a distinct long-shot. The second was the challenge, already mentioned, of raising $25 million before a single delegate was selected. And so, one by one, Gore's major rivals took themselves out of the running, until by late March, only one was left: Bill Bradley.[17]

Among early handicappers of the 2000 Democratic contest, the general consensus was that Bradley ranked a notch or two below Dick Gephardt (who, in turn, was several notches below Al Gore). Bradley had several important strengths: he had spent eighteen years in the U.S. Senate, where he was generally regarded as a thoughtful and hard-working legislator, and, prior to that, he had built a life outside of politics, as a legitimate sports hero. But there were also some decided weaknesses: Bradley was almost universally regarded as a loner, uncomfortable with many of the rituals of politics; partly as a consequence, he had remarkably little support among other Democratic officials. On the stump, Bradley was generally rated as an even less exciting speaker than Al Gore. He also had very little experience in waging a long, hard-fought election campaign, having rarely faced stiff competition in his runs for the Senate.

The one exception was 1990: Bradley's near loss that year left him, by all accounts, angry, shaken, and disillusioned.[18] Although he had once contemplated running for president in 1992, he not only declined to make that race but also announced, in August 1995, that he would not seek reelection to the Senate. In a speech that would eventually create problems for his presidential candidacy, Bradley declared that "politics is broken" and then criticized both parties for their ideological rigidity and for failing to speak "to people where they live their lives."[19] To further complicate his relationship with the Democratic Party establishment, Bradley also told reporters in 1996 that he had "not ruled out" running for president as an Independent. As it was, Bradley spent the next two years teaching, writing, traveling, and working in private business. By mid-1998, he claimed to be re-energized and ready to seek the White House.

DEFINING THE FIELD: THE REPUBLICANS

Meanwhile, the Republicans were going through similar gyrations. As in the Democratic Party, a large number of potential candidates expressed interest in the campaign or were frequently mentioned in press reports, but unlike the Democrats, most of the Republican prospects actually got into the race. Two factors may have accounted for the difference. First, when most of the candidates were assessing their chances, it seemed less likely that the Republicans would have a single, overwhelming favorite. Also, it is easier to raise large sums of campaign money in the Republican Party than among the Democrats. Whatever the causes, there were, in all, twelve announced candidates for the 2000 Republican presidential nomination, though an unusually large number of them would withdraw well before the first delegates were selected.[20]

As a matter of chronological accuracy, the first two names on the list should be Lamar Alexander, former Tennessee governor and secretary of education, and multimillionaire publisher Steve Forbes. Both had also been candidates for the 1996 nomination and, in a real sense, had never stopped running. Even by the standards of contemporary presidential campaigns, each had established an unusually active and visible presence in such key early battleground states as Iowa and New Hampshire. Alexander's appearances in New Hampshire began during the fall of *1996,* when he was nominally campaigning for Bob Dole and the rest of that year's Republican ticket. A few weeks after the November election he was back on his own.[21]

By all accounts, Forbes matched Alexander visit for visit — and then went him one better. In 1997 Forbes began airing radio ads in Iowa, New Hampshire, and a number of other early-voting states. While the ads were ostensibly not about the candidate but about an issue then pending before Congress (tax reform), the chief spokesman and prime mover in the commercials was, of course, Forbes himself. Alexander, being less well-heeled, did not begin his issue ad campaign until August 1998.[22]

Ten other Republican aspirants eventually joined the race: Texas Governor George W. Bush; former Secretary of Labor and Transportation Elizabeth Dole; former Vice President Dan Quayle; U.S. Senators John McCain of Arizona, Orrin Hatch of Utah, and Robert Smith of New Hampshire; Representative John Kasich of Ohio; media commentator Pat Buchanan; Gary Bauer, a Reagan administration appointee who later became head of the Family Research Council; and former ambassador Alan Keyes.

As in the Democratic race, a May 1998 Gallup poll provides a nice window on how the Republican presidential nomination was shaping up. Even at that early date, George W. Bush had opened up a modest lead over the rest of the field (see table 2.3). In second place was Elizabeth Dole; a notch below her were Dan Quayle and Jack Kemp, the party's 1996 vice-presidential candidate (who never did join the fray). Conspicuously, neither Forbes nor Alexander, in spite of their early and constant campaigning, came close to the front-runners.

Such was the early line on the 2000 Republican nomination race. But over the next nine months, the Republican contest would be gradually but thoroughly transformed. By mid-March 1999, *Time* magazine would declare, "George W. Bush is so far ahead in the race for the G.O.P. nomination, some call him a sure bet."[23]

How Bush became such a prohibitive early favorite for his party's presidential nomination is considerably more difficult to explain than Al Gore's ascendancy among the Democrats. Obviously, one starts off with his name. (Indeed, there is some evidence — though it is less definitive than it is sometimes alleged to be — that Bush showed well in the early polls primarily because survey respondents confused him with his father, the former president.)[24] Given the generally low level of public interest in and knowledge of public affairs, it has always been an advantage in electoral politics to have a famous name — witness the Democratic presidential candidacies of Robert and Edward Kennedy. And in Bush's case (as in the Kennedys'), it wasn't just the name, but the remarkable network of friends, contacts, and long-time supporters that went with it.

Bush had also, by this time, begun to attract a certain amount of favorable attention for his record as governor of Texas. How much of this early coverage filtered down to the ordinary voter is difficult to say; but for those who were paying

Table 2.3 Presidential Nomination Preferences of National Republican Identifiers (in percentages)

Sampling Dates	Bush	McCain	Forbes	Dole	Buchanan	Quayle	Hatch
All Republicans							
8–10 May 1998	30	4	7	14	3	9	–
23–25 October	39	–	7	17	–	12	–
8–10 January 1999	42	8	5	22	–	6	–
12–14 March	52	3	1	20	4	9	–
13–14 April	53	5	6	16	7	4	–
30 April–2 May	42	4	6	24	6	5	–
23–24 May	46	6	5	18	7	6	–
4–5 June	46	5	5	14	9	6	–
25–27 June	59	5	6	8	6	3	2
16–18 August	61	5	4	13	6	3	1
10–14 September	62	5	5	10	5	3	2
8–10 October	60	8	4	11	–	3	2
21–24 October	68	11	8	–	–	–	3
4–7 November	68	12	6	–	–	–	2
18–21 November	63	16	6	–	–	–	4
Registered Voters							
18–21 November 1999	63	16	6	–	–	–	4
9–12 December	64	18	7	–	–	–	2
20–21 December	60	17	9	–	–	–	1
7–10 January 2000	63	18	5	–	–	–	2
13–16 January	61	22	5	–	–	–	1
25–26 January	65	15	7	–	–	–	–
4–6 February	56	34	2	–	–	–	–
14–15 February	58	31	–	–	–	–	–
20–21 February	58	31	–	–	–	–	–
25–27 February	57	33	–	–	–	–	–

Source: Gallup polls, various dates.

Note: Candidates are dropped from the survey question when they withdraw from the race. McCain and Buchanan were omitted from some early surveys by mistake.

attention, the reviews were generally quite positive.[25] But it was the 1998 elections that really sent Bush's stock into orbit. On one level the 1998 results helped to polish his credentials as a successful governor and an attractive vote-getter. Not only was Bush the first Texas governor in twenty-four years to be reelected; he also won 68 percent of the vote, a total that included, according to the network exit polls, 27 percent of the black vote, 49 percent of the Hispanic vote, and 31 percent of the votes cast by Democrats and liberals.

Equally important, the 1998 returns removed whatever luster remained on the image of the Republican Congress. In the leadup to the 1996 presidential campaign, the most important source of political and policy leadership within the Republican Party had unquestionably been its congressional contingent, especially the Republican membership in the House of Representatives. By 1998 the "geniuses" who had taken back Congress for the first time in forty years had given way to the "idiots" who had misplayed the Clinton sex scandal.

In one instance, the impact was particularly direct. Throughout 1997 and 1998 there had been repeated indications that Newt Gingrich, the controversial Speaker of the House, was quietly laying the groundwork for a presidential bid in 2000.[26] If so, the 1998 elections brought these plans to a crashing halt. Three days after the election, Gingrich announced that he was resigning both the Speakership and his House seat and returning to private life.

More broadly, the message of 1998, as many Republicans saw it, was that the party would have a far better chance of winning the presidency in 2000 if it fielded a candidate who could not be tarnished by close association with the congressional Republicans. There were, of course, thirty-one other Republican governors, but in addition to having a famous name, Bush stood out from this group because of his unusually broad appeal to all segments of the party. He had not taken liberal positions on so many social and cultural issues as to be unacceptable to large numbers of southern and western Republicans. Yet, though generally conservative on subjects such as abortion, gay rights, and gun control, he did not emphasize social issues or talk about them in a strident way. Above all, Bush had practiced a very inclusionary style of politics. In 1994, for example, when many other Republicans had attacked bilingual education or tried to deny state aid to illegal immigrants, Bush had resisted the trend. By 2000, with both parties increasingly solicitous of the growing Hispanic vote, Bush plainly had a greater prospect of winning such votes than many other Republican governors.[27]

And once the Bush bandwagon was set in motion, several other dynamics came into play that helped give it further momentum. To begin with, Republicans of every stripe were, by all accounts, desperately anxious to win back the White House in 2000. Without the presidency, Republicans found themselves unable to articulate a clear policy agenda; they were all too prone to be dominated by the most extreme elements of their congressional leadership. Above all, they prized the potential of the next president to appoint three or four new justices to the Supreme Court. Second, Republicans have long had a lower tolerance than Democrats for intra-party conflict.[28] Believing that a protracted nomination battle would only hurt their ticket in the general election, Republicans clearly hoped to avoid open warfare and settle the whole matter by consensus.

Both dynamics favored the early front-runner. Even the Republican-allied interest groups seemed to be on their best behavior. The Christian right, in particular, was often credited with showing an unaccustomed measure of pragmatism, generally refusing to demand that Bush toe the line on all of their favorite issues.[29]

Yet, even after all these factors are taken into account, it is hard not to feel that the Republican establishment made a remarkable rush to judgment in early 1999, putting a lot of eggs in a very uncertain and untried basket. If there were a number of reasons to think that Bush might make a strong standard-bearer in the general election, there were also surely a large number of question marks hovering over his candidacy: How well would he stand up under the rigors of a national campaign? How would the American public react to his almost complete lack of foreign policy experience — or to the widespread rumors that he had used drugs as a young adult? Did he have the intelligence and "gravitas" necessary to be an effective candidate? For whatever reason, most Republicans never waited to get solid answers. By early spring 1999 an aura of invincibility had already begun to envelop the Bush candidacy.

EARLY SKIRMISHES: THE DEMOCRATS

By April 1999 Bill Bradley was, for a long-shot candidate, in an enviable position. Though far behind in money, endorsements, and the polls, he was the only candidate running against Al Gore, and therefore Bradley became the official anti-Gore candidate. Any Democrat who disliked Gore — for whatever reason — or who simply had doubts about his electability had only one real option. And for quite a while, it appeared that Bradley just might pull it off.

The Bradley campaign marched to its own peculiar rhythm, a rhythm set by the candidate himself.[30] For the first nine months of 1999, Bradley spent most of his time speaking and listening to small groups, outlining a broad vision and philosophy, but generally refusing to talk about specific programs. In the first post-Lewinsky presidential election, Bradley seems to have concluded — just as John McCain would on the Republican side — that the public was tired of handlers and spin control and carefully packaged media events, that it craved spontaneity and "authenticity," that the most compelling image a campaign could project was that of a candidate unconcerned about his image. In the early going, Bradley's campaign style played to generally positive reviews, though as the race wore on, he was increasingly criticized for being aloof, sanctimonious, and inflexible.

Eventually, the specifics came, too. Beginning in late July and culminating in late September and early October, Bradley unveiled a series of detailed proposals on all the major issues on which he hoped to stake his campaign: health care, child poverty, campaign finance reform, gun control, and gay rights. If the list was not especially long, it can reasonably be described as ambitious. As Bradley himself described his agenda, "We will do fewer things. But they will be essential things, and we will do them more thoroughly."[31] Although Gore and Bradley were generally seen as occupying very similar positions on the ideological spectrum, Bradley clearly tried to position himself to the left of Gore, repeatedly criticizing the vice president for the small-scale character of many of his ideas and for his unwillingness to take on "the big challenges."[32]

If observers were often uncertain what to make of the Bradley campaign, their judgment about the Gore effort was decidedly less ambivalent. It is difficult to find a newspaper or magazine article from the first eight months of 1999 that provided a favorable review of the Gore campaign. By early spring, there was a widespread perception that the campaign was floundering, that it lacked a clear sense of direction, that it was failing to connect with the voters.[33] By mid-May, even President Clinton publicly admitted that he was concerned that Gore's campaign was off to "a sluggish start."[34]

To make matters worse, once the campaign had acquired a negative image, it made repeated attempts to redesign or "reinvent" itself, generally in rather cosmetic ways, always claiming that the latest crop of innovations would finally allow the real, "authentic" Al Gore to shine forth. As one reporter commented at the end of the year, "It is hard now to think of a candidate who has tried more transformations in a shorter period."[35]

Having been mistaken all too often in the past, reporters, pundits, and other observers inevitably look for more objective ways to measure each candidate's progress during the so-called invisible primary period. In the 2000 campaign, the three principal indicators they used were polls, endorsements, and money-raising figures. Of the three, only the endorsement battle provided the Gore campaign with a clear advantage. Bradley endorsements by major Democratic leaders were sufficiently rare that when one did occur, it generally made the headlines. Even in his own home state, not one Democrat in the New Jersey congressional delegation supported Bradley.[36]

Unfortunately for Gore, the pattern of elite endorsements is the least electorally important of the three indicators: no one has ever been able to show that congressional or gubernatorial endorsements carry much weight in a presidential primary. Gore's deep support among Democratic Party leaders had one other potential significance: under current party rules, all Democratic governors, members of Congress, and members of the Democratic National Committee become automatic delegates to the Democratic National Convention. According to some reports, this gave a Gore a huge early lead in the delegate hunt.[37] But this advantage also tended to dissolve on closer inspection. These superdelegates, as they were called, were likely to stick with Gore only if he won or at least did well in the primaries and caucuses. If ordinary Democratic voters expressed a clear preference for Bradley, there was no reason to think that the superdelegates would try to countermand that verdict.

The polls presented a more mixed picture. In national surveys of Democratic Party identifiers, Gore still held a clear lead over Bradley, but it was declining: from about 35 percentage points in early 1999 to about 15–25 points in the last three months of the year (see table 2.2, p. 18). More worrisome for the Gore campaign was the trend in New Hampshire. By early September, polls were showing the race there tied or Bradley narrowly ahead. Bradley also had a modest lead in the state of New York, which was scheduled to vote on 7 March.

Given Bradley's image as an outsider and reformer, his most impressive performance came, ironically enough, in the fund-raising derby. When the campaign began, it was widely assumed that Gore would have a huge financial advantage over Bradley, but by late summer, as the Bradley fund-raising operation shifted into high gear, the Gore machine began to falter. In the final six months of 1999, the former senator clearly outperformed the sitting vice president, and the year-end fund-raising totals showed the two campaigns all but even (see chapter 5).

Fund-raising aside, in the last few months of 1999, the momentum of the Democratic presidential nomination contest finally began to shift back in Gore's favor. Several developments probably contributed to the change. First, the vice president moved his campaign headquarters from Washington, D.C., to Nashville, Tennessee, enabling the campaign to reduce its overhead expenses and jettison many of its high-priced consultants. Second, in early October, Gore won the backing of a number of major labor organizations, culminating in the endorsement of the AFL-CIO. In contrast to those of party leaders and elected officials, union endorsements have some weight behind them: they provide the favored candidate with such valued commodities as soft money, field workers, and a well-established communications network. Third, Gore's top advisers made one final attempt to retool the vice president's much-maligned campaign style. Their strategy was to have the candidate dress more casually, get rid of the usual stump speech and most of the visible symbols of the vice-presidential office, and then fill Gore's schedule with town-hall forums and intimate question-and-answer sessions. Though it was difficult to credit his repeated assertions that he was now ignoring all his pollsters and consultants and speaking "directly from my heart," the "new Gore" did play to considerably better reviews.[38]

Most important, after months of basically ignoring Bradley, in early October the Gore campaign launched a sustained and aggressive attack on the former senator and his policies. Gore questioned Bradley's loyalty to the Democratic Party, his sincerity as a reformer of the campaign finance system, his concern for farmers, and his commitment to education. Gore attacked Bradley for supporting vouchers and Ronald Reagan's original package of budget cuts and for deciding to quit the Senate in 1996 rather than "stay and fight" the new Republican Congress.[39] Above all, Gore hammered at Bradley's proposal to extend health insurance coverage to millions of poor and middle-class Americans, charging that the plan cost too much, used up too much of the federal budget surplus, and might require increased taxes. At the same time, the vice president claimed that Bradley wanted to eliminate Medicaid and thereby "shred the social safety net."[40]

Some of these attacks were reasonable; others were widely condemned as inaccurate or misleading. In either case, Bradley was notably slow and reluctant to respond. Though Bradley had taken his share of shots at Gore, he now seemed to regard Gore's criticisms of him as somehow illegitimate. "I am simply not going to deal with the darts that are being thrown," he said at one point. To another group of reporters, he declared, "I think the American people are tired of negative politics."[41] But like it or not, press coverage from the final three months of 1999 suggests that it was Gore, not Bradley, who was setting the campaign agenda. Equally important, as we will see, Bradley's long rise in the polls came to an end around this time. In Iowa, New Hampshire, and the nation, the Gore campaign had at last managed to stanch the bleeding.

EARLY SKIRMISHES: THE REPUBLICANS

Meanwhile, the Bush juggernaut rolled on. Between November 1998 and July 1999, George W. Bush enjoyed nine months of essentially uninterrupted good news. It wasn't just that he was the front-runner; on almost every measurable dimension, Bush dominated the competition more completely than any other nonincumbent candidate in the modern history of presidential nominations.[42]

The most publicized demonstration of the Bush campaign's prowess was its fund-raising. Having waited until the comparatively late date of 8 March to establish its exploratory committee, in early July the Bush campaign stunned the political world by announcing that it had already raised $36.3 million in contributions.[43] This figure was almost six times as much money as had been raised by Bush's nearest competitor[44] and almost twice as much as had been raised by the eleven other Republican presidential candidates combined (see chapter 5). Even after allowing for inflation, the 2000 Bush campaign was easily the most successful fund-raising operation since the Federal Election Commission began keeping records.

By the summer of 1999 Bush had opened up a huge lead in the national polls of Republican identifiers. In late June almost 60 percent of Republicans wanted Bush to be their party's presidential candidate, a level of support that he never lost (see table 2.3, p. 21). Not until August did the Bush campaign begin to show a few faint signs that it might be mortal after all. For reasons that defy rational explanation, the first major "test of strength" for the Republican presidential hopefuls was the Iowa straw poll. The turnout was small, the results had no effect on delegate selection, and no one could vote without first paying a $25 entry fee. Nevertheless, several different campaigns had targeted the event as a key opportunity to demonstrate their popular support and organizational muscle and thus shake up the race a bit.[45] In the end, after spending about $800,000, Bush won the Iowa straw poll, but his relatively narrow margin of victory—he won 31 percent of the votes cast, to 21 percent for Forbes and 14 percent for Dole—failed to match the soaring expectations raised by every other aspect of his campaign.[46]

A potentially more serious stumble came less than a week later, when Bush himself helped reignite concerns about whether he had ever used illegal drugs. Ever since his first run for governor in 1994, Bush had declined to answer this question, saying only that "I've made mistakes in the past, and I've learned from my mistakes." But on 18 August a reporter broached the issue in a new way:

Could Bush pass the background question posed to all potential employees of the Clinton White House, whether they had used drugs at any time in the past seven years? Bush replied that, yes, he could meet that standard. But that answer only opened up a floodgate of further questions. After saying that he could also have passed the fifteen-year standard that was in force when his father was president, Bush retreated to his original position: that this was one subject he just would not talk about. The controversy hung around in the press for a few more days and then effectively disappeared. If this was the first "crisis" of the Bush campaign, as some reports claimed, they weathered it with surprising ease.[47]

The Early Withdrawals

One of the more noteworthy features of the 2000 Republican nomination contest was the large number of candidates who withdrew between July and October 1999, well before a single vote was cast or a single delegate selected. Many recent nomination races have seen one or two early withdrawals,[48] but nothing on this scale. By late fall of 1999 the original field of twelve Republican contenders had already been reduced to six.

Candidates dropped out for a number of reasons. In some cases, those who withdrew had never had much chance of winning the nomination, and their final decision is best seen as a simple recognition of the inevitable. But the early retirees also included some people who were — or should have been — taken more seriously. If there is a common thread that seems to underlie most of the early withdrawal decisions, it is money. By raising so much money so quickly, Bush not only guaranteed himself the resources to wage a long and vigorous campaign; he also made it considerably more difficult for his rivals to get the money they needed. As one national Republican official commented, "Bush is sucking the wind out of everybody's sails."[49] Political scientist John Pitney employed a different metaphor: "This is the political equivalent of bombing the supply lines. There's only so much political money out there, and every dollar that goes to [Bush] is a dollar that doesn't go anywhere else."[50]

The candidacy of Lamar Alexander seems to have been hit particularly hard by Bush's success: so many of the traits and qualities that had helped Alexander attract support in 1996 — his claim to be a Washington "outsider," his image as a moderate and a pragmatist, the argument that he would make a very strong candidate in the general election[51] — seemed in 2000 to apply with much greater force to the governor of Texas. After lagging behind his own 1995 fund-raising levels in the first two quarters of 1999 and then finishing a weak sixth in the Iowa straw poll, Alexander dropped out of the race.

As the last Republican vice president, Dan Quayle was, at least on paper, a natural candidate for the 2000 presidential nomination. But Quayle's, of course, had not been a normal vice presidency. From the day his selection was announced, Quayle had faced a torrent of ridicule and abuse, centering on whether he had the intelligence and ability to serve as president. These attacks left Quayle with an extraordinarily negative public image. Nevertheless, he soldiered on against long odds until September, when the combination of an eighth-place finish in the Iowa straw poll, defections from within his own organization, and the inevitable money troubles finally drove him from the race.[52]

In contrast to Quayle, Elizabeth Dole was taken seriously as a presidential candidate.[53] By most reckonings, in fact, she was one of the two early front-runners for the Republican nomination, definitely behind Bush, but not that far behind. Yet, for a variety of reasons — many of them reflecting the fact that Dole herself had never run for elective office before — the Dole campaign never quite got off the ground. Initial expressions of interest from potential supporters were never followed up; many key staff positions (including national finance chairman) remained vacant for extended periods of time or suffered from a high turnover rate; the candidate herself, accustomed to delivering carefully rehearsed, meticulously choreographed speeches, was uncomfortable with the spontaneity and chaos of a contemporary presidential campaign.[54]

Tactics aside, Dole's principal problem may have been that she was simply running in the wrong party. There are lots of people who would thrill to the prospect of a serious woman presidential candidate; unfortunately for Elizabeth Dole, most such people are Democrats. While some anecdotal evidence suggests that Dole's candidacy attracted a number of women and young people who were new to electoral politics,[55] there was nothing like the outpouring that greeted Hillary Clinton's New York Senate campaign. To the end of her candidacy, Dole remained in second place in the national polls, but it was an increasingly distant second. As with Alexander and Quayle, it was fund-raising that administered the coup de grâce. On 20 October, she quit the race.

Just five days later, it was Pat Buchanan's turn. Buchanan, of course, had also been a candidate for the Republican presidential nomination in 1992 and 1996. He must have enjoyed the experience, because in early 1999, he was back at it. This time, however, there were early signs that he might not find the ride so rewarding. In his two previous campaigns, Buchanan had been virtually the only candidate trying to appeal to the large number of cultural and religious conservatives within the Republican Party. In 2000 at least four other candidates — Bauer, Quayle, Keyes, and Forbes — were targeting the same constituency. By May Forbes had hired away the entire Buchanan '96 campaign staff in New Hampshire. In the Iowa straw poll, Buchanan finished fifth, behind both Forbes and Bauer.

Buchanan was unwilling to quit the race entirely, however. Instead, by early August, he and Bay Buchanan, his sister/campaign manager, had begun to think about seeking the presidential nomination of the Reform Party, the third-party vehicle that Ross Perot had created in 1995.[56] Joining the Reform Party had several attractions for Buchanan: it was already on the general election ballot in twenty-one states and, more important, the party's nominee would automatically receive $12.6 million in federal funds for his campaign. After testing the extent of his support within the Reform Party, and ignoring a series of pleas from top Republican officials, on 25 October Buchanan made it official: he was no longer a Republican.

A 2 1/2-Man Race

By early November, then, the battle for the Republican presidential nomination had narrowed to just two — or maybe it was three — serious candidates. At the top of the totem pole, of course, was George W. Bush. Second place belonged just as clearly to John McCain, who had become Bush's chief rival partly as a result of simple attrition. As a sitting senator, McCain's fund-raising through the first three quarters of 1999 had at least allowed him to stay in the race; and with Alexander, Dole, and Quayle all getting out, McCain was almost the only person left who had actually held a high government office.

But McCain had two other important factors working in his favor. First, McCain had easily the most compelling personal story of any candidate in either party. As a Navy pilot during the Vietnam War, he had been shot down over North Vietnam in 1967 and held as a prisoner of war for almost six years. Though tortured and kept in solitary confinement for long periods of time, McCain had declined to take advantage of his father's position as an admiral to gain early release. His book about these experiences, *Faith of My Fathers,* published in September 1999, quickly became a national bestseller.

Second, though it might not have worked very well in a general election, McCain ran a campaign that was almost perfectly suited to the particular circumstances of the New Hampshire presidential primary. Given his lack of resources, McCain concentrated almost all of his early campaigning in three states: bypassing Iowa altogether, he became a fixture in South Carolina, California, and, especially, New Hampshire.[57] Even by New Hampshire standards, McCain ran an exceptionally open campaign — between April 1999 and the end of January 2000, he held a total of 114 town meetings in the Granite State. At each one, he made a few introductory comments and then, for ninety minutes or more, took questions from ordinary voters on any and all subjects. As word got around, his audiences grew progressively larger and more enthusiastic.[58] He was also unusually accessible to the press, which tended to make his newspaper and television coverage more favorable. By early November, at a time when he was barely breaking double digits in the national polls, McCain had pulled even with Bush in New Hampshire.

But McCain also had one major liability, which would ultimately play a major role in determining the fate of his candidacy. Simply put, the Arizona senator received almost no support from other Republican leaders. In the Democratic race, as we have seen, most party leaders preferred Al Gore as their party's candidate — but most of them also regarded Bill Bradley as an acceptable substitute.[59] The same cannot be said for McCain, whose presidential candidacy excited considerably more active, even vehement opposition from within his own party. Part of the problem lay in McCain's policy positions. Although his overall voting record in the Senate was irreproachably conservative, he had broken with his party on a number of crucial issues, most notably campaign finance reform. To many Republican leaders and Republican-allied interest groups, the much-publicized McCain-Feingold bill, which sought to outlaw the use of "soft money" in federal elections, was not just bad policy, but a threat to their very existence.

McCain had also alienated many of his fellow Republicans by his style and temperament. As one experienced Congress-watcher noted, "Republican senators have long griped about his [McCain's] low tolerance for alternative viewpoints, his 'my-way-or-the-highway' approach to making legislation."[60] If being a "maverick" is not a disabling quality in a senator, it is a considerably more problematic trait in a president, who must generally serve as both the leader of his party and one of the chief assemblers of legislative coalitions. As a result, where George W. Bush always received strong support from other Republican governors, GOP senators were notably less enthusiastic about McCain. Even in February 2000, at the height of his campaign, McCain was endorsed by only four of the fifty-four Republican senators; thirty-seven supported Bush.

The wild card in the Republican race was Steve Forbes. By most measures, Forbes looked to be well out of the running. In New Hampshire, where he had been campaigning nonstop for almost four years, Forbes was a distant third. He was second in Iowa, but only because McCain had decided not to contest that state. In the country as a whole, only 6 percent of Republicans wanted him to be their party's presidential candidate. Add in his wooden speaking style, his unimpressive performances in televised debates, and the fact that he had never held elective office before, and it was difficult to argue that Forbes had a realistic shot at winning the nomination.

Yet, most commentators were never quite willing to write him off entirely.[61] Forbes was the one candidate who might be able to compete with Bush in the money wars. As in 1996, he financed his presidential candidacy almost entirely out of his own deep pockets. By the end of 1999, Forbes had given his campaign $28.7 million; he had also raised $5.5 million from outside sources. Moreover, even if Forbes couldn't win, there was always the fear that he might have a major impact on the candidate who did. In the 1996 election cycle, he had launched a barrage of negative advertising directed principally at Bob Dole. Many Republicans believed that the Forbes ads had crippled the eventual nominee's chances in the general election, dramatically raising his negatives in a number of states and, even more important, forcing the Dole campaign to spend its own money so rapidly in the early primaries that it was left almost entirely without funds between April and July.[62] (Indeed, this was one of the major reasons that the Bush campaign had decided not to accept federal matching funds. By turning down the federal money, Bush was also released from the spending limits established in the campaign finance laws.)

In the end, however, the expected Forbes negative ad campaign never materialized. After receiving repeated warnings from Republican Party leaders, and after its own research apparently showed that voters were fed up with negative advertising and reacted very unfavorably to the candidate who used it, the 2000 Forbes campaign was considerably kinder and gentler than the 1996 edition. By early January, one major theme in media commentary on the Republican race was how civil and genteel (and boring) it was turning out to be.[63]

THE CAUCUS AND PRIMARY SEASON: THE DEMOCRATS

Among the many "What if's" of Bill Bradley's presidential campaign, one of the most tantalizing was his decision to devote so much time and money to the Iowa caucuses. The Hawkeye State had never looked like particularly fertile ground for Bradley's message. In November, when Bradley was running even with or slightly ahead of Gore in New Hampshire, he still trailed the vice president by 22 percentage points in Iowa.[64] And the fact that Iowa had caucuses, rather than a primary, would only seem to magnify the advantages Gore derived from his support among unions and top party officials. But the conventional wisdom going into the 2000 campaign held that *both* Iowa and New Hampshire were essential proving-grounds for the serious national candidate, and Bradley, unlike McCain, chose not to put this nostrum to the test. Instead, he spent $2.2 million and half of January campaigning in Iowa. To add one more obstacle to what was already an uphill struggle, on 20 January Bradley was compelled to admit that, over the past month, he had had four episodes of irregular heartbeat, an apparently nonlethal health problem that nevertheless obscured his message for several days and raised questions about how well he would hold up in a general election campaign. On 24 January, Gore won the Iowa caucuses by a decisive margin, 63 percent to 35 percent for Bradley.

The scene now shifted to New Hampshire. According to the polls, Bradley had been leading in New Hampshire through most of the fall, but by early or mid-January, Gore had narrowly reclaimed the lead. In the days immediately after Iowa, Gore's lead widened but then began to narrow again as Bradley finally became more aggressive in attacking and responding to the vice president. But it was too little too late: on 1 February Gore eked out a slender 4-percentage-point win (see table 2.4, p. 32).

Though it may not have been immediately apparent, the competitive phase of Bill Bradley's presidential campaign came to an end with his narrow loss in New Hampshire.[65] Already running 30 points behind Gore in the national polls, Bradley had had only one chance of success: to pull off an upset victory in Iowa and/or New Hampshire and then hope that momentum would propel him to a series of more substantial triumphs in early March. Though he had lost New

Table 2.4 Democratic Primary Results (in percentages)

Date	State	Gore	Bradley	Total Vote
1 February	New Hampshire	49.7	45.6	154,639
5 February	Delaware	57.2	40.2	11,141
29 February	Washington	68.2	31.4	297,001
7 March	California	81.2	18.2	2,654,114
7 March	Connecticut	55.4	41.5	177,301
7 March	Georgia	83.8	16.2	284,431
7 March	Maine	54.0	41.3	64,279
7 March	Maryland	67.3	28.5	507,462
7 March	Massachusetts	59.9	37.3	570,074
7 March	Missouri	64.6	33.6	265,489
7 March	New York	65.6	33.5	974,463
7 March	Ohio	73.6	24.7	978,512
7 March	Rhode Island	57.2	40.6	46,844
7 March	Vermont	54.3	43.9	49,283
10 March	Colorado	71.4	23.3	88,451
10 March	Utah	79.9	20.1	15,687
11 March	Arizona	77.9	18.9	86,762
14 March	Florida	81.8	18.2	551,995
14 March	Louisiana	73.0	19.9	157,551
14 March	Mississippi	89.6	8.6	88,602
14 March	Oklahoma	68.7	25.4	134,850
14 March	Tennessee	92.1	5.3	215,203
14 March	Texas	80.2	16.3	786,890
21 March	Illinois	84.3	14.2	809,648
4 April	Pennsylvania	74.6	20.8	704,150
4 April	Wisconsin	88.5	8.8	371,196
2 May	District of Columbia	95.9	—	19,417
2 May	Indiana	74.9	21.9	293,172
2 May	North Carolina	70.4	18.3	544,922
9 May	Nebraska	70.0	26.5	105,271
9 May	West Virginia	72.0	18.4	253,310
16 May	Oregon	84.9	—	354,594
23 May	Arkansas	78.6	—	230,197
23 May	Idaho	75.7	—	35,688
23 May	Kentucky	71.3	14.7	220,279
6 June	Alabama	77.0	—	278,527
6 June	Montana	77.9	—	87,867
6 June	New Jersey	94.9	—	378,272
6 June	New Mexico	74.6	20.6	132,280
	TOTAL	75.7	20.0	14,024,664

Source: Rhodes Cook Letter, July 2000, 18.

Hampshire by just 7,000 votes, Bradley's showing there was evaluated according to the expectations raised by the late fall polls, not by the expectations that had prevailed one year earlier.

And now the calendar became important. Without a single Democratic primary or caucus between 1 February and 7 March, Bradley had no other opportunity to demonstrate his viability on a small scale. Instead, he would need to wage an aggressive, come-from-behind campaign in New York and California and Ohio and eight other states. To make matters worse, most media outlets were now concentrating on the Republican race and the McCain phenomenon, while ignoring the struggling Bradley campaign. Bradley's last strategic gambit was, in effect, to create a contest where none existed. On 29 February, the state of Washington was holding a non-binding Democratic primary. Though both campaigns had previously ignored this event, Bradley now decided to spend five full days campaigning in Washington, hoping that a victory there, even if it yielded no delegates, would at least convince the nation's Democrats that the presidential nomination race was not over, and that the former New Jersey senator deserved another look. But even in Washington, Gore beat Bradley by almost 40 percent. The vice president then won every one of the eleven primaries held on 7 March, all by margins of 10 percent or greater. On 9 March Bradley bowed to the inevitable and withdrew from the race.

For all his early missteps, Gore did very well in the Democratic nomination race, winning every primary and caucus he contested, the first non-incumbent candidate to have an unblemished record since Richard Nixon in 1960.

Did Bill Bradley ever have a realistic shot at winning the Democratic presidential nomination? Particularly in retrospect, one is struck by the long odds that always confronted the former New Jersey senator. Had Bradley run a somewhat better campaign, he clearly could have won the New Hampshire primary, which almost certainly would have given him a better prospect of winning at least some of the early March primaries. But even in the early fall of 1999, when almost everything seemed to be going right for Bradley and everything seemed to be working against Al Gore, several important groups in the Democratic Party remained strikingly resistant to Bradley's appeal, including blacks, Hispanics, and southerners. The South, in particular, seemed to provide Gore with an almost impregnable firewall: on 7 March, when Gore averaged just 56 percent in five New England primaries, he won 84 percent of the vote in Georgia, the only southern state to vote that day.

Given the condition of the macroeconomy and the president's high approval ratings, it was always going to be difficult to defeat a candidate so thoroughly identified with the incumbent administration. If these factors worked to Gore's advantage in the general election, they should have helped him even more among Democratic primary voters, whose assessment of the economy and opinions about Bill Clinton were even more lopsidedly positive. While large segments of the Democratic electorate clearly had reservations about the Clinton presidency, Bradley was not, given his Senate record, the natural candidate to exploit these openings. Organized labor, for example, strongly disagreed with the general thrust of Clinton's trade policy — but Bradley was just as much a free trader as Gore and Clinton were.

THE PRIMARY AND CAUCUS SEASON: THE REPUBLICANS

From the moment McCain announced that he would not be competing in the Iowa caucuses, first place in that event had been conceded to Bush, second place to Forbes. The only remaining question was, How close would it be? Though the January polls generally showed Bush with a lead of 25–30 percent, the final result was considerably closer: Bush, 41 percent; Forbes, 30 percent. It was the first sign — more were soon to come — that for all its easy successes during the so-called invisible primary, the Bush campaign would face a much more difficult struggle during the real primary and caucus season.

If the Bush campaign hoped that it would get a substantial "bounce" out of its Iowa victory, or that McCain would find his campaign hamstrung by the decision not to compete there, these hopes were quickly dashed. According to the CNN/Gallup tracking polls, the Iowa results did have some measurable impact on the race in New Hampshire, but the effect was both small and temporary.[66] By late January McCain had reestablished the lead he had held before Iowa, and then considerably widened it in the final few days before the New Hampshire primary. McCain's efforts were almost certainly aided by a strange miscalculation on the part of the Bush campaign. In a state that prides itself on requiring the candidates to engage in a substantive, personal dialogue with the voters, the Bush team inexplicably decided to run a glitzy, vacuous, high-media campaign in the final week.[67] The result was a stunning win for McCain: 48 percent to Bush's 30 percent. For all the time and money he expended, Forbes limped in a poor third, at 13 percent (see table 2.5).

Suddenly, the Republican presidential nomination race was turned upside down. As *Time* declared, "No one was prepared for what happened to American politics last week. A man almost no Republican in Washington likes, John McCain, suddenly stood a chance to grab the party's nomination from the... Governor of Texas."[68] Perhaps the best way to capture the tide of momentum that now surged behind McCain's presidential candidacy is to observe its effect on the candidates' standing in the national polls. From mid-November through late January, Bush had led McCain by an average margin of 45 percentage points. In the first Gallup poll conducted after New Hampshire, Bush still led, but by only 22 points (see table 2.3, p. 21). More ominous still were the samplings from South Carolina, where the next major primary would take place: in November, Bush had led McCain there by 62 percent to 15 percent; three days after New Hampshire, it was McCain, 44; Bush, 40.[69]

One week after New Hampshire was the Delaware primary. Bush won it quite comfortably, with 51 percent of the vote, but Delaware was significant chiefly for what happened below the top spot. McCain, who had never set foot in the state, nevertheless came in second with 25 percent, while Forbes, who had devoted considerable time and effort to Delaware, finished third. Two days later, Forbes dropped out of the race.

Table 2.5 Republican Primary Results (in percentages)

Date	State	Bush	McCain	Total Vote
1 February	New Hampshire	30.4	48.5	238,206
8 February	Delaware	50.7	25.4	30,060
19 February	South Carolina	53.4	41.9	573,101
22 February	Arizona	35.7	60.0	322,669
22 February	Michigan	43.1	51.0	1,276,770
29 February	Virginia	52.8	43.9	664,093
29 February	Washington	57.8	38.9	491,148
7 March	California	60.6	34.7	2,847,921
7 March	Connecticut	46.3	48.7	178,985
7 March	Georgia	66.9	27.8	643,188
7 March	Maine	51.0	44.0	96,624
7 March	Maryland	56.2	36.2	376,034
7 March	Massachusetts	31.8	64.7	501,951
7 March	Missouri	57.9	35.3	475,363
7 March	New York	51.0	43.4	720,000
7 March	Ohio	58.0	37.0	1,397,528
7 March	Rhode Island	36.5	60.2	36,120
7 March	Vermont	35.3	60.3	81,355
10 March	Colorado	64.7	27.1	180,217
10 March	Utah	63.3	14.0	91,053
14 March	Florida	73.8	19.9	699,503
14 March	Louisiana	83.6	8.9	102,912
14 March	Mississippi	87.9	5.4	114,979
14 March	Oklahoma	79.1	10.4	124,809
14 March	Tennessee	77.0	14.5	250,791
14 March	Texas	87.5	7.1	1,126,757
21 March	Illinois	67.4	21.5	736,857
4 April	Pennsylvania	73.5	22.7	643,085
4 April	Wisconsin	69.2	18.1	495,769
2 May	District of Columbia	72.8	24.4	2,433
2 May	Indiana	81.2	18.8	406,664
2 May	North Carolina	78.6	10.9	322,517
9 May	Nebraska	78.2	15.1	185,758
9 May	West Virginia	79.6	12.9	109,404
16 May	Oregon	83.6	—	349,831
23 May	Arkansas	80.2	—	43,755
23 May	Idaho	73.5	—	158,446
23 May	Kentucky	83.0	6.3	91,323
6 June	Alabama	84.2	—	203,079
6 June	Montana	77.6	—	113,671
6 June	New Jersey	83.6	—	240,810
6 June	New Mexico	82.6	10.1	75,230
6 June	South Dakota	78.2	13.8	45,279
	TOTAL	63.2	29.8	17,146,048

Source: Rhodes Cook Letter, July 2000, 19.

All of which only heightened the sense that the single most important showdown between Bush and McCain would take place in the South Carolina primary. McCain, as we have seen, had targeted this state from the very beginning. To become a legitimate national contender, the Arizona senator had to show that New Hampshire was not an aberration, and South Carolina, with its large population of military veterans, seemed like a favorable venue for him. On the other side, the Bush campaign desperately needed a win to restore its hard-earned aura of inevitability; to aid him in that task, Bush had the support of almost every major leader in the South Carolina Republican Party.

The primary that followed was hard-fought and sometimes nasty. Stunned by the magnitude of its loss in New Hampshire, the Bush campaign abandoned its previous resolution to run a "positive campaign" and attacked McCain as a Washington insider who preached campaign reform but then raised money from lobbyists involved in business before his committee. McCain, having previously raised questions about whether Bush could both enact a large tax cut and protect Social Security, now criticized Bush for the tone and honesty of his campaign, including one controversial ad that accused Bush of "twist[ing] the truth like Clinton." McCain soon did an about-face, stopped running the ad that compared Bush to Clinton, and vowed to run a strictly positive campaign from then on; the Bush campaign, however, continued to pound away. Bush also received assistance from a number of independent-expenditure groups, which attacked McCain for his positions on taxes, abortion, and tobacco.

In the end, McCain learned what Gary Hart had learned in 1984 and Paul Tsongas found out in 1992: that with enough time and money — and a determined opposition — even the strongest tide of momentum can be stopped. On 19 February Bush won the South Carolina primary by 53 percent to 42 percent.

With its victory in South Carolina, the Bush campaign expected to sail smoothly through the rest of the primaries. But just three days later, the Republican race took another unanticipated twist. The Michigan primary had once been considered a safe bet for Bush, largely because it occurred on the home turf of Governor John Engler, one of Bush's earliest and most enthusiastic supporters. But in almost every other respect, the Michigan primary was ideally designed for John McCain. State law allowed Independents and Democrats to vote in the Republican primary; and since there was no Democratic primary to speak of that day,[70] any politically active resident of the Wolverine State had little reason not to get involved in the Republican race. Indeed, some of Engler's political opponents were actively encouraging Democrats to vote for McCain, as a way of embarrassing the Michigan governor. The result was a huge turnout of Democrats and Independents in the Republican primary — and a major victory for McCain. The Arizona primary was also held that day; and though polls had once shown Bush doing very well in McCain's home state, that was before New Hampshire. The final vote gave McCain a comfortable win.

McCain's triumphs in Michigan and Arizona gave the senator renewed momentum and a modest lead in the delegate tallies. But surface appearances notwithstanding, the 2000 nomination race was taking on a general shape that clearly did not bode well for McCain. In both South Carolina and Michigan, according to the Voter News Service exit polls, Bush had beaten McCain by better than 2 to 1 among those voters who considered themselves Republicans. McCain was managing to hold his own only because he was racking up similarly lopsided majorities among Independents and Democrats. Once the Democratic primaries resumed and primaries took place in states with more restrictive participation rules, however, the McCain bubble would collapse — unless the Arizona senator could quickly and dramatically increase his support among hard-core Republicans. His campaign clearly appreciated its predicament, and immediately began to tout its candidate's credentials as a "proud conservative Republican" and a devoted adherent of Ronald Reagan. But McCain himself may have undercut these efforts by delivering several highly publicized attacks on the "evil influence" of the Christian right within the Republican Party.[71]

As table 2.5 shows, McCain's victories in Michigan and Arizona were the last good moment for his campaign in the 2000 nomination race. A week later, Bush handily beat McCain in the Virginia and Washington primaries and trounced him in the North Dakota caucuses. On "Titanic Tuesday," 7 March, McCain won four of the eleven Republican primaries, but the number sounds more impressive than it was. McCain's victories occurred entirely in New England, and mostly in small states. Elsewhere, McCain came close only in Maine and New York, while losing California, Maryland, Missouri, Georgia, and Ohio by margins of 20 percent or greater. The most relevant summary statistic that night were the delegate totals, which read: Bush 433, McCain 113.

Running out of money, and knowing that 14 March was likely to be an even better night for Bush (six southern states were to vote that day, including Texas and Florida), McCain withdrew from the race on 9 March, the same day on which Bill Bradley exited the Democratic contest.

Like Bradley, McCain had always faced an uphill battle to win his party's presidential nomination. Indeed, in at least two important respects, McCain's challenge was even more daunting than Bradley's. First, where Bradley and Gore raised essentially equal amounts of money during the preprimary period, Bush had a huge financial advantage over McCain. Second, McCain had aroused substantially more opposition from other elected officials and power centers within his own party. That McCain went as far as he did is a striking tribute to his own personal strengths and the quality of the campaign he ran, especially in New Hampshire, as well as a series of significant mistakes committed by the Bush campaign. Like Al Gore, however, Bush enjoyed enormous early advantages that gave him plenty of room for error.

FROM MARCH TO AUGUST

There is no name yet for the kind of political season that took place between 10 March and 17 August. The presidential nominations had been settled, but not yet officially conferred. A number of primaries were still to be held, and many delegates were yet to be selected, but most of this activity was now fairly mechanical; the candidates and their top advisers had clearly turned their attention to the general election. The pace of the campaign during this period was plainly different from what it would become after Labor Day, in part because the campaigns understood that neither the voters nor the media were ready yet for an intense, full-throttle effort, in part because both campaigns were still compelled to live under the campaign finance regime that had governed the nomination race and thus did not have a lot of money available.

At the beginning of this interim period, the momentum of the 2000 race clearly seemed to favor Al Gore. After stumbling through the first nine months of 1999, the vice president had apparently managed to whip his campaign organization into shape, find his rhythm, and dispatch Bill Bradley with comparative ease. Bush, by contrast, had looked surprisingly weak in the early primaries and caucuses. The trial-heat polls showed the same trend: where Gore had been running well behind Bush throughout 1999, by mid-March he had pulled even with or slightly ahead of the Texas governor.

Yet, within a few weeks, the events and experiences of the past two months had apparently been ignored or forgotten, and the campaign took on a complexion very much like the one it had borne during the preelection year. On the one side, Bush began delivering a series of fairly specific and well-conceived policy speeches, which helped move him back to the political center and reassure those who wondered about his seriousness and command of the issues. Gore, meanwhile, spent most of his time reacting to Bush's agenda and fighting signs of dissension from within his own campaign. His most significant policy initiative of this period — his decision to break with the Clinton administration and support political asylum for Cuban refugee Elian Gonzalez — was roundly criticized as a blatant attempt to pander to the Cuban-American community in Florida.[72] By early April, Bush had reclaimed the lead in the national polls, a position he then held until the end of the Democratic National Convention. By late spring, news reports were regularly describing the Gore campaign with such terms as *flagging, flailing, ebbing,* and *wrongheaded.*[73]

The one task performed during the late spring and early summer that would most clearly seem to belong to the nomination phase of the campaign is the selection of a vice-presidential candidate. Although this was once a helter-skelter affair performed almost entirely in the twenty-four hours after the presidential candidate had formally been nominated, an actual selection process has gradually evolved over the past two decades.[74] Both candidates established vice-presidential search teams that were responsible for compiling initial lists of prospects, interviewing the major contenders and then carefully scrutinizing a mountain of information about each aspirant's political, financial, medical, and personal history.

As often happens, the person whom George W. Bush finally selected as his running-mate was never mentioned in the early press speculations about the position. Richard Cheney was, after all, the person Bush had tapped to direct the vice-presidential search. By convention, this implied that Cheney himself was not a possible candidate for the second spot. But as the search progressed, it became apparent that Bush and Cheney got along very well together. Bush pressed Cheney to add his own name to the list, and in early July, Cheney relented.

Besides having a good working relationship with the presidential candidate, Cheney was an attractive vice-presidential choice for a number of reasons. Though Cheney had never described himself as a "compassionate conservative," he and Bush actually had quite similar ideologies and operating styles. Both were conservatives but pragmatists, who had always prided themselves on maintaining cordial relations with the other party. Given the cloud that had always hovered over his father's vice-presidential choice, George W. Bush was also determined to select someone whose capacity to serve as president was not in doubt, and on this score, he could hardly have done better than Cheney. The Wyoming native had an extraordinary diversity of experience in Washington, as chief of staff to President Gerald Ford, ten years in the House of Representatives, and four years as former President George Bush's secretary of defense.

On the whole, the Cheney selection worked out well for the Bush campaign. Above all, it greatly bolstered Bush's own credentials as a person of substance and "gravitas"; there was also a wide consensus that Cheney performed very well in his debate with Joseph Lieberman. The major shortcoming of the Cheney selection, paradoxically, was that it was insufficiently vetted. Though Cheney had spent several months minutely examining the records of every other vice-presidential prospect, when he himself became a candidate, no one was ever assigned to perform the same task for him. As a result, the Bush campaign was noticeably unprepared to deal with the attacks that the Democrats launched against Cheney in the days immediately after he was selected.[75]

The Republican National Convention, held in Philadelphia from 31 July through 3 August, was a strangely apolitical affair. Anxious to bolster Bush's credentials as "a uniter not a divider," and still blaming their 1992 loss on a controversial convention speech given that year by Pat Buchanan, the Republicans spent four full days determinedly projecting the image of a tolerant and inclusive party. But everyone's party is no one's party: when the convention was over, it had certainly not antagonized anyone, but neither was it clear that it had offered a compelling statement about what the party stood for or what distinguished it from the Democrats.

Four days later, Al Gore announced his vice-presidential choice: U.S. Senator Joseph Lieberman of Connecticut. Like Cheney, Lieberman filled a number of specific needs for his running-mate. Devoutly religious, and one of the first Democrats to criticize Bill Clinton's affair with a White House intern, Lieberman helped Gore distance himself from the president's personal scandals and reclaim the values and integrity issue from the Republicans. In naming the first Jew ever nominated for a major-party presidential ticket, the Lieberman selection also won Gore plaudits for being *bold* and *exciting* — two adjectives not often applied to the vice president. Ideologically, the Connecticut senator was clearly to the right of Gore; at various points in his Senate career, he had voted for or made favorable comments about school vouchers, privatizing Social Security, and limiting corporate liability in civil damage suits. While this helped enhance Gore's credentials as a "new Democrat," it also gave the Republicans ammunition to answer many of the charges that Gore would level against them in the general election.

The Democratic convention, which took place in Los Angeles on 14–17 August, started out rather poorly for the Gore campaign. The first night was given over to the Clintons; the president gave a speech that did a wonderful job of extolling his own administration but mentioned Al Gore only in passing. The second night, or at least the televised portion of it, was largely a celebration of the Kennedy family. Both nights, according to the tracking polls, did nothing to help the Democrats' presidential ticket. Fortunately for the Democrats, the speeches given by Lieberman and Gore were considerably better received. Gore's speech, in particular, was an effective evocation of what has long been the Democrats' most potent appeal — economic populism — though to judge by subsequent media coverage, the most memorable aspect of the night was the prolonged kiss that Gore gave his wife before speaking.

A NOTE ON THE REFORM AND GREEN PARTIES

The Reform Party, as already noted, was the vehicle that Ross Perot created for his 1996 presidential candidacy. For the first several years of its existence, the new party was all but a wholly owned subsidiary of Perot, Inc. The Texas billionaire was the party's principal spokesman, the source of its money, the keeper of all its records. But this cozy arrangement was suddenly and dramatically overturned in November 1998, when another candidate running under the Reform Party banner, a former professional wrestler named Jesse Ventura, somehow managed to get elected governor of Minnesota. Now the party had a second power center — and this one could actually claim that he had won an election.

For the next year and a half, the "Dallas group" and the "Minnesota group" struggled for control of the Reform Party and its 2000 presidential nomination. In fall 1999 a number of people described as "close Perot advisers" decided to back Pat Buchanan as the party's next presidential standard-bearer.[76] Ventura, meanwhile, tried to encourage former Connecticut Governor Lowell Weicker and then celebrity and real estate developer Donald Trump to enter the race.

In mid-February, however, Ventura announced that he was resigning from the Reform Party. Trump officially ended his flirtation two days later.

With Buchanan now apparently having an uncontested path to the Reform Party nomination, many of the old Perot loyalists began to have second thoughts about the direction the party would take with Buchanan as its principal spokesman. Shortly before the party's national convention in August, these old-line members came up with an alternative candidate: John Hagelin, a physicist and advocate of transcendental meditation who had previously run for president as the candidate of the Natural Law Party. The battle between these two factions proved so divisive that two different conventions were eventually held, both of which claimed to be the successor to Perot's 1996 presidential candidacy and, thus, the proper recipient of $12.6 million in federal funds. (The Federal Election Commission later ruled in favor of Buchanan; see chapter 5.)

While the Reform Party's chaotic wrangling received prominent news coverage, remarkably little attention was being paid to another third-party venture that ultimately proved to be considerably more influential. Both Ralph Nader's announcement in February 2000 that he would be seeking the Green Party's presidential nomination and the final decision of the party's national convention to endorse him (on 25 June) were almost entirely ignored by the national media. Not until late summer did the press begin to notice that Nader was doing far better than Buchanan in the polls — and might pose serious problems for the Gore campaign.

CONCLUSION

How well did the presidential nomination process work in the 2000 election cycle? Perhaps the most natural way to answer this question is to judge the process by its product: the quality of the people who were finally nominated. Unfortunately, it is notoriously difficult to render objective judgments in this area, or even, at times, to say what counts as relevant evidence. In particular, there is an all-too-common tendency in this sort of analysis to belittle the present in comparison to the past: to argue that, where once we nominated "giants" for the presidency, today we always seem to select "midgets" for the position.

Legitimate questions can be raised about whether George W. Bush had sufficient experience and substance to make an effective president. Generally speaking, our society has demanded that its presidential candidates have a bit more than five or six years' experience in governmental office. But unlike Jimmy Carter, another recent presidential nominee whom many observers thought ill-prepared for the office, Bush received a remarkable level of early support from Republican Party leaders and elected officials, including his fellow governors. If some sort of "peer review" is a good way of assessing a presidential candidate's fitness for office, as many scholars have argued, Bush hardly fell short in this regard.

Bush's slight experience aside, both Bush and Gore proved to be reasonably plausible and effective candidates for the White House. When compared to his party as a whole, each man was clearly a centrist. Both were able to arouse some degree of support and enthusiasm from the more extreme segments of their parties, while also competing for the support of the more moderate, "swing" voters who usually decide the fate of general elections.

The most troubling questions about the 2000 nomination process, then, are not about the candidates it finally selected, but about the way it arrived at those decisions and about all the potential candidates who were excluded from consideration before the process really began. The major culprit here is front-loading, which had at least two important consequences for the 2000 race. First, it meant that both parties had, by the time of the Iowa caucuses, a surprisingly small number of serious candidates. In recent years, the general tendency has been that, unless a party has an incumbent running for reelection, a large number of candidates actively campaign for their party's presidential nomination. In 2000, however, only two candidates entered the Democratic race; the Republicans had twelve announced candidates, but six had dropped out by the end of October 1999. While a number of factors may have entered into these decisions, one of the most important was the perceived difficulty of raising $25 million and constructing a national campaign organization in the year before the election.

The second disturbing consequence of front-loading was that it brought a premature end to both races, compelling both Bradley and McCain to withdraw much earlier than they would have in a system that started up more slowly. Some leaders in both parties actually seem to have regarded this as a good thing: long nomination campaigns, according to this line of thinking, only stir up divisions within the party and deplete the winner's financial resources. But the 2000 nomination races suggest that there is another side to the story: both Bush and Gore were significantly better candidates in the general election because of the opposition they had had to face in the primaries. Gore made at least some efforts to hone his message, improve his style, and retool his organization, while Bush learned some useful lessons about the importance of preparation and the dangers of complacency. In both cases, however, this education was cut short, with the result that many of their mistakes would be repeated in the general election.

NOTES

The author would like to thank Alan Silverleib, Jill Zuckman, Tami Buhr, Andy Smith, Craig Tufty, Rhodes Cook, Bob Biersack, Tony Corrado, Jane Caplan, Gerald Pomper, and Amy Logan for their assistance with this chapter.

1. For a more detailed account of front-loading and other important trends in the presidential nomination process, see Michael G. Hagen and William G. Mayer, "The Modern Politics of Presidential Selection: How Changing the Rules Really Did Change the Game," in *In Pursuit of the White House 2000: How We Choose Our Presidential Nominees,* ed. William G. Mayer (New York: Chatham House, 2000).

2. The fullest account of the 1996 Republican task force, on which the following account draws, is Andrew E. Busch, "New Features of the 2000 Presidential Nominating Process: Republican Reforms, Front-Loading's Second Wind, and Early Voting," in Mayer, *In Pursuit of the White House 2000.*

3. Position in the calendar is defined here in terms of weeks in a month. Thus, the Massachusetts primary is classified as having the same position in both years because it was held in the first week in March, even though the actual date in 2000 (7 March) was two days later than the 1996 date (5 March).

4. See *New York Times,* 29 September 1998, A1. Since 1984, the Democratic Party's national rules have required states to hold all delegate selection activities between the first Tuesday in March and the second Tuesday in June, but specific exemptions have been granted to Iowa and New Hampshire.

5. The $20–25 million figure is cited by various candidates, consultants, and reporters in *Time,* 27 April 1998, 36; *Congressional Quarterly Weekly Report,* 23 January 1999, 197; and *New York Times,* 5 December 1998, A8; 12 January 1999, A17; 16 January 1999, A8; 19 January 1999, A12; and 22 January 1999, A17.

6. *New York Times,* 5 September 1998, A10 (emphasis added).

7. A few states held advisory Democratic primaries during this period; but since these primaries played no role in selecting delegates, they were, with one exception to be discussed later, almost completely ignored by both the candidates and the media.

8. For a fuller discussion of this point, see William G. Mayer, "A Brief History of Vice Presidential Selection," in Mayer, *In Pursuit of the White House 2000,* 341–45.

9. This argument is made with particular force in Arthur M. Schlesinger Jr., "On the Presidential Succession," *Political Science Quarterly* 89 (Fall 1974): 475–505.

10. At one point in the 2000 campaign, Gore was remarkably upfront about his priorities, openly telling reporters that, "Running for president of this country is far more important than being the best vice president I can possibly be." See *New York Times,* 13 November 1999, A11.

11. For a particularly good description of just how far the Clinton White House went in supporting Gore's candidacy, see Richard L. Berke, "The Gore Guide to the Future," *New York Times Magazine,* 22 February 1998, 30.

12. Though there is some evidence of increased friction between Gore and Clinton as the 2000 campaign progressed, it does not seem to have affected Clinton's fervent support for Gore's candidacy. See *New York Times,* 17 April 1999, A13; 26 May 1999, A28; 26 June 1999, A1; 11 August 1999, A14; 25 September 1999, A11; 12 October 1999, A28; and 27 January 2000, A1.

13. See *Gallup Poll Monthly,* No. 392, May 1998, 30.

14. For reports on early candidate activity within the Democratic Party, see *New York Times,* 9 April 1998, A20; 28 June 1998, I, 15; 12 July 1998, I, 22; 27 November 1998, A23; and 29 November 1998, I, 1. For declarations of noncandidacy, see table 2A at www.chathamhouse.com/pomper2000

15. On Gephardt's decision, see *Congressional Quarterly Weekly Report,* 23 January 1999, 197–98; and *New York Times,* 15 January 1999, A20, and 3 February 1999, A10.

16. See *New York Times,* 10 January 1999, I, 13; 24 March 1999, A24; and 25 March 1999, A26.

17. See table 2A at www.chathamhouse.com/pomper2000 For further coverage of these early withdrawal decisions, see *New York Times,* 14 December 1998, A20; 10 January 1999, I, 13; and 27 February 1999, A9.

18. See, in particular, *New York Times,* 15 December 1999, A1.

19. Excerpts from Bradley's retirement speech are reprinted in *New York Times,* 16 October 1999, A14.

20. See table 2B at www:chathamhouse.com/pomper2000

21. *New York Times,* 31 January 1999, 12.

22. On the nonstop campaigns of Alexander and Forbes, see *New York Times,* 15 August 1998, A7; 6 December 1998, A25; 31 January 1999, A12; 10 March 1999, A17; and 17 March 1999, A19.

23. *Time,* 15 March 1999, 42.

24. On this controversy, see *New York Times,* 14 June 1998, IV, 1; and the letter from T. Keating Holland in *New York Times,* 20 June 1998, A10.

25. *New York Times,* 29 May 1999, A1. For a similarly laudatory assessment, see *Time,* 16 November 1998, 60–62.

26. On the possibility of Gingrich running for president in 2000, see *Time,* 20 April 1998, 28–29; and *New York Times,* 14 January 1998, A14; 3 March 1998, A14; and 7 June 1998, IV, 4.

27. Bush's potential appeal to Hispanic voters particularly enhanced his standing among California Republicans, while diminishing the chances of former California Governor Pete Wilson. See *New York Times,* 16 January 1999, A8; 21 January 1999, A14; and 23 February 1999, A19.

28. For an extended demonstration of this point, see William G. Mayer, *The Divided Democrats: Ideological Unity, Party Reform, and Presidential Elections* (Boulder, Colo.: Westview, 1996).

29. See, for example, *New York Times,* 21 June 1999, A1; 2 October 1999, A1; and 7 November 1999, I, 1.

30. On the extent to which Bradley served as his own campaign manager, see *New York Times,* 21 November 1999, I, 30; and 16 January 2000, I, 22; and *Time,* 31 January 2000, 32.

31. As quoted in *New York Times,* 9 September 1999, A22.

32. See, for example, *New York Times,* 11 April 1999, I, 26; and 9 September 1999, A22.

33. For some early indications of this, see *Time,* 5 April 1999, 42–43, and 24 May 1999, 47; and *New York Times,* 11 May 1999, A20, and 14 May 1999, A1.

34. *New York Times,* 14 May 1999, A1.

35. *New York Times,* 28 December 1999, A1.

36. See, for example, *New York Times,* 24 April 1999, A20; 24 September 1999, A22; 16 November 1999, A22; and 19 December 1999, I, 53.

37. *New York Times,* 21 September 1999, A22; 28 December 1999, A22; and 20 January 2000, A1.

38. See, for example, *New York Times,* 11 October 1999, A12; 27 October 1999, A22; 8 November 1999, A25; 2 December 1999, A1; and 16 January 2000, I, 22.

39. For a sampling of Gore's attacks, see *Time,* 1 November 1999, 42–45, and 20 December 1999, 60–63; and *New York Times,* 11 October 1999, A1; 16 October 1999, A14; 29 October 1999, A29; 14 November 1999, I, 28; 3 December 1999, A29; 10 December 1999, A32; 20 December 1999, A1; and 21 December 1999, A26.

40. For coverage of Bradley's health care proposal and the controversy that ultimately developed around it, see *New York Times,* 29 September 1999, A1; 29 October 1999, A29; 8 November 1999, A18; 9 November 1999, A23; 11 November 1999, A27; 14 November 1999, I, 28; and 3 December 1999, A29.

41. See *New York Times,* 11 October 1999, A12; and 17 October 1999, I, 26.

42. For a historical comparison of the fund-raising and polling success of the Bush campaign with that of other early front-runners in contested presidential nomination races, see table 2C at www:chathamhouse.com/pomper2000

43. $36.3 million was the figure that the Bush campaign announced in early July and that was most often cited in subsequent press coverage. In fact, this turned out to be a slight underestimate: in its mid-year report to the Federal Election Commission, the total was listed as $37 million.

44. The candidate referred to is John McCain, who raised $6.3 million during the first half of 1999 — but this figure includes $2 million that McCain transferred from his Senate campaign. McCain raised only $4.3 million in new contributions.

45. On the importance that various Republican campaigns attached to the Iowa straw poll, see *New York Times,* 25 June 1999, A21; 11 July 1999, I, 14; 29 July 1999, A16; 10 August 1999, A1; 13 August 1999, A1; and 14 August 1999, A1.

46. See, for example, *New York Times,* 16 August 1999, A15.

47. For accounts of the drug controversy and its aftermath, see *Time,* 30 August 1999, 32–34; and *New York Times,* 19 August 1999, A14; 20 August 1999, A14; 21 August 1999, A8; 22 August 1999, I, 28, and IV, 13; 26 August 1999, A12; and 28 August 1999, A13.

48. Since 1980, five candidates have formally announced that they were running for president and then suspended their campaigns before the delegate selection season began: in the 1988

Democratic race, Gary Hart (who later reentered the race) and Joseph Biden; in the 1992 Democratic race, Douglas Wilder; in the 1996 Republican race, Pete Wilson and Arlen Specter.

49. Mel Sembler, as quoted in *New York Times*, 10 June 1999, A24.

50. As quoted in *Time*, 12 July 1999, 28.

51. On Alexander's near miss in 1996, see William G. Mayer, "The Presidential Nominations," in Gerald M. Pomper et al., *The Election of 1996: Reports and Interpretations* (Chatham, N.J.: Chatham House, 1997), 56–57.

52. On the denouement of the Quayle campaign, see *New York Times*, 17 August 1999, A14; 27 September 1999, A16; and 28 September 1999, A22.

53. See *New York Times*, 10 August 1999, A1.

54. On the problems of the Dole campaign, see *New York Times*, 11 March 1999, A1; 10 August 1999, A1; 7 October 1999, A28; and 21 October 1999, A22.

55. See, for example, *New York Times*, 22 July 1999, A16.

56. So far as I can determine, Buchanan's interest in the Reform Party nomination was first mentioned in the *New York Times* on 10 August 1999, at A14.

57. For discussions of the McCain strategy, see *New York Times*, 15 August 1999, I, 24; 28 September 1999, A22; 17 October 1999, I, 26; and 17 November 1999, A22.

58. This description of McCain's town meetings is based partly on contemporary news coverage, but also on several of these meetings attended by the author in December 1999 and January 2000.

59. See, for example, *New York Times*, 21 September 1999, A22; 26 September 1999, I, 34; and 16 January 2000, I, 1.

60. Charles E. Cook Jr., "Bush's Secret Weapon: Congress," *New York Times*, 24 February 2000, A27.

61. A good example is the *New York Times*, which profiled five presidential candidates in the final days of 1999: Gore, Bradley, Bush, McCain — and Forbes.

62. For a good account of how Forbes's spending spree depleted the resources available to the Dole campaign, see Anthony Corrado, "Financing the 1996 Election," in Pomper et al., *Election of 1996*, 143–45.

63. See, for example, *New York Times*, 20 November 1999, A8; 6 December 1999, A1; and 1 January 2000, A28.

64. See table 2D at www:chathamhouse.com/pomper2000

65. Among those who misread the situation was R.W. Apple Jr., "A Beginning, Not an End," *New York Times*, 2 February 2000, A1.

66. See table 2F at www:chathamhouse.com/pomper2000

67. For an account of one particularly vacuous Bush rally witnessed by the author, see William G. Mayer, "Turning a Candidate Into a Lightweight," *New York Times*, 4 February 2000, A29.

68. *Time*, 14 February 2000, 28.

69. Both polls are reported in *Time*, 14 February 2000, 36.

70. Actually, there was a Democratic presidential primary on 22 February, but not only was it nonbinding, neither Gore nor Bradley was even listed on the ballot.

71. See, in particular, *New York Times*, 29 February 2000, A1; and 1 March 2000, A18.

72. In light of the importance that Florida would eventually play in the 2000 vote, one wonders if, in retrospect, Gore's decision was politically shrewder than it was thought to be at the time.

73. See, for example, *Time*, 15 May 2000, 42; 5 June 2000, 44; and 26 June 2000, 29.

74. On the recent evolution of vice presidential selection, see Mayer, "Brief History of Vice Presidential Selection," 352–63.

75. The same point is made in *Time*, 7 August 2000, 28–29.

76. See *New York Times*, 24 September 1999, A1.

CHAPTER 3

The Campaign and the Media

Marjorie Randon Hershey

> Hamlet: *Do you see yonder cloud that's almost in shape of a camel?*
> Polonius: *By the mass, and 't is like a camel, indeed.*
> Hamlet: *Methinks it is like a weasel.*
> Polonius: *It is backed like a weasel.*
> Hamlet: *Or like a whale?*
> Polonius: *Very like a whale.*
>
> — Hamlet (III, 2)

THE TALL, SANDY-HAIRED MAN on the television screen looked befuddled. That was fitting, because he was a member of a highly prized species in media coverage of the 2000 presidential race: the Undecided Voter. "If I were choosing a friend," he said, "I'd choose Bush. If I were choosing somebody to administer the federal government, I'd choose Gore." The CNN interviewer smiled. But nobody pursued the point: in voting for president, did this Undecided Voter — and millions of others who went to the polls — really think he was choosing a friend, or the man who would head the powerful federal executive branch for the next four years?

Many voters feel they have good reason to search the media coverage for information about candidates' personalities. A candidate with a lot of personal charm, who can win the trust and respect of peers and reporters, may have an advantage in bridging party and issue divisions in Washington. The issues faced by governments can change, and probably will. All presidents deal with crises and decisions they did not anticipate. When that happens, presidents are not bound by their preelection promises, their parties' platforms, or the commitments of their co-partisans in Congress. Their personal qualities, however — intelligence, likeability and persistence — are more enduring and can be valuable in managing the extraordinary demands of the presidency.[1]

Alternatively, some voters may try to get a measure of the candidates' personalities because they don't know or care enough about politics to be able to draw on any other criteria in selecting a president. Or voters may pay attention to the candidates' personal qualities — or to policy issues or strategic moves — because that is what they see in media coverage of the campaign. For most of us, the combination of media coverage and media advertising *is* the campaign; few voters see the candidates in person or involve themselves directly in campaign events. What the broadcast and print media choose to cover and what candidates decide to emphasize in their media ads can make a real difference in our views of the candidates.

How the Media "Frame" Campaign Coverage

In their coverage of presidential elections, journalists can report any of a multitude of bits of information: the issues candidates discuss, their charges and countercharges, their styles of presentation, their strategic choices about where to campaign at particular times, their experience in politics, their personal backgrounds, their families, the activities of their political parties. But there is not enough space to report on *all* these pieces of the campaign picture, and media people know that they are in a competitive business, so they must report stories that people want to see and read if they are to keep selling air time to advertisers and newspapers to readers.

Naturally, then, media coverage tends to limit its focus to a few of the many possible stories — those most likely to interest its audience. Further, many students of media suggest, journalists don't just throw facts at us but rather present information in a sort of *media frame* — a story line or central organizing idea that calls attention to some aspects of the story, connects events to one another, and thereby helps us understand what they mean. A media frame offers an answer to the question: What is most significant about this story? Consider a candidate who announces a new proposal to regulate abortions. If the media report stopped at that statement, it would be a very short story indeed. Normally the reporter will go on to frame the story in a way that helps readers make sense of it: has the candidate offered this new proposal because abortion is at the top of her legislative agenda, or because she feels her opponent is getting too much of the pro-life vote — or because her religious beliefs lead her to reject abortion, or she needs a dramatic event to stop her slide in the polls, or she wants to demonstrate that she is an independent thinker and will not be swayed by party pressures?[2]

The way a campaign story is framed can affect the dynamics of the campaign. Any reader or viewer holds many different opinions about politics at any given time, including some conflicting opinions. The frame a reporter assigns to a story can pull one of those opinions to the forefront of the individual's thinking.[3] When a fact or an interpretation is more accessible to us — when it comes to mind easily because it has been featured in media coverage — we are more likely to draw on it in interpreting a campaign, just as researchers have found that when a particular issue gets greater emphasis on television news, viewers attribute greater importance to it, at least in the short run.[4]

Because media frames can be influential, candidates and other political actors work hard to affect the interpretation reporters give to particular events. The frame, then, can be seen as "the imprint of power" in a high-stakes game; it represents the outcome of a competition over how any given event is defined in the media.[5] As two media observers put it, candidates and other political actors "wage a war of frames because they know that if *their* frame becomes the dominant way of thinking about a particular problem, then the battle for public opinion has been won."[6] In the same way, candidates' paid media ads are their effort to frame the campaign so as to convince voters to support them and not their opponents.

Framing is not all-powerful, of course. Viewers may draw meaning from a news story or a TV ad that is completely unrelated to the way it is framed. Someone watching the candidate's speech on abortion could, for instance, ignore her words and those of the reporter, note the candidate's clothing and tone of voice instead, and draw the conclusion that she is too "shrill" to deserve the viewer's vote.[7] A study by the Pew Research Center for the People and the Press, released just before the 2000 Republican convention, argued that the content of media coverage during the presidential primaries was not closely mirrored in public opinion polls.[8] Pew Center director Andrew Kohut concluded, "Clearly, a lot of what we regard as spin for one candidate or the other is just lost on the public."[9]

There is evidence, however, that media framing can often make a difference in campaigns and in debate on public policies as well.[10] When a particular frame becomes The Story of a campaign, it can "turn into a self-reinforcing plot that shapes public perceptions of the race."[11] Readers and viewers can interpret new information in relation to this "plot" (meaning a story line, not a conspiracy) or frame. In this way, it is accurate to say that media people are not just the chroniclers of a campaign but participants in the way it unfolds.

The frames that dominate presidential campaign coverage have changed over time. In 1968, researchers found, press coverage of the election emphasized the candidates' personal attributes, such as their ability to inspire confidence, their compassion, and their integrity.[12] Citizens, when questioned by pollsters, mentioned the candidates' personal qualities even more.[13] It may be, one political psychologist suggested, that as social groups were becoming less powerful in determining individuals' preferences, more people looked for personal qualities as bases for choosing leaders, to "seek in leaders the same qualities they seek in friends."[14]

Since the mid-1970s, however, media coverage of campaigns has been dominated by the "game frame" — a focus on candidates' strategic moves, their travels, and their standings in the polls (the so-called horse race). Policy issues typically get less attention from the media and from poll respondents as well.[15] Campaign events, including candidates' statements about issues, are often framed as strategic choices intended to win votes rather than as the candidates' real policy preferences.[16] In an online story about the Gore presidential campaign, for example, a *Washington Post* reporter led with Gore's announcement that he would agree to a set of presidential debates. But the lead was not, "Vice President Gore's campaign chairman today formally endorsed the Commission on Presidential Debates plan for a series of prime-time televised forums this fall." Instead it began, "*Seeking to put pressure on George W. Bush,* Vice President Gore's campaign chairman today...."[17] Campaign coverage in recent years has tended to highlight anything that could be seen as an attack (and therefore overstates this aspect of campaigning), to put pressure on the candidate who is behind in the polls, and, in short, to pay greater attention to candidates as manipulators and to their personality and style than to their political experience, records in office, and positions on issues.

Some reporters insisted that things were different in 2000. *Washington Post* writer Howard Kurtz acknowledged that in each presidential campaign, "critics come out of the woodwork to complain that the media are spending too much time panting after the presidential horse race and ignoring — yes — The Issues." He claimed that the major networks were trying to change their approach in 2000, and running a "striking number of stories on issues, rather than personalities, polls, and prognostication," even though news directors considered issue coverage to be a "hard sell," because there was so little public interest in the race.[18]

Other observers thought the 2000 race was business as usual. Poll findings were splashed all over television, newspapers, and the Internet. Personalities were analyzed in minute detail; as *Newsweek* writers framed the contest, "The race seems, at first glance, like the world's largest student-body election, a low-stakes affair pitting the gregarious chairman of the Inter-Fraternity Council against the earnest president of the Science Club."[19] At least in the view of many commentators, voters, too, were fixed on the candidates' personalities as ways to decide who would be the best president. An Associated Press writer summed up reactions to the parties' conventions by noting that "many voters insist they want to focus on issues — but their comments quickly slide back to considerations of the personal," quoting viewers' opinions such as "It seems like Gore was more sincere. Bush gave a good speech, but it seemed more rehearsed — like they weren't his own words," and reporting that another felt "he doesn't like 'that half-grin' on Bush's face."[20] If this was so, media framing could help voters decide whether they thought of Al Gore as hard-working and smart or overbearing and pushy, and of George W. Bush as easygoing and self-assured or just cocky and a bit dim.

Given that media framing matters, let us take a closer look at the events of the 2000 presidential campaign and their coverage by the broadcast and print media and the Internet. How did the campaigns use the media to get out their messages? How did journalists frame these messages for the public? How effective was the result as a means for voters to learn about the people who wanted to govern them?

THE CAMPAIGNS OF SUMMER

From the primaries until the end of the Democratic convention, George W. Bush had the look, and the coverage, of a hands-down winner. Al Gore's campaign appeared to be fumbling and boring, and Bush led consistently in public opinion polls. That in itself was a puzzle. Voters tend to support incumbents in good economic times. And these were good economic times. The stock market was soaring, inflation remained low, and so did unemployment. Vice President Al Gore had served in the Clinton administration throughout the economic prosperity of the mid- to late 1990s.

Why, then, was Bush so confident that he could beat Gore? He had three good reasons to support his hopes. One was that vice presidents traditionally do not get much voter credit for an administration's successes. Second, reporters and pollsters had found ample evidence of "Clinton fatigue." Public opinion was ambivalent on the subject of President Bill Clinton. Majorities approved of Clinton's job performance and the strong economy but disapproved of his private behavior, and particularly of his long dalliance with a young White House intern, which he had publicly denied. If Gore ran as a vital part of the Clinton Team, he might be able to capitalize on public satisfaction with the economy. But he might also be hurt by an association with scandal and deceit — and although Gore was known as a devoted family man, he had been tainted with just enough scandal (a 1996 appearance at a Buddhist temple, at which Gore denied knowing that campaign funds were being raised) to link him to this media frame. Finally, Gore seemed to be known to the public, if at all, through a personal image that caught the worst of both worlds: as a stiff and pedantic bore who nonetheless exaggerated the truth to make himself attractive to voters.

Consistent with that image, Gore's campaign coverage throughout the summer was generally framed as the inept effort of an unlikeable man. The allegations that Gore had been involved in questionable fund-raising in 1996 were not going away. The Pew study reported that during the primaries, a full 76 percent of Gore's coverage focused on the themes that he is tainted by scandal and that he lies and exaggerates. The most common frame in Bush's coverage was a much more promising one: that he is a "different kind of Republican."[21] As E.J. Dionne wrote in the *Washington Post* on 30 May,

> The "Al Gore Is in a Huge Mess" story line is at least a month-and-a-half old. It's reaching its crescendo right about now as Democrats go public with criticisms of Gore's campaign, his failure to engage voters and his ceding public attention to George W. Bush.... To hear critiques of Gore these days, you don't have to talk to a single Republican. You hear his Democratic friends mourn the lack of uplift in Gore's speeches, his tendency toward micromanaging....[22]

Gore's response to his weak standing in the polls was to change his campaign message several times, which did little more than reinforce the theme that the vice president was not a man of principle and was a lousy campaigner to boot.

It was not perfectly smooth sailing for the Bush campaign during the summer months either. Bush had been pushed farther toward the right wing of his party than he had hoped, due to the primary challenge from Senator John McCain. His campaign tried to counter that image by stressing the first half of his slogan — "*compassionate* conservative" — and by focusing on issues in keeping with that frame: education, health care, retirement security.

Neither Bush nor Gore had locked up the states that should have been his base: those in which his party was traditionally strong at the presidential level. Throughout the summer the Gore campaign spent millions of dollars on media in Democratic-leaning states such as Illinois and New Jersey and even in the candidate's home state of Tennessee. Bush, although not as hard-pressed as Gore, was also spending large sums in states such as Florida, which had recently (although not in 1996) been safe Republican territory, and of which his brother Jeb was governor.[23] Like two aspiring alpha males, each challenging the other on his home turf, Gore went to Texas on the eve of the Republican convention to criticize Bush's budget management and the inadequacy of health care for Texas's poor, while at the end of the Democratic convention, Bush responded with a campaign swing to Tennessee, where he claimed he would win that state.

Convention Surprises

Gore, the underdog, needed to shake up the race — to change the media frames — as the two parties' conventions approached. So when Bush announced that he would nominate former Senator and Defense Secretary Dick Cheney for vice president, Gore's campaign jumped into action. The Gore team pointed to Cheney's very conservative record as senator from Wyoming and to his post-government years as chairman of an oil services company, Halliburton Co. A few weeks later, news broke that Cheney would receive an extremely generous retirement package from Halliburton, including stock options whose value would depend on the maintenance of high energy prices — an awkward situation for a vice president elected to serve a nation of energy consumers. Bush himself had spent several years as an oilman; Democrats cracked that the Republican idea of diversity was that these two middle-aged white men worked for *different* oil companies.

This effort to change the media focus, however, did not seem to derail the front-runner. Bush came out of the Republican convention flying high. The well-choreographed show was meant to demonstrate the inclusiveness of the party by featuring groups generally thought to be Democratic in their leanings. There were speeches by African Americans (including General Colin Powell), Hispanics, and even a gay member of Congress. Long-standing intraparty battles between right-wingers and relative moderates were downplayed in favor of a vision of the

Republican Party as centrist and diverse. "After eight years on the outside," wrote Richard Berke of the *New York Times,* "even Republican delegates who were not pleased with the inclusive tone of their program were so desperate to return to power that it took little, if any, prodding to corral them behind Mr. Bush."[24] The tone of the convention reflected the style of its candidate: relentlessly upbeat and expansive in preempting signature Democratic issues such as Medicare and schools.

The Wired Convention

This was the first presidential convention — in fact, the first election — in which the Internet played a prominent role. A few candidates had made use of web sites as early as 1995,[25] but Internet usage became much more sophisticated very quickly. In the 2000 primaries, John McCain and Bill Bradley proved that it is possible to raise a lot of money fast and at surprisingly little cost on the Internet. McCain, for example, raised more than $1 million on his web site in about 24 hours after his win in the New Hampshire primary (see chapter 5). Soon after the primaries ended, the Bush campaign released an ad focusing entirely on the candidate's improved web site. The site contained live, interactive chats with campaign personnel, video clips of Bush, and three "channels" of video on issue positions and other topics. It also provided the means for visitors to register to vote, volunteer or donate to the campaign, visit a state campaign site, and download screen savers and "virtual" yard signs. CNN covered the unveiling of this new, upgraded web site as a headline news story and convened a focus group to compare the site with Al Gore's (even though it wasn't a slow news day).

The Gore site was just as elaborate, featuring news articles, video and audio outtakes from Gore speeches (and the various rock stars who "opened" for him), messages on a series of issues, links for contributing to the campaign, volunteering and registering to vote, and fliers to download and distribute in the community. There were pages designed especially for various groups ("Law Enforcement Officials, Native Americans, Nurses, . . ."), Gore T-shirts and other products for sale, and Internet tools for parents to screen their children's web-surfing. There were even quizzes for kids (such as a challenge to "find Daisy," one of the Gore family's dogs, whose picture was hidden in several places on the site).

By the time of the conventions, both campaigns had developed e-mail lists with which to maintain regular contact with local supporters. A typical "issue" of *Gore Mail* or *Bush News* contained links to web sites carrying the candidate's most recent proposals or attacking the opponent as well as bits of commentary. Later the Gore campaign set up an Instant Message program to connect supporters with one another, and by the end of the campaign the Republican National Committee had assembled almost half a million e-mail addresses in order to generate a virtual get-out-the-vote drive just before Election Day. Both parties hoped that the Internet — by offering these remarkably cost-effective ways to reach prospective voters — could make the difference if the race proved to be tight.

The campaigns were finding, however, that the Internet posed major challenges as well as opportunities. They had to be sure, for example, that their own web sites would come up on search engines when a viewer looked for them, rather than a web site with a similar name created by an opponent (such as [candidate's name]sucks.com) with very different content. The Democratic National Committee got the jump on the Bush campaign, for instance, by grabbing the domain name www.bush-cheney.net the day Bush announced his choice of Cheney as his running-mate and then using it to post material attacking Cheney's Senate voting record ("Bush-Cheney Is Dream Team for U.S. Oil Industry"), accompanied by a picture of an oil well gushing dollar signs.

Internet coverage filled a gap for viewers interested in the parties' conventions. The major television networks largely ignored the conventions in favor of their regular schedules of summer reruns. (The networks were proven right from a profit-making standpoint; NBC, which ran a *Third Watch* rerun one evening during the convention, got almost twice as many viewers as the other two traditional networks, which carried up to an hour of the proceedings.) In contrast, more than fifty-five Internet outlets ranging from tiny operations to media giants had a presence at the Republican convention. AOL's site, one of the larger Internet outlets, not only included live feed from the convention and the protesters outside but also let viewers click on background material about the speakers, the text of the Republican platform, and even a link in which they could participate in live polls, the results of which could be used to frame interview questions for analysts featured on the site. More than one site used a 360–degree camera from which the viewer could choose a camera angle day or night.

Despite all the hoopla, the Internet bells and whistles often fell short of their advance publicity. Most of the news sites did little original reporting; many simply re-posted wire service stories concentrating on the "game frame." One observer complained, "The promised 360–degree cameras often returned a prolonged 'loading' message or warnings about missing software. Web browsers occasionally crashed; some sites were busy. And one chat room degenerated briefly into a discussion about porn."[26] The audience on the web was only a small proportion of the numbers watching on television. Most home computers lacked the high-speed Internet connections needed to take advantage of the most sophisticated broadband video feeds provided by such sites as AOL. The webcasts certainly hinted at the great potential of Internet convention coverage, but as of the 2000 conventions, as one PBS analyst wondered, "Why would somebody want to go on the Internet to watch bad TV?"

Internet and other media outlets looked forward to greater drama and conflict at the Democratic convention. The Democrats didn't have the luxury of making inclusive appeals; elements of the party were restive and Gore would not be able to appeal to the crucial Independents until all the Democratic ducks were in a row. The problem, journalists and activists agreed, was the candidate himself. For a nation used to the easy empathy projected by Bill Clinton, Al Gore seemed formal, unexciting, and a bit holier-than-thou. The challenge for Gore's advisers was "to create a compelling portrait of an often-awkward man who, in trying on various fashions in the political wardrobe, seems uncertain just what his public persona should be."[27] Even committed supporters were nervous. "It will be a difficult campaign," one Democratic convention delegate was quoted as saying. "Gore has one of those personalities you have to develop a relationship with."[28] Too few Democrats, it seemed, were committed to trying; the most common media frame was still that Gore's campaign was dead in the water and only an act of God could revive it.

Gore Revives

The first break in the "Al Gore Is in a Huge Mess" story line came when Gore made a historic choice for his running-mate by selecting Connecticut Senator Joseph Lieberman, who became the first Jewish candidate on a major-party ticket in U.S. history. While Dick Cheney started out as a lackluster campaigner with little enthusiasm for the task, Lieberman proved to be an engaging and warm speaker, frequently invoking images of faith and religious commitment (an appeal not normally found in Democratic campaigns). Lieberman was able to draw on his background as the grandchild of immigrants to celebrate the same sunny story as Bush did: "Only in America!"

The real test, however, would be Gore's acceptance speech at the Democratic convention. Earlier, reporters and commentators had set a fairly low standard of expectations for Bush's acceptance speech; if Bush could appear presidential, which often seemed to be defined as not smirking for the duration of the speech, he would be considered to have "met expectations." Gore, on the other hand, was warned in print and on television that to take the lead in the polls, he'd need to change nothing less than his personality: to become a warm, lively, relaxed and entertaining speaker. As one reporter wryly summed it up: "Al Gore, here's some advice from your fellow Democrats: Make it the speech of your lifetime. Get personal. Get specific. Give your campaign a lift. And, oh yes, shake free 'of all the second-guessing and criticism' and just be yourself."[29] Take lots of advice. But be yourself. Gore had a major task ahead of him.

That wasn't all (though it certainly would have been enough). Bush had already identified some winning campaign themes: a promise to avoid personal scandal and political partisanship, an appeal to centrists on traditionally Democratic issues, and his own upbeat personality. What would be Gore's themes? It was risky for him to run on his record; voters probably wouldn't give him credit for the strong economy anyway, and trying to get it would just remind voters of Gore's link with the scandal-dogged Clinton. So Gore decided to make a virtue out of his much-criticized wonkishness. I may not be an exciting politician, Gore said, but just listen to what I'll do for you on the issues. From Social Security to health care, from education to jobs, the candidate promised, "You ain't seen nothin' yet!" He identified himself as a coauthor of the national economic boom, but managed to avoid explicitly mentioning his eight years as vice president. He stressed that he was "his own man," and set his course with an intense, populist promise to represent "the people, not the powerful." It was a rhetorical feat that even President Clinton might have found difficult to pull off. (It *would* prove difficult later in the campaign, when *Slate* reporter Michael Kinsley parodied Gore's message this way: "You've never had it so good, and I'm mad as hell about it. Keep the team that brought you this situation, and I'll fight to take back power from the evil forces that have imposed it on you.")[30]

The immediate media assessment leaned negative: that Gore's acceptance speech hadn't demonstrated enough personality change. But the polling reaction politely disagreed; Gore got the "convention bounce" in the polls that presidential candidates hope to get. The speech increased people's perceptions of Gore as a leader, as having a policy agenda that made sense, and as having emerged from Clinton's shadow. Just as important, his favorability ratings, until then lagging well behind Bush's, now matched those of his rival. His enthusiastic embrace of his wife Tipper — a kiss clocked at three seconds, with considerably more gusto than is usually seen on a convention podium — helped to humanize him in viewers' minds (not to mention the fodder it provided for Jay Leno and David Letterman's monologues).

This was the high point of Gore's campaign. The unflattering media frames of the candidate as a near-certain loser and a dull and ineffective campaigner quickly faded. An analysis of media frames in the convention coverage demonstrates the shift, which took place in a mere two weeks.[31] In the wire service, "elite" press (*New York Times* and *Washington Post*), and broadcast coverage of the Republican convention, stories about Bush were most likely to be framed in "game" terms, emphasizing his standing as the front-runner in the "horse race" and his likelihood of winning in November (see figure 3.1, p. 56). Frames that centered on Bush's political experience and personal background, his personality, and leadership skills were less frequent.

In contrast, during the Democratic convention, issue frames were most common in the widely-disseminated wire service coverage of Gore (almost half of these referring to the economy). Further, the broadcast media and stories in the elite press framed fully one-fifth and one-fourth of their stories, respectively, with the theme of Gore establishing himself as "his own man." Coverage of the Democratic convention put much less emphasis on strategy and poll standings than had the coverage of Bush during the Republican convention. For the first time in the campaign, then, the frames that Gore was trying to get across to voters were actually dominating his coverage. Themes relating to Gore's personality and character,

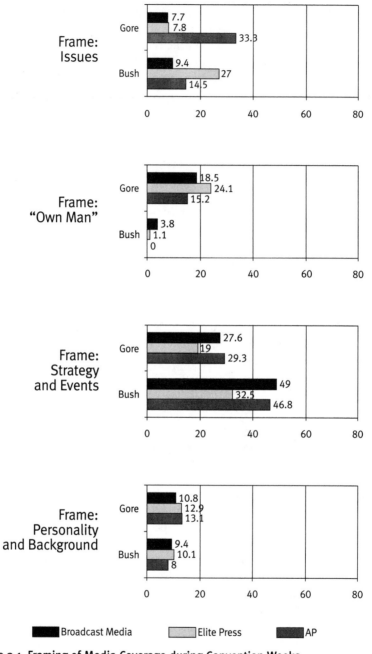

Figure 3.1 Framing of Media Coverage during Convention Weeks

Source: Compiled by the author.

which in Gore's case had generally been unflattering, were used to frame only 10 percent of the Associated Press stories and only 6 percent and 5 percent of the elite press and the broadcast reports.

The story line had clearly changed. And a good thing, too, for the reporters covering the candidates. A genuinely boring campaign, in which the leader remained ahead in the polls and the opponent continued to drag along in impressive ineptitude, was not very interesting to cover, not to mention its effect on political reporters' ability to get their stories on the front pages and into the headline news. Gore's convention bounce took effect in his media coverage as well as in public opinion, and the positive coverage continued in the days following his speech. The vice president seemed to draw energy from his and Lieberman's post-convention riverboat trip down the Mississippi River, finding enthusiastic crowds and seeming to relax and enjoy them.

Once Bush no longer had the momentum, problems that had dogged the Bush campaign from the beginning began to attract reporters' attention. Governor Bush had long been known as a speaker capable of mangling his words (as in his statement that "Republicans understand the importance of bondage between a mother and child"). His slips of the tongue, rarely reported when he was ahead in the polls, now became a more frequent frame for stories about his campaign. Most candidates trip over their words occasionally. Gore did. Spotting a community band while on his riverboat cruise, for example, the vice president asked whether they could play "On Wisconsin." Bystanders yelled back, "THIS IS IOWA!" Had the speaker been Bush, the incident might well have made headlines, but because it didn't fit the Gore frame, it got relatively little coverage.

Labor Day: Gore Rides the Wave

By Labor Day weekend, the Gore camp's confidence was growing day by day. He was solidifying the support of his party's base, so he could turn more of his attention to swing voters. "The optimism may be overstated. . . . But Gore's upswing is coming at one of the best possible times for a presidential candidate: at Labor Day, when important polls are taken, vacationing voters start tuning in and the psychological terrain of the race is marked. 'The wind is at our backs and it's filling our sails,' Gore said in an interview. . . . "[32]

Bush's campaign, in contrast, was having trouble with more than just the candidate's slips of the tongue. Gore put heavy stress in late August on his proposal to add partial prescription drug coverage to Medicare. It was an issue he expected to resonate well with middle-aged and older voters. Bush's campaign had not yet come up with the details of its own health care plan and found itself in the embarrassing position of having to say, in effect, "give us another few days" to figure one out. Further, Bush advertising specialists were complaining that their candidate was getting cranky about the demands of a full-fledged campaign; he wanted more time to relax and to be home with his family, whereas Gore was keeping to a schedule of seven or eight campaign events — and opportunities for media coverage — a day.

Bush was caught in other awkward incidents in these early weeks of the fall campaign. In one, he was overheard on a live microphone calling *New York Times* correspondent Adam Clymer a "major-league a------." Soon after, Gore staffers pointed reporters to information that an allegedly subliminal message had been included in a Bush television ad produced by the Republican National Committee (RNC). The ad, which claimed that Gore's plan for expanding Medicare would turn health care decisions over to bureaucrats, contained a split-second frame of the word *Rats,* described by the ad's creator as a "visual drumbeat." The Gore campaign decried what they called an effort at subliminal persuasion. Bush dug a deeper hole for himself by repeatedly agreeing that he was opposed to "subliminable" advertising; that fit easily into the new media frame of the Republican candidate as a dim bulb. Another ad for Bush, also by the RNC, tried to skewer Gore as a defender of Clinton's indiscretions, but the ad was pulled before it was aired, after the Gore campaign called attention to the fact that it used misleading excerpts from an interview taped six years before those scandals arose.

The Bush campaign struggled to break its fall. Greater effort was made to draw explicit contrasts between Bush's proposals and Gore's. There was a new campaign slogan: "Real Plans for Real People." A busier campaign schedule was developed for both Bush and Cheney, including local town meetings and other means of direct contact with voters and local media. Bush's staff, seeking to avoid the tough questions posed by the national press, discovered the advantages of talk shows. Bush appearances were scheduled on *Oprah, The Tonight Show,* and *Live with Regis,* which offered him access to huge audiences of undecided voters at no cost to the campaign. Gore countered with *Rosie O'Donnell* and his own appearance on *Oprah.* These were ideal settings for the candidates to demonstrate their most winning personal qualities and tell their most appealing personal stories. No major-league reporters were on hand to ask tough questions about the candidate's plans for the Strategic Petroleum Reserve; the grilling Bush and Gore faced from Oprah included requests to name their favorite cereal and their best gift.

It would be standard practice for a struggling campaign to put some negative messages in its advertising mix. That was risky for the Bush campaign. Its candidate had made a major point in his acceptance speech of presenting a different kind of political voice, one committed to conciliation and bipartisanship rather than personal attack. So most of the Bush advertising begun in the early fall was positive. The attack ads, however, could come from another source. Thus the Republican National Committee put $7.5 million into an ad showing footage of Al Gore at the fabled 1996 fundraiser at a Buddhist temple in California, asking whether the real Al Gore was the one who advocated campaign finance reform or the one who had "misstated" his 1996 fundraising.[33] Republican ads also made fun of Gore's claim to have, more or less, invented the Internet. (Gore responded a few weeks later in an appearance on *The David Letterman Show* by warning, tongue firmly in cheek, "Remember, America, I gave you the Internet, and I can take it away.")

On the other side, moving up in the polls helped the Gore camp to confirm an important strategic decision. From the beginning, his campaign had kept its distance from President Clinton. Clinton's role in the campaign, for the Gore strategists, was like that of a beloved but eccentric aunt with a taste for the cooking wine; the president could dominate any event he attended, and he fascinated journalists and viewers alike, but in doing so, he inevitably stole the spotlight from their candidate. The decision to keep Clinton at arm's length had costs. In addition to limiting Gore's ability to link himself to the economic prosperity of the Clinton years, it also kept the president from adding his personal appeal to the personality-challenged Gore effort. The president was an engaging campaigner and he clearly had a way with Republican opponents. As a columnist put it, "Clinton fairly specializes in driving Republicans to Rumpelstiltskinian fits of self-destructive rage. The greatest political feats of his presidency — the government shutdown that effectively ended the Newt Gingrich revolution, Clinton's narrow escape from impeachment — have involved leveraging Republicans' hatred of him in such a way that they are left, Wile E. Coyote to his Road Runner, with their exploded grenades clutched in their blackened fists."[34] But with the Gore campaign on the upswing, there was no reason to rethink this central decision.

DUELING FRAMES

Things that bounce tend to bounce again. From the preconvention period, when network television coverage seemed to portray Bush more favorably than Gore[35] to the month after the Democratic convention, when stories focused on the Gore campaign's strengths and improved fortunes, media frames had followed the same pattern as the public opinion polls. As the fall campaign geared up, however, the number of story lines expanded and both candidates' media coverage became much more negative than positive. Media analysts seemed to be developing serious cases of buyer's remorse — a familiar pattern in presidential campaigns in which reporters appear to be asking, "Out of 280 million Americans, how did we get stuck with a choice between these two guys?" A *Washington Post* writer offered these descriptions of three of the candidates: "As a campaigner, Al Gore periodically plugs in and amps up, in the manner of a man self-administering a defibrillator. George W. Bush shouts and drawls a lot, but his conceit is that he'd rather be jogging. Dick Cheney is the corporate possum dragged blinking into the harsh sunshine of the presidential trail."[36]

Reporters picked up on Republican charges that Gore and Lieberman were hypocritical in trying to raise big money from the entertainment industry while at the same time criticizing the violence portrayed in movies and TV. Then a Gore misstatement made headlines when the candidate said he paid much less for arthritis medication for his dog than his mother-in-law paid for the same medicine. The tale turned out to be largely true, but the numbers Gore cited were drawn from a congressional study rather than from his family's checkbook. For most candidates, this would probably not have been judged banner-headline news, but because it fit into the frame of Gore as a politician who stretches the truth, it became a big story as well as a focus of Bush campaign advertising.

The variety of media frames was accompanied by a big increase in media advertising. In addition to the campaigns and the national parties, "issue ads" produced by dozens of independent groups, many with obscure names designed to hide their origins, flooded the airwaves. The campaigns themselves concentrated their fire on fifteen to seventeen so-called battleground states — big states near the Mississippi and in the Rust Belt — in which they believed the election would be decided. Voters in the other states were exposed to very little advertising from either campaign.

Debates: The Sighs of Gore's Difficulty

The race was extremely close, according to published polls, by the time of the first presidential debate in early October. That made the debates seem likely to be even more vitally important than usual. The television audience would be larger than that for the parties' conventions, and the election was only five weeks away. Yet the challenges for the two candidates remained the same as they had been in the summer. Could Bush convince women voters that he was indeed a *compassionate* conservative rather than a hard-right clone, and did he have the brains and the maturity to fill the big chair in the Oval Office? (Ralph Nader, Green Party presidential candidate, referred to the major-party candidates as "Gore Tweedledum and Bush Tweedledumber.") Did Gore seem to lecture or talk down to the audience, and could he be trusted?

"It's nearly impossible to win a debate but it is possible to lose one," said political scientist Nelson Polsby. "Therefore, whoever is perceived going in as having the higher level of expectations is the one that's most at risk. I would say that's Gore."[37] As a result, both the Bush and Gore campaigns spent the last two weeks of September trying to raise expectations for their opponent's performance and to lower expectations for that of their own candidate. Bush's advisers called Gore no less than "a world-class debater" and referred to the dozens of times Gore had bested a debate opponent. Gore's team gathered some "ordinary people" at a "debate camp" to advise their candidate on how to act, in part to demonstrate that he was not overconfident.

The first debate was an intense, issue-oriented ninety minutes in which both candidates played to their strengths. Their different strategies practically jump off the page in table 3.1, which shows a content analysis of all three debates. Bush

Table 3.1 What the Candidates Emphasized in the Presidential Debates

	Debate 1		Debate 2		Debate 3	
	Bush	Gore	Bush	Gore	Bush	Gore
BUSH'S MAIN THEMES						
Fairly consistent themes:						
Bipartisanship, consensus, work with both Republicans and Democrats	19	1	12	1	12	4
Squabbling, finger-pointing, Washington politics	7	0	3	0	11	0
Introduced, then dropped:						
Fuzzy math, phony numbers	5	3	0	0	0	0
Different kind of leader, new approach	8	0	4	1	1	0
Gore exaggerates, credibility	2	0	12	1	2	0
Gore's trying to scare people	5	0	0	0	0	0
Mentioned increasingly:						
Accountable, responsible, consequence	11	6	8	3	18	2
Gore catches up:						
Strong military, strength, rebuild military	8	1	14	13	6	4
Government size, government making decisions for people	10	2	7	3	8	7
GORE'S MAIN THEMES						
Fairly consistent themes:						
Wealthiest 1 percent, rich, wealthy Americans	4	16	1	4	3	9
Family, strengthen family	8	15	0	0	3	12
Middle class	2	10	0	0	1	11
Introduced, then dropped:						
Prosperity	1	14	1	1	0	2
Important choice, right choice, wrong choice	0	9	4	1	0	1
Big oil companies	0	4	0	2	0	1
Mentioned increasingly, Bush catches up:						
Values	0	0	1	8	4	3
BOTH CANDIDATES' THEMES						
Gore dominates:						
Social Security, retirement security	22	30	2	1	5	9
Bush catches up:						
Education	5	11	7	8	9	4
Medicare, health care, prescription drugs, Patients' Bill of Rights	21	45	18	16	40	27
Cut taxes, tax relief	12	22	7	9	13	15

Source: Compiled by the author.

put his greatest emphasis on the themes of bipartisanship (contrasted with visions of Washington "squabbling" and "finger-pointing," both presumably linked with Gore), his promise to offer a different kind of leadership, opposition to big government, and, in terms of policy issues, the need for a strong military. Bush also gained from what he failed to do: he didn't smirk, get tangled up in his own syntax, or seem intimidated by his opponent's longer resume. Gore, in turn, was able to stress his best issues, using a hard-charging approach. He made bushels of references to the traditional Democratic concerns of Social Security, education, and health care and to the not-so-traditional Democratic issues of tax cuts and prosperity. Especially prominent in Gore's debate language were mentions of middle-class families, which Gore claimed to defend, and to the "wealthiest 1 percent" of the public, which, he charged, would get the bulk of Bush's proposed tax cuts.

The immediate post-debate polls showed a slight Gore advantage. That disappeared within the next few days, however. The Bush campaign had sent out e-mail alerts on the day of the debate, warning supporters to watch for and publicize any lies or exaggerations that Gore might make. It was a matter of trust, they said; if Gore was prone to embellish during the campaign, didn't that remind voters of you-know-who while in office? Gore obliged the Bush campaign by overstating two points. One was a story Gore repeated about a high school student in Florida who had had to stand up in a science class because of the lack of classroom space. The other was Gore's claim that he had visited Texas with Federal Emergency Management Agency director James Lee Witt after several serious fires.

In fact, the Florida story proved to be accurate, if over-stated, because the student in question had had to stand for only a day (though others remained without desks for weeks), and Gore's Texas trip had taken place, but with Witt's regional director rather than Witt himself. And ironically, Bush had told a bigger whopper in the first debate by claiming that the Gore campaign had outspent him in the race. But the media frame of Gore as a "serial exaggerator," as Bush advisers called him, was much more firmly established than that of Bush as a stretcher of the truth, so it was Gore's misstatements, not Bush's, that received front-page treatment. Gore was also ridiculed on *Saturday Night Live* and by a number of commentators for his eagerness to interrupt Bush and get the last word and for the exasperated sighs with which he responded to many of Bush's debate statements. In this way, too, Gore's performance fit the existing media frame of the vice president as a condescending know-it-all. Within a very few days, then, the Gore debate "victory" had been reinterpreted as a major defeat.

The format of the second debate was not expected to help Gore much, either. As the campaigns had previously agreed, this time the two candidates sat at a table with moderator Jim Lehrer in a more conversational setting. Gore, more at home in a formal debate, tried earnestly to break out of his "smartypants" frame. He toned down his normally aggressive speaking style. He treated Bush more respectfully, even agreeing with him several times on foreign policy and almost matching Bush's references to the need for a strong military (see table 3.1). Gore muted his emphasis on the "wealthiest 1 percent" and on the nation's prosperity, changing his approach markedly, in short, in response to the media criticism. Ironically, however, it was again Bush who seemed to benefit; by getting respectful treatment from the vice president of the United States in a discussion of world politics, the Texas governor appeared to gain stature. So media coverage again judged Gore the loser; he had come across in this debate not as less irritating but as less dominant and sure-footed.

In the third, town-meeting-style debate in mid-October, Gore returned to a forceful approach — and to his mentions of middle-class families' needs and to charges that Bush's policies would mainly help the wealthy. Bush continued to stress the need for bipartisan consensus, and he dropped his critical references to Gore's "exaggerations" and "credibility" in favor of the milder terms "accountability" and "responsibility" (both, however, still aimed at Gore). Despite a strong performance in this debate, Gore continued to slip a little in the polls.

The Ground War

The race remained too close to call as the election drew nearer. As many as a quarter of likely voters were telling pollsters that even now, after months of media attention to the race, they might still switch their vote by Election Day.[38] Neither Bush nor Gore, in the words of so many journalists, had "closed the deal" yet. Gore came out ahead in the polls on issues such as Social Security, health care, and the economy, but the debates had intensified many swing voters' doubts about his personality. Bush, who had the advantage in the polls on personality characteristics such as honesty and likeability, still faced questions about his inexperience and his intellect.[39]

In short, then, it would come down to the "ground war" — the one-on-one drive to get each candidate's supporters to the polls. Both the Bush and Gore campaigns put major effort into get-out-the-vote activities throughout the country. Labor unions, which would normally be spending most of their money on media ads at this point in a campaign, instead spent heavily on communications with their members to increase their turnout. The closeness of the race brought a wide range of independent groups into the ground war as well, and the results were not pretty. Charlton Heston, the head of the National Rifle Association, for example, was quoted ten days before the election as suggesting that a "lynching mob" was the best answer to Gore's gun control policy.

In the closing days of the campaign, however, it was Green Party candidate Ralph Nader who emerged as the chief obstacle to Gore's chances of overtaking Bush, thanks in large part to the Internet. In the summer, Gore's campaign had not worried much about the Nader challenge. Although it was assumed that Nader would draw 4 or 5 percent of the vote mainly from among people who otherwise would have supported Gore, the Reform Party candidacy of right-winger Pat Buchanan was expected to draw a similar share of the vote mainly from pro-Bush conservatives. But Buchanan's candidacy — and the Reform Party — collapsed in a bizarre heap even before the fall campaign started. That left the only spoiler on Gore's side of the fence. Arguing the controversial position that Gore was no better than Bush on environmental and consumer issues, Nader was attracting just enough votes in such traditionally Democratic states as Washington, Oregon, Minnesota and Wisconsin to deny Gore their electoral votes.

A week before Election Day, some worried Gore supporters devised an ingenious plan. Suppose that a Gore backer in an uncontested state — Massachusetts, for instance, whose electoral votes would go to Gore under any circumstances short of mass hypnotism — could offer to vote for Nader instead. The Nader vote would not hurt Gore in Massachusetts, and it would bring Nader closer to 5 percent in the popular vote, which determines whether a third party qualifies for federal funding in the next election. In return, suppose a Nader supporter in a battleground state agreed to vote for Gore, his or her second choice, to keep that state from tilting to Bush. More than a dozen Internet sites popped up within days to act as brokers for these "Nader traders." The sites generated a lot of media interest and a lot of "hits," though there is no way to know how many of these trades were actually carried out in the privacy of the voting booth. At least one such site closed down before the election after a warning from the California secretary of state that it was illegal in that state to broker any exchange of votes. The result was a reminder of the potency of the Internet; it would have been "virtually" impossible to conduct such an exchange through any other means.

Despite all the online excitement, however, a more homely device had greater impact at the end of the campaign: the telephone. Campaigns had long used volunteer phone calls to get out the vote. By 1998 congressional campaigns had begun to use automated calls rather than live volunteers, and this technique was further refined in 2000. With the help of polls that identified voters' concerns, a campaign could target a particular message to each individual voter, using a recorded message by someone with credibility on that issue for that voter. The Gore campaign, for example, delivered calls recorded by Whoopi Goldberg to black women in many areas, while messages on abortion recorded by Barbra Streisand were targeted to Florida voters. Robert Redford, Bill Cosby, and other well-known entertainers also lent their voices. Both parties are estimated to have placed 50 to 60 million such calls, mainly during the last week of the campaign. Actual numbers are hard to come by because these calls do not need to be reported to the Federal Election Commission; they generally take place "under the radar" — an ideal channel for making campaign claims that cannot be verified or rebutted.

And Then, the "November Surprise"

Just as the intensity of the conflict was reaching a peak, a small shock wave emanated from Maine. Five days before the election, a police officer in that state overheard an interesting conversation in the local courthouse and informed a reporter for the local newspaper. A lawyer and a judge, the officer said, were discussing an old case — a visitor to Maine in 1976 who was charged by a police officer with driving while under the influence of alcohol. The driver was George W. Bush, then staying at his family's home in Kennebunkport. The lawyer was a Democratic activist who had previously obtained court documents on the case and had tried to give the information to the Gore campaign, but he said he had not been able to make contact.

After verifying the Bush conviction, the reporter went national. A media feeding frenzy ensued. Bush quickly confirmed to reporters that the incident had occurred but advised voters to pay no attention to it; it had happened twenty-four years ago, he had learned his lesson, and the last-minute story could be seen only as a campaign dirty trick, he said. Whenever the candidate had been asked about past problems with alcohol, his communications director insisted, Bush had responded with a generic statement about having been wild and irresponsible in his youth, so although he had never admitted to drunk driving before, technically he had not lied either.

Gore staffers stayed as far from the story as they could, fearing that they would be blamed for having planted it. Instead, Gore closed his campaign by making fun of a Bush speech in which the Republican seemed to suggest that he didn't consider Social Security to be a federal program. By calling attention to this slip, the Gore campaign hoped to elicit the Bush-as-dim-bulb frame in journalists' stories and thus in voters' minds. For Gore, it was an ideal time to raise questions about Bush's readiness to serve as president. Despite Gore's avoidance of the story, however, news about the drunk-driving conviction caused frames relating to Bush's background and character to be raised more than twice as frequently in media coverage during the last five days of the campaign as they had been during the convention weeks (see figure 3.2, p. 66; compare with figure 3.1, p. 56).

The other main change in media coverage involved the "game frame." By the end of the campaign, more than half of each candidate's coverage in each medium — and about three-quarters of the coverage in the broadcast media — focused on strategy, most notably candidates' standings in the polls and chances of winning. Thus at the crucial time when voters who would compose the margin of victory were making up their minds about the candidates, the dominant media frame pointed them to this question: Who is most likely to win? These vital swing voters may have regarded information about candidates' personality and character to be especially valuable in choosing a president. Or they may have been looking for clues as to whether Bush or Gore would give them a bigger tax cut or more prescription drug coverage. What they got from media coverage, instead — and perhaps what they preferred to get — was a good story.

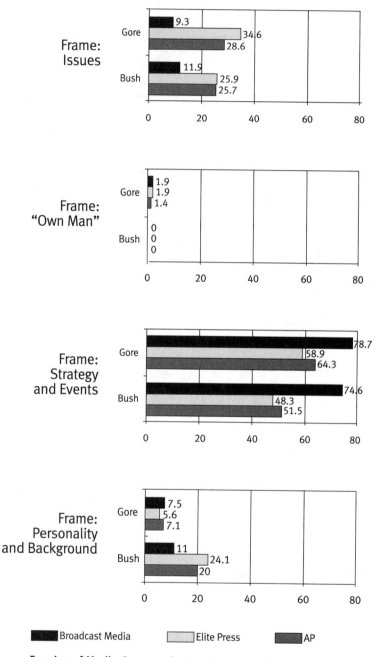

Figure 3.2 Framing of Media Coverage in Last Five Days of the Campaign

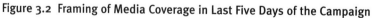

Source: Compiled by the author.

The Election Night That Wouldn't Die

As Election Day dawned, Bush's lead in the polls was so small that it fell within the statistical margin of error. The election was too close to call. Amazingly, that was still true after all the votes had been cast. The first editions of many newspapers carried the headline "Bush Wins!" after that media consensus was reached at about 2 A.M. on the day after the election. Some of those newspapers had to be snatched from delivery trucks an hour or two later and headlines such as "Cliffhanger" and "Bush Wins?" were hastily substituted. Large numbers of newspaper editors, including those from some of the nation's most august print institutions, were eating king-sized meals of crow by the break of dawn.

The voting, as chapter 6 describes, was quickly followed by the recounts. In the state of Florida, whose twenty-five electoral votes were the last to be decided (and would therefore determine the outcome of the 2000 presidential race), teams of lawyers promptly took the places of the campaign strategists, developed lines of argument, chose their venues, and marched on courtrooms from Tallahassee to Washington, D.C. Polls continued to chart the public's reactions to this novel experience: the postelection campaign. Perhaps inevitably, journalists were reminded of an overtime game, so the game frame continued to dominate the coverage of this month-long "election night."

Another media frame that transferred easily to the courtroom phase of the election was the personality and character frame. As *Newsweek* reported, "the candidates' transparent posturing and legal maneuvering reminded voters of just what they disliked about each one: Gore's merciless hunger, Bush's smirking arrogance."[40] As in the earlier election months, the candidate most negatively affected by this frame was Gore. He had won the popular vote but he was narrowly trailing Bush in the effort to win Florida's electoral votes. Unless a recount took place, Bush would win Florida and the presidency. Gore's only hope was to demand recounts in counties where he could claim his votes had been undercounted, due to either carelessness or fraud. That would require tenacious effort by an aggressive group of Gore attorneys. But aggressiveness, tenacity, and insistent argument were exactly the qualities that poll respondents liked least about Gore. Unless he won a quick and definitive court decision — an unlikely outcome — the actions that Gore would have to take to keep his hopes alive were exactly those that would weaken his standing in public opinion.

DOES MEDIA FRAMING MATTER?

Media coverage of this presidential campaign, then, was dominated by a short list of frames that had the potential to affect voters' choices. Once a frame has become well-established in the coverage, it can serve as a filter through which journalists assess and report later campaign events. Presidential campaigns work hard, planning events and leveling charges, to influence media coverage by eliciting the media frames that they consider helpful to their candidate at a particular time. Recall the example of the Bush campaign during the presidential debates: it e-mailed friendly viewers and asked them to watch for instances when Gore made exaggerated claims and to alert friends and reporters to these overstatements. The purpose was to remind journalists of the established frame of Gore as a "serial exaggerator," a candidate not trustworthy or appealing enough to be president, and thus to encourage use of that frame in media reports of the debate. Candidates have the same goal in their paid media advertising, where they hope to plant certain themes or frames in voters' minds that will attract them to the candidate (or repel them from the opponent), and then call forth those frames in later ads.

Some candidates are more effective than others at influencing their media coverage; that was true in the 2000 campaign. Throughout the primaries and the summer, Gore's coverage was dominated by two frames that did not make it easy for the vice president to nail down his Democratic base: a personality frame emphasizing his stiffness, ambition, and possible ethical lapses; and a strategic frame focusing on the inability of his campaign to organize effectively and catch fire with the public. It was not until the end of the Democratic convention in August that Gore's changed media frames no longer presented so much of a hurdle for his campaign to overcome.

Reporters do not have the freedom to "make up" these frames out of whole cloth, of course, to suit either their own political leanings or, more likely, their desire for a good story. The candidates and the campaigns provide the raw material that sets boundaries on media framing. The media were covering a Democratic candidate who would not have been mistaken for a happy-go-lucky talk-show host, any more than the Texas governor's academic record and public pronouncements could have been attributed to Albert Einstein. Both candidates and their campaigns, however, had hundreds of different attributes, and it is a simple function of limited time and space that when one set of attributes makes its way into the lead of a large proportion of news stories, other, different — and arguably, equally important — attributes do not.

The result is that these media frames screen what voters learn about their candidates for president. Bush was not the only presidential candidate who made verbal stumbles. If it had been Bush instead of Gore who temporarily mistook Iowa for Wisconsin on the postconvention riverboat tour, the embarrassing incident probably would have made headlines, because it would have fit into the media frame of Bush as dim bulb. In reality, it was Gore who made that mistake, but he paid a very small price for it in media publicity because the incident did not make sense in relation to the story line of Gore as a slippery, manipulative candidate. Similarly, Bush got a free pass on some self-serving exaggerations — as in the first debate when he claimed his campaign had been outspent by Gore's — because reporters were more accustomed to seeing and portraying him as the dim candidate than as the liar.

Framing, like any other heuristic or guide, has advantages that help to compensate for its limits. By providing a "lead" and a frame, journalists can tell us what is most important about an event when we have neither the time nor the inclination to find out everything about it. The true test of a guide is whether it takes us where we need to go. Did the framing of the 2000 presidential campaign give citizens the information they needed to cast a vote on whatever grounds they chose?

We can see in figure 3.2 (p. 66) that issue-based frames were available in the coverage, even more in the days immediately prior to the vote than during the convention weeks. True, learning about a candidate's stands on various issues may not provide voters with an accurate blueprint of the actions a president will take; many other forces also affect an elected official's priorities and decisions. But news dealing with candidates' positions on "The Issues" can at least offer citizens some helpful clues as to what to expect if they choose one candidate rather than another. In this campaign, citizens who wanted to vote on the basis of various issue preferences could have found the information to do so, as long as they were reading newspapers; they would have had a much harder time finding out about issues if they had relied on broadcast coverage of the race.

More common in the coverage, however, were the strategic or game frames, just as they have been in media coverage of politics during the past two decades. A large proportion of stories in this category referred simply to the candidates' standing in the polls and chances of winning the election; others reported events or strategic decisions (such as campaign advertising or fund-raising) designed to affect the election result. It is possible that in the primaries, when some voters might be trying to choose the strongest candidate for their party on the basis of the "horse race" results alone, this frame may have some limited use.[41] In the general election, however, how does information about a candidate's chance of winning help a voter decide who would do a better job as president? Strategic coverage may be useful to voters who want to associate themselves with winners, but it does little to ensure responsive government after the election is over.

Even more important is the timing involved. Strategic frames were much more dominant in the closing days of the campaign than they were during the convention weeks. It is certainly understandable that the last few days of a close race would be filled with speculation about the outcome. But such coverage carries a risk for a democracy. The final days were the time when undecided voters — those who often tend to have the most limited stock of information about politics and the candidates — were just tuning in to the race (literally, because they were likely to take more of their information from television than from newspapers).[42] So when undecided voters were at the point of making up their minds, most of the coverage they found in the media, and especially in the broadcast media, focused on little more than which candidate was more likely to win. In an election finally decided by a few hundred votes in Florida, this emphasis on strategy gave the late-deciders little meaningful information with which to pick a president for the rest of us.

Frames dealing with the candidates' personal qualities may be at least as useful to the voting public as any others, as long as they communicate information about a prospective president's management skills and other aspects of his or her experience and abilities. With the exception of the candidates' intelligence, however, these are not the kinds of references that appeared in the "personality and background" frames shown in figures 3.1 and 3.2. Instead, the references utilized terms such as *stiff, self-confident,* and *boring* — qualities more relevant for judging a prospective entertainer than a president.

By the time of the 2000 campaign, then, the idea that presidential candidates ought to be evaluated on the basis of their entertainment value had become well entrenched in media coverage as well as in public opinion. Coverage of a presidential election was more and more difficult to distinguish from the prime-time dramas and sports events on network television, except that the personal clashes and competitive action took place in an assortment of settings rather than in an emergency room or an athletic stadium. The frequent use of the personality and game frames certainly makes sense for the media because they attract a bigger audience, which produces bigger profits for publishers and broadcast media owners. It may even help stem the decline in voter turnout, presuming that viewers and readers find the candidate "cast" appealing and the conflict suspenseful enough.

Realistically, however, despite journalists' and campaigners' best efforts, "Presidential Election — The Miniseries" is not likely to be Emmy material. Instead, the emphasis on game and personality frames serves to construct a comforting illusion, just as entertainment programs usually do. In this case, the illusion is that an American presidential election in the twenty-first century — which has the potential to determine matters ranging from the composition of the Supreme Court to the state of our nuclear arsenal — *can be* about nothing more weighty than whether the gregarious chairman of the Inter-Fraternity Council will beat the earnest leader of the Science Club.

NOTES

1. See Doris A. Graber and David Weaver, "Presidential Performance Criteria: The Missing Element in Election Coverage," *Harvard International Journal of Press/Politics* 1 (Winter 1996): 7–32.

2. For discussions of media framing, see Robert M. Entman, "Framing: Toward Clarification of a Fractured Paradigm," *Journal of Communication* 43 (Autumn 1993): 51–58; William A. Gamson and Andre Modigliani, "Media Discourse and Public Opinion on Nuclear Power: A Constructionist Approach," *American Journal of Sociology* 95 (July 1989): 1–37; Amos Tversky and Daniel Kahneman, "The framing of decisions and the psychology of choice," *Science* 211 (30 January 1981): 453–58; Dennis Chong, "How People Think, Reason, and Feel about Rights and Liberties," *American Journal of Political Science* 37 (August 1993): 867–99; and, on the effects of framing, William G. Jacoby, "Issue Framing and Public Opinion on Government Spending," *American Journal of Political Science* 44 (October 2000): 750–67. A useful critique can be found in Paul Sniderman and Sean Theriault, "The Dynamics of Political Argument

and the Logic of Issue Framing," paper presented at the annual meeting of the American Political Science Association, Atlanta, September 1999.

3. See Stanley Feldman and John R. Zaller, "The Political Culture of Ambivalence: Ideological Responses to the Welfare State," *American Journal of Political Science* 36 (February 1992): 268–307; and Chong, "How People Think."

4. See Shanto Iyengar and Donald R. Kinder, *News That Matters* (Chicago: University of Chicago Press, 1987), 33.

5. The quoted phrase is Entman's, in "Framing: Toward Clarification," 55.

6. Thomas E. Nelson and Donald R. Kinder, "Issue Frames and Group-Centrism in American Public Opinion," *Journal of Politics* 58 (November 1996): 1058.

7. A classic example of the conflicting impact of a television news story's visuals and its audio is discussed in Darrell M. West, *Air Wars: Television Advertising in Election Campaigns, 1952–1996,* 2d ed. (Washington, D.C.: CQ Press, 1997), 5–6, 96.

8. See Howard Kurtz, "Pew Poll: Voters Reject Media Message," *Washington Post* on the Web, 27 July 2000. The content analysis included newspaper, television, and Internet coverage during five weeks between February and June 2000, compared with a public opinion survey taken at one time point.

9. Ibid.

10. See Tversky and Kahneman, "Framing of Decisions"; Nelson and Kinder, "Issue Frames"; and Jacoby, "Issue Framing." On public policy, Jamieson and Cappella tell a fascinating story about the effects of media norms on the nature and outcome of the public and congressional debate over the Clinton health care reform proposals in 1993–94. See Kathleen Hall Jamieson and Joseph N. Cappella, "The Role of the Press in the Health Care Reform Debate of 1993–1994," in *The Politics of News; The News of Politics,* ed. Doris Graber, Denis McQuail, and Pippa Norris (Washington, D.C.: CQ Press, 1998), 110–31.

11. Howard Kurtz, "The Media, Swinging with the Polls," *Washington Post,* 12 September 2000, C1.

12. Doris A. Graber, "Personal Qualities in Presidential Images: the Contribution of the Press," *Midwest Journal of Political Science* 16 (February 1972): 46–76.

13. On this point, see also David P. Glass, "Evaluating Presidential Candidates: Who Focuses on Their Personal Attributes?" *Public Opinion Quarterly* 49 (1985–86): 517–34; Iyengar and Kinder, *News That Matters,* 1987, 73; and, on an earlier election, Donald E. Stokes, "Some Dynamic Elements of Contests for the Presidency," *American Political Science Review* 60 (March 1966): 19–28.

14. Robert E. Lane, "Interpersonal Relations and Leadership in a 'Cold Society,'" *Comparative Politics* 10 (July 1978): 447.

15. See Thomas E. Patterson, *The Mass Media Election* (New York: Praeger, 1980).

16. Kathleen Hall Jamieson, *Everything You Think You Know about Politics…and Why You're Wrong* (New York: Basic Books, 2000), 13, and chap. 3.

17. Dan Balz, "Gore Endorses Commission's Debate Plan," *Washington Post,* 30 August 2000, A8 (italics added).

18. Howard Kurtz, "On TV, Covering 'The Issues' from A to Zzzzzz," *Washington Post,* 3 July 2000, C1.

19. Howard Fineman and Bill Turque, "How Al Will Fight Back," *Newsweek,* 14 August 2000, 26.

20. Associated Press, "American Voters Consider Their Choices," *Sunday Herald-Times* (Bloomington, Ind.), 27 August 2000, A4.

21. Kurtz, "Pew Poll."

22. E.J. Dionne Jr., "Meet Upbeat Al," *Washington Post,* 30 May 2000, A19.

23. Associated Press, "Democrats Try to Protect Turf, Swing States with Ads," *New York Times* on the Web, 12 July 2000.

24. Richard L. Berke, "A Man of Many Tasks," *New York Times,* 18 August 2000, A1.

25. See Derek Willis and Anne Perra, "The Future of Fundraising," *CQ Weekly,* 1 January 2000, 28–30.

26. Anick Jesdanun, "Convention Coverage All Over Web," Associated Press on the Web, 31 July 2000.

27. Howard Kurtz and Ceci Connolly, "Gore's Spin Team Set to Play Tough," *Washington Post,* 20 July 2000, A1.

28. Quoted in Berke, "Man of Many Tasks."

29. Mike Feinsilber, "Advice Aplenty for Gore," Associated Press on the Web, 16 August 2000.

30. Michael Kinsley, "The Art of Finger-Pointing," *Slate,* 30 October 2000, http://slate.msn.com/Readme/00-10-30/Readme.asp

31. I coded all articles on the Bush and Gore campaigns (other than those that mentioned the campaign merely in passing) in the *New York Times* and *Washington Post* (the "elite press") from Tuesday through Friday of the two parties' national convention weeks plus all Associated Press articles (taken from the Web) at 2 P.M. on the same days. I also coded campaign and convention stories on these dates in a sample of news programs and convention coverage on ABC, NBC, CBS, CNN, Fox News, and on MTV and Comedy Central, both of which had considerable viewership at this time (see Marshall Sella, "The Stiff Guy vs. the Dumb Guy," *New York Times Magazine,* 24 September 2000, *New York Times* on the Web: www.nytimes.com/library/magazine/home/20000924mag-comedy.html). Content analysis was conducted again in each of these media from 2 to 6 November (the day before the election); see figure 3.2, p. 66. Full data and coding conventions are available from the author. When stories began with a conglomeration of several different points, more than one frame was coded.

   N's for convention weeks: AP - Bush 62, Gore 99; Elite Press - Bush 89, Gore 116; Broadcast Media - Bush 53, Gore 65. N's for 2–6 November: AP - Bush 70, Gore 70; Elite Press - Bush 116, Gore 107; Broadcast Media - Bush 118, Gore 108. I am grateful to Lori Poloni-Staudinger for her help and to Lissa Hershey for graphing these data.

32. Mike Allen, "Gore Camp's Confidence Takes Flight," *Washington Post,* 2 September 2000, A1.

33. Ibid.

34. Marjorie Williams, "Baiting the Bushes," *Washington Post,* 4 August 2000, A29.

35. Associated Press, "Study: Coverage Favors Republicans," *New York Times* on the Web, 13 August 2000.

36. Michael Powell, "The Running Mate with Stand-Up Timing," *Washington Post,* 27 September 2000, C1.

37. Quoted in Richard L. Berke, "Debate Stakes Seen as Critical by Candidates," *New York Times,* 1 October 2000, A1.

38. Associated Press, "Voters Seen Uneasy About Gore, Bush," *New York Times* on the Web, 25 October 2000.

39. Ibid.

40. Howard Fineman, "A Whiff of Victory...But Now It's War," *Newsweek,* 20 November 2000, 14.

41. On the effects of "momentum" (changes in candidates' likelihood of winning) in presidential primaries, see Larry M. Bartels, *Presidential Primaries and the Dynamics of Public Choice* (Princeton, N.J.: Princeton University Press, 1988), chap. 6.

42. On political knowledge in the U.S. and its impact on political behavior, see Michael X. Delli Carpini and Scott Keeter, *What Americans Know about Politics and Why It Matters* (New Haven: Yale University Press, 1996).

CHAPTER 4

Public Opinion in the 2000 Election: The Ambivalent Electorate

Kathleen A. Frankovic and Monika L. McDermott

> *The people will remain uncertain whilst*
> *'Twixt you there's difference; but the fall of either*
> *Makes the survivor heir of all.*
> —Coriolanus (V, vi)

THE 2000 ELECTION CAMPAIGN began in December 1998, on the day that President Bill Clinton was impeached by the U.S. House of Representatives. Republicans expected to run a campaign that would eventually turn on public concern about morals in the Clinton White House, while Democrats hoped to invoke public dismay about the Republican Congress's impeachment of the president for behavior that most Americans viewed as a private matter.

As it turned out, the Clinton impeachment formed part of the 2000 electoral landscape, but it was not the pivotal issue that both sides expected it to be. Other expectations were also not met. Vice President Al Gore was supposed to benefit from the strong economy, and on that basis should have been the front-runner. As it turned out, while he ended up after the election with a 500,000-vote plurality nationwide, Gore never led in the polls until after the Democratic convention in Los Angeles in August.[1] At that point he did take a slight lead, but the contest quickly settled back into the dead heat that lasted through Election Day, and even beyond.

Why did Gore run far behind Texas Governor George W. Bush for most of the year, and then lose one of the closest elections in U.S. history while winning a popular-vote plurality? Three factors help to explain the results: an electoral landscape that gave neither candidate a clear advantage, two candidates who highlighted their similarities as much as their differences, and voters who were ambivalent about their desires for the future.

The landscape of the 2000 election provided a background for both complacency and conflict in the electorate. On the one hand, the strong economy led to complacent attitudes about economic performance and little concern over who could best continue the prosperity. On the other, American voters were conflicted over basic ideology — what they believed to be the appropriate role for government. And finally, President Bill Clinton, while by no means the determining factor in the election, posed a dilemma for the many voters who felt he had done a fine job as president but had concerns about his morality. This uneven terrain made it difficult for Gore to use his position as an incumbent vice president to advantage.

The candidates were strikingly similar in many ways, and in a time of peace and prosperity, voters were not eager to rock the boat. In each party's primary, voters chose the establishment politician over opponents who portrayed themselves as mavericks and reformers. As a result, the candidates' images, including their weaknesses, were established early, and these perceptions were difficult to change. It was especially difficult for Gore, who only managed to turn things around after his August convention.

Finally, the voters who went to the polls on 7 November were ambivalent about key issues in the campaign. Many held contradictory opinions and had reservations about the individuals they voted for. Those feelings were especially prevalent among the "swing voters" each campaign had worked hard to lure. This was a close election; in all probability, it could have gone either way. As Harry Truman remarked, "Popularity and glamour are only part of the factors involved in winning presidential elections. One of the most important of all is luck."

THE ELECTORAL LANDSCAPE

On first glance, the electoral landscape in the 2000 campaign was primarily one of voter contentment. The economy was the best that voters had ever seen, the government was projecting a record budget surplus (which meant candidates could talk about how to spend money, not how to save it), and the sitting president — despite the impeachment scandal — enjoyed widespread public job approval. That combination made many political scientists assume that Gore would coast to an easy victory.

But instead, these positive circumstances made voters both complacent and conflicted — and their preferences difficult to predict. A long-running, stellar economy left many thinking that economic prosperity would continue regardless of who became president, and as a result, the economy did not play the role in the race that many thought it would. In contrast, issue preferences were often apparently contradictory. Voters supported the idea of smaller government, but, in prosperous economic times, they also wanted programs that would expand the federal government's problem-solving role. And finally, Clinton's relative popularity as president was not without controversy: many approved of his job performance, but many were also ready to see him (and those associated with

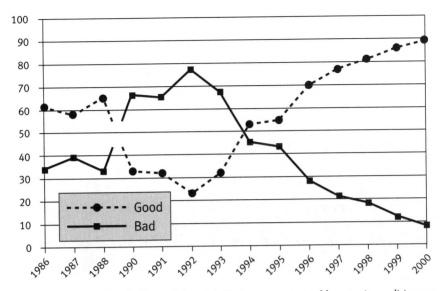

Q: *How would you describe the condition of the U.S. economy—would you say its condition was very good, somewhat good, somewhat bad, or very bad?*

Figure 4.1 Public Opinion of Economic Performance

Source: CBS News polls, 1986–2000.

Note: There are no data for 1989.

him) go. All of these factors combined to offer no clear advantage for either Gore or Bush.

The Economy

The 2000 election took place during the best economic atmosphere in at least a decade and a half. Since the CBS News Poll began asking its national economy question in 1986, public attitudes toward national economic performance had never been higher than they were during the 2000 election, as figure 4.1 indicates. In October 2000, less than one month before the presidential election, nine in ten Americans viewed the national economic performance as "good."

This optimistic attitude stands in stark contrast to the 1992 elections, when economic confidence was at a nadir, and voters chose to bring in a newcomer — Bill Clinton — rather than continue with the incumbent George Bush. At that time, three-quarters of the public — the highest proportion ever — described the economy as "somewhat bad" or "very bad." Also in contrast to 1992, when the Clinton campaign theme could be simplified to a wall poster that read "It's the economy, stupid," the economy did not play a central role in 2000.

Table 4.1 Who Is Responsible for the Economy?

Q: How much of the economy's current condition has to do with the economic policies of (the Clinton administration/Congress)—a lot, a little, or nothing at all?

Credit for National Economic Performance	Clinton's Policies	Congress's Policies
A lot	45%	47%
A little	41	37
None	8	5

Source: CBS News poll, August 2000.

While voters consistently acknowledged the good economic times they had enjoyed under the Clinton/Gore administration, these same good times may have made them complacent about the economy. Throughout the year, less than 5 percent answered "the economy" when asked what problem they wanted the government to address first. And voters believed the economy would continue to do well regardless of who became president.

This was clear early in the election season. In May 2000 voters were giving the Clinton administration some credit for the economy, but they were giving nearly equal credit to the Republican-led Congress. At that time, 43 percent of voters said that the Clinton administration deserved a lot of credit for economic performance, but an almost identical number—40 percent—said Congress deserved a lot of credit. By August, Congress had even overtaken the administration by a narrow margin: 45 percent of voters said the Clinton administration deserved a lot of credit, and 47 percent said Congress did (see table 4.1). In other words, throughout the election, voters were convinced that the economy is influenced by various factors, and not just presidential policies.

As voters left the polls on Election Day, they confirmed the marginal role played by the economy. Only 18 percent of voters said the economy was the top issue in their vote in 2000, compared to 43 percent who had said so in 1992. During that campaign, the economy ranked as the country's most important problem throughout the year. But the political science forecasting models that center on the economy had never been tested in such prosperous times as 2000.[2] Those forecasts may work better when the economy is failing than when it is thriving, because voters cite the economy as the reason for their decision-making most often when it is in bad shape.

Attitudes about Government

Attitudes about the federal government were decidedly ambivalent in this election. Voters expressed their long-term support for the idea of a smaller government that offered fewer services while at the same time favoring specific programs that would expand the federal government's role. They also came down firmly on the side of spending the budget surplus on new or existing programs, rather than on tax cuts.

For the past few decades, Americans have had a penchant for reducing the size of government, at least in the abstract. The 2000 election season was no different. In a late October survey, 57 percent of voters said they preferred a smaller government that offered fewer services, while just 32 percent expressed a preference for larger government offering more services. But this support for the idea of downsizing did not always square with the policy preferences expressed. Specifically, in the areas of education and health care, voters said they wanted continued, or even expanded, federal government involvement.

On education, a September 1999 survey demonstrated voters' belief that the federal government should have a strong role. Education was the first issue voters wanted the campaigns and the candidates to address. When asked what was the most important thing a president could do to improve education in this country, voters' top answer was increasing government funding. Three of the top four suggestions for what a president could do about education involved government funding — increasing funding in general, adding more money for teachers, or increasing college funding and scholarships — while other voters said they would like the president to do something about teacher quality. Hardly any suggested school vouchers, which were an integral part of the Bush campaign's education plan.

On health care, voters even supported an *expanded* federal role — providing prescription drug coverage to seniors. In a test of the competing Gore and Bush plans on prescription drug coverage, voters were asked in September 2000 to choose whether such coverage could better be provided by the government or by the private sector (insurance companies). The federal government was a decisive winner: 51 percent of registered voters chose the federal government, while only 29 percent chose insurance companies.

Conflicting views about the role of government were not just a matter of different majorities for each question. Many individual voters were also clearly personally ambivalent, unable to reconcile their desire for government programs with their preference for smaller government. In September 1999, registered voters were in favor of smaller government (by 48 percent to 40 percent), but many of those who supported reducing the size of government also supported the idea of an activist government that takes care of people. Table 4.2 (p. 78) shows this voter conflict: 61 percent of those who preferred smaller government also thought that the government should be responsible for people who cannot take care of themselves. In addition, a narrow 43 percent plurality of voters who wanted smaller government said they would prefer to see the budget surplus used to pay for social programs — such as education and welfare — rather than to cut taxes.

Voters continued this preference for government program support over tax cuts throughout the election season. When asked to prioritize spending of the

Table 4.2 Government Program Support among Voters Who Support Smaller Government

Q: If you had to choose, would you rather have a smaller government providing fewer services, or a bigger government providing more services? Do you agree or disagree with the following statement: It is the responsibility of the government to take care of people who can't take care of themselves. If you had to choose, would you prefer using the budget surplus to cut taxes or to pay for social programs such as education and welfare?

Supporters of Smaller Government	Favor Programs
Government should help those who can't help themselves	61%
Government should spend surplus on programs over tax cuts	43%

Source: CBS News poll, September 1999.

budget surplus, voters consistently showed overwhelming support for programs such as Social Security and Medicare. In October 2000, 47 percent of voters chose shoring up Social Security and Medicare over cutting taxes and paying down the debt, while only 17 percent chose tax cuts, and 15 percent chose paying down the debt as the top priority for the budget surplus.

The Clinton Administration

President Bill Clinton was yet another source of voter contradiction. His approval ratings were higher than those for any modern president in his eighth year of governing — and they only improved during the Lewinsky scandal — but many voters felt dismay at his personal behavior. Voters were happy with the way the country was going and wanted the pattern to continue, but they were not as supportive of the idea of continuing the Clinton era. (See the discussion in chapter 1 of the Clinton administration's role in setting the stage for the election.)

Large majorities of voters approved of the job Clinton was doing as president throughout the election season. On Election Day itself, 57 percent of voters gave him a positive approval rating. On that same day, however, a full 60 percent of voters said they viewed the president unfavorably "as a person." Overall, one in five voters said they approved of Clinton's job performance, but disapproved of him personally.

Opinions of the Clinton *administration* divided along similar lines. While people thought the administration had done a good job, they were less thrilled with the notion of continuing the Clinton regime. When asked about the direction of the country, a majority of voters said they would like things to continue as they were, but when Clinton was mentioned, many more voters called for change. In an August 2000 CBS News poll, 60 percent of voters said they liked the direction in which the country was headed and they hoped it would continue,

Table 4.3 The Clinton Legacy?

Q: Do you think things in this country today are generally going in the right direction or seriously off on the wrong track? Considering the moral climate of the country today, do you think things are generally going in the right direction, or seriously off on the wrong track?

	Generally	Morally
Right direction	65%	39%
Wrong track	31	57

Source: CBS News National Exit Poll, 7 November 2000.

while only 33 percent said they did not like the direction and would like to see it changed. At the same time, however, an NBC News poll affixed Clinton's name to a similar question, and discovered much more mixed results. Forty-five percent of voters in the NBC News poll said that after eight years of Clinton-Gore it was time for a change, while 47 percent said that with the economy strong and the nation at peace, they would like to continue with Democrats in the White House.

Similarly, voters on Election Day were divided over the nature of the country's success, arguably a defining feature of the Clinton era. As table 4.3 demonstrates, in the 2000 national exit poll voters felt by a 65–31 percent margin that the country was headed in the right direction. When asked about the "moral" direction of the country, however, by a 57–39 percent margin voters said the country was on the wrong track.

Gore's Dilemma

This uneven electoral landscape presented Al Gore with a dangerous dilemma. Given voters' complacency over the economy, and their conflicted views over Clinton and the administration, the vice president had to walk a fine line in taking credit for Clinton administration accomplishments and yet distancing himself from the unpopular image of Clinton the person. Facing the worst of both worlds, Gore had difficulty separating himself until well into the election season, and he never managed to turn the good economy into a big advantage (see chapter 6 on Gore's failure to capitalize on this issue).

Clinton seemed loath to leave the spotlight to his second-in-command — witness the long (135 steps) televised corridor walk preceding Clinton's speech to the Democratic convention — so it was not until his turn at the convention podium that Gore finally managed to establish himself in his own right. Figure 4.2 (p. 80) tracks the voters' opinions of Gore over the course of the 2000 campaign. Clearly, Gore's image changed dramatically after the August convention. Up to that point, unfavorable opinions predominated, with negative views peaking at the culmination of the Democratic primary campaign in March, when four in ten voters viewed the vice president unfavorably. But directly after Gore

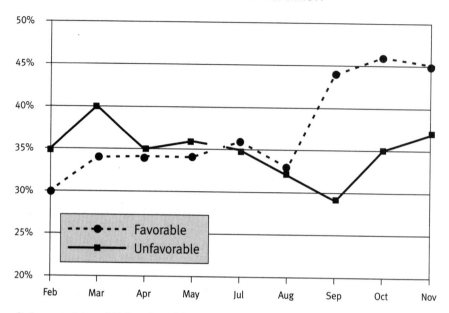

Q: Is your opinion of Al Gore favorable, not favorable, undecided, or haven't you heard enough about Al Gore yet to have an opinion?

Figure 4.2 Voters' Opinions of Al Gore throughout the Campaign

Source: CBS News polls, February-November 2000.

Note: There are no data for June.

stood up at the convention and proclaimed himself "my own man" (and planted a long wet kiss on his wife's lips), opinions reversed, and Gore headed into the fall campaign with favorability ratings rivaling those of George W. Bush, who had maintained a positive voter assessment throughout the year.

Gore's convention bounce was the second highest in recent history — surpassed only by former President George Bush's bounce in 1988. Before the 1988 Republican convention, Bush had trailed his Democratic opponent Michael Dukakis by 17 points; directly following the convention, Bush led Dukakis by 6 points. Gore's bounce was nearly as impressive: between the two party conventions Gore trailed the former president's son by 16 points, but after the Democratic convention Gore was up by 1.

While this comparison would seem to bode well for Gore as the incumbent vice president, the differences between 1988 and 2000 were much larger than their similarities. Both George Bush and Al Gore had served as vice presidents to popular incumbents, and both had found it difficult to emerge from the shadows. But unlike Bush in 1988, Gore faced an opponent whose campaign

Table 4.4 The Candidates on the Issues

Q: If (Al Gore/George W. Bush) is elected president, do you think he is likely or not likely to (preserve Social Security/improve education/make sure the country's economy remains strong)?

Issue	Gore	Bush
Preserve Social Security	71%	56%
Improve education	66	64
Keep economy strong	75	66

Source: CBS News polls, September–October 2000.

was well-organized, well-financed, and in control of the candidate's public image. And while the 1988 Bush campaign could demonize Dukakis as an unabashed liberal, Gore faced an opponent whose campaign had strategically moved to the middle of the ideological spectrum, labeling its candidate a "compassionate conservative," making inclusiveness the visual image of the Republican convention, and appropriating Democratic issues. While 51 percent of voters saw George W. Bush as a conservative, more than a quarter viewed him as a moderate, thus mirroring the view of Gore — nearly half described Gore as liberal, while 30 percent said he was a moderate.

In 2000 Bush and the Republicans were able to weaken the traditional Democratic advantages on issues such as Social Security and education (see table 4.4). In addition, voters' complacency about the economy meant that they viewed both candidates as likely to continue the prosperity. The end result was that while Gore did have a natural issue advantage, Bush did not necessarily have a large issue weakness: by making himself acceptable on what should have been Democratic issues, Bush neutralized them.

With the exception of education, Gore retained substantial leads on important issues. By a margin of 15 points voters thought Gore more likely to preserve Social Security, and by 9 points they thought he would be more likely to keep the economy strong. But these advantages did not necessarily make Bush weak: substantial majorities of voters also thought Bush could handle these issues — 56 percent said Bush would be likely to preserve Social Security, and 66 percent thought he could keep the economy prosperous. And on education, the two candidates were virtually tied, with 64 percent and 66 percent respectively saying that Bush or Gore would be likely to improve education if elected.

TWO SIMILAR CANDIDATES

Voters in the 2000 election were not looking for a president who would shake things up. Enjoying a strong economy and relative peace in the world, and clearly believing that the country was on the right track, voters saw little need to change the status quo. As a result, in the nominating contests, voters chose the most familiar, most "establishment" candidates available. Because of their familiarity, the two major-party candidates—both scions of political families and both claiming the middle of the road — established their images early, and there was little opportunity to change these strikingly similar images later. And this was what the voters wanted—as will be seen later, by the end of the election more were satisfied choosing among this year's field of candidates than has been true for any presidential electorate in the past two decades.

The Devil You Know

Voters' satisfaction with the status quo was clearly reflected in their primary election choices. While voters said early on that they were looking for reformers, or candidates who would try new ways of doing things, they actually preferred two candidates who they believed were unlikely to do so. Bush and Gore were familiar to voters — both had strong ties to Washington and the establishment (despite the Bush campaign's protestations to the contrary), and those ties drove voters' early images of the candidates.

In June 1999, well before the primary elections but after each party's respective fields had formed, voters expressed the desire for a president who would "try new ways of solving the country's problems," rather than following familiar approaches. A 59-percent majority of registered voters said they would prefer new ways, while only 30 percent said they preferred familiar approaches to problems.

At the same time, voters labeled both Bush and Gore as candidates who would follow familiar approaches. While they were still unsure of many of the other candidates, the trend was clear — Bush and Gore were the familiar establishment politicians, while Bradley and McCain were the candidates who could bring change. As table 4.5 shows, 55 percent of voters thought Gore would follow familiar approaches to addressing problems, and only 25 percent thought he would try new ways. Bush's image was similar: only 28 percent thought he would be likely to try new ways of problem solving, but 45 percent thought he would rely on familiar approaches. In contrast, the less familiar candidates, McCain and Bradley, were more likely to be seen as candidates who would try new ways of problem solving.

Voters also viewed Bush and Gore as typical politicians, who would tailor their words to suit the perceived preferences of their audience. In early February 2000, more than six in ten voters said that Gore and Bush were more likely to say what they thought people wanted to hear than what they really believed. In contrast, both Bradley and McCain were viewed as candidates who more often said what they believed.

Both of the eventual nominees' ties to other presidents were likely responsible for these judgments about them. Gore's association with Clinton, by virtue of his vice presidency, and Bush's ties to his father, were the factors that voters most readily associated with each candidate. In fact, early in the process, some

Table 4.5 Candidates' Approaches to Problems

Q: Do you think (Al Gore/George W. Bush/John McCain/Bill Bradley) is someone who will try new ways of solving the country's problems, or is he someone who will follow generally familiar approaches and try to do them better?

Candidate	Candidate will...	
	Try new ways	Follow familiar approaches
Al Gore	25%	55%
George W. Bush	28	45
John McCain	13	21
Bill Bradley	22	24

Source: CBS News poll, June 1999.

voters actually confused George W. Bush with his father: in October 1999, 38 percent of voters mentioned the fact that the current candidate was former President George Bush's son as the first thing they thought of when they heard his name, but 6 percent volunteered that he *was* the former president (12 percent had thought so two months earlier, in August), and only 5 percent mentioned his governorship of Texas first.

Similarly, early in the election season, when asked the first thing that came to their minds when they heard the name Al Gore, voters most frequently responded that he was the vice president. In October 1999, 18 percent of voters named the vice presidency as the first thing they thought of when they thought of Gore (in June 1999, 24 percent had mentioned it), and another 9 percent mentioned Clinton himself.

Persistent and Shared Images

Because Gore and Bush were so familiar to voters, their images were determined early on. Questions about Gore's veracity and Bush's readiness persisted throughout the election season, regardless (or perhaps even because) of what the candidates did, and the media's tendency to dwell on these widely accepted images only served to reinforce them in the public mind (see chapter 3).

The issue of pandering (or exaggerating, versus speaking truthfully) proved to be a more persistent problem for Gore than it was for Bush. Voters consistently viewed the vice president as a candidate who said what people wanted to hear, rather than what he really believed. In October 1999, 54 percent of voters said that Gore more often said what he thought people wanted to hear, and as noted earlier, this number was 61 percent in February. But even after a positive image of Gore began to dominate after his party's convention, voters had not changed their minds about this impression. In October 2000, 58 percent of voters said that Gore more often said what people wanted to hear.

Table 4.6 Shared Images

Q: Do you think (Al Gore/George W. Bush) shares the moral values most Americans try to live by or doesn't he? Regardless of how you intend to vote, do you think (Al Gore/George W. Bush) has the skills needed to negotiate with both Democrats and Republicans in Congress or doesn't he have these skills? Do you think (Al Gore/George W. Bush) has strong qualities of leadership or not? Do you think (Al Gore/George W. Bush) cares about the needs and problems of people like yourself? Do you think (Al Gore/George W. Bush) has more honesty and integrity than most people in public life? Do you think (Al Gore/George W. Bush) can be trusted to keep his word as president, or not? How many of his campaign promises do you think (Al Gore/George W. Bush) will try to keep: all of them, most of them, some of them, or hardly any of them?

Characteristic Strengths	Gore	Bush
Shares moral values of most Americans	72%	70%
Has bipartisan skills	68	60
Has strong qualities of leadership	67	70
Cares about people like you	66	55
Characteristic Weaknesses	Gore	Bush
Has more honesty and integrity than most	42	48
Can be trusted to keep his word	46	48
Will keep most campaign promises	41	45

Source: CBS News/*New York Times* polls, August–October 2000.

Questions also dogged Bush throughout the election, reflecting a suspicion that he was not quite up to the job of president. Specifically, voters had long-standing concerns about Bush's ability to deal with foreign affairs. In October 1999 voters were evenly divided over his ability to deal wisely with international crises — 40 percent thought he could, but 41 percent were afraid he could not. A full year later, in October 2000, voters remained divided — 45 percent thought Bush could deal with international crises, but 46 percent were uneasy about his approach. And in general, voters had questions about Bush's preparedness: as early as August 2000 and continuing on through the election, only half of voters thought Bush was "prepared" for the presidency. In contrast, over two-thirds of voters regularly rated Gore as prepared for the job.

With the exception of these two qualities, Bush and Gore had comparable strengths and weaknesses in the eyes of the voters. As table 4.6 demonstrates, both candidates were viewed as sharing most Americans' moral values, as well as being strong leaders. And while Gore ranked higher on bipartisanship and caring about people's needs and problems, Bush was still viewed by a majority as having those characteristics as well. The candidates also shared many weaknesses. Voters were skeptical about the honesty and integrity of both, and whether they could trust either man to keep his word or his campaign promises as president.

While Bush and Gore's images were set early and stayed similar, the candidates did have opportunities to polish and even improve their images in the presidential

Table 4.7 Which Candidate Won the Debates?

Q: Who do you think did the best job — or won the debate?

	Debate 1 3 October	Debate 2 11 October	Debate 3 17 October
Bush	42%	51%	45%
Gore	56	48	55

Q: If the presidential election were being held today, and the candidates were Al Gore, the Democrat, George W. Bush, the Republican, Pat Buchanan, the Reform Party candidate, and Ralph Nader, the Green Party candidate, would you vote for Al Gore, George W. Bush, Pat Buchanan, or Ralph Nader?

	Before Debate 1	After Debate 3
Bush	41%	44%
Gore	45	42
Nader	4	4
Buchanan	2	1

Source: For debate winner question: CBS News/Knowledge Network polls on night of each debate. For presidential preference question: CBS News/*New York Times* polls before (27 September–1 October) and after (18–21 October) debates.

debates in October 2000. But overall, the debates resulted in a sort of draw: according to CBS News surveys conducted each debate night by Knowledge Networks, Gore won the first and third debates, while viewers saw Bush as the winner of the second. Not surprisingly, the debates had little effect on the race overall — neither candidate substantially altered his position in the race as a result.

Indeed, the only real effect of the debates was to reverse some of Gore's postconvention gains in voter preference (as shown in table 4.7). While Bush's favorable ratings did not budge, Gore's negatives began to rise again after the debates, having dropped directly following his successful convention speech (see figure 4.2, p. 80).

Voter Satisfaction

Bush and Gore were exactly what the voters wanted. Content with the state of the country, they willingly chose candidates who represented the status quo. Despite early indications that they might be interested in change, in October 2000, 63 percent of voters said they were satisfied to choose among Gore, Bush, Nader, and Buchanan for president (see figure 4.3, p. 86). Voter satisfaction levels in other recent elections do not come anywhere close to this level: in 1996 and 1980, voters may have been the most satisfied in the past two decades, but even then just 50 percent of voters claimed to be satisfied with their choices. And in 1988, the election that, as discussed earlier, seemed most similar to 2000, voter satisfac-

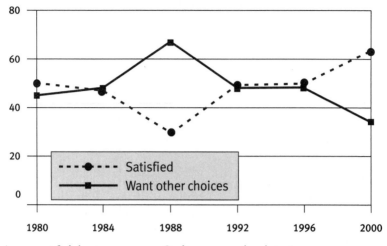

Q: Are you satisfied choosing among..., Or do you want other choices?

Figure 4.3 Voter Satisfaction with Candidate Choices

Source: CBS News/*New York Times* polls.

tion reached a recent low-point, as just 30 percent were satisfied with the choice between Dukakis and Bush.

Given the similarities between the two major-party candidates — both in background and in image — as well as voters' complacent but conflicted attitudes on major issues, it should come as little surprise that the electorate that turned out on 7 November was one of the most closely divided in history. The ambivalence voters expressed throughout the election season was carried into the voting booth.

THE AMBIVALENT DESIRES OF A DIVIDED ELECTORATE

Voters' ambivalence on some key campaign themes — such as the importance of issues versus character, the role of morality, and the role of government — may have contributed to some ambivalence in the vote as well. The choices were not clear-cut: many voters left the polls with reservations about the choice they had just made, indicating that both candidates had some soft support and that the ambivalent, mushy middle may have contributed to a tight election.

Issue Ambivalence

Voters' issue ambivalence was illustrated by three main conflicts. They were split over the relative importance of character and issues in the election, they were divided over the role of morality in politics and the presidency, and they had mixed preferences over the size and role of the federal government. Given these conflict-

Table 4.8 Candidate Support by Issues and Qualities

Q: Which was more important in your vote for president today—My candidate's position on the issues, or my candidate's leadership and personal qualities?

Presidential Preference	Issues Positions	Personal Qualities
Al Gore	55%	35%
George W. Bush	40	62

Source: CBS News exit poll, 7 November 2000.

ing attitudes, it is no surprise that the votes were so closely divided between the two major-party candidates.

Issues and Character. While voters frequently professed to find a candidate's issue positions to be the most important element in determining their vote, they also wanted specific personal qualities. In a survey in March 2000, CBS News asked voters, in two separate questions, which they thought was more important in a president — the candidate's positions on issues or the candidate's qualities. Half of voters were asked whether "issue positions" or "personal qualities" were more important to their vote. The other half were asked which was more important for a president: "to be very honest and fair, to favor policies you think are good, or to have strong qualities of leadership."

By a 2-to-1 margin — 61 percent versus 30 percent — voters reported that issues positions were more important than personal qualities. But when asked which of various characteristics was more important for a president to have, voters ranked issues last. Only 7 percent chose policy positions, while 43 percent said being honest and fair, and another 42 percent said leadership was most important.

These apparently contradictory preferences indicate the voters' own inner conflicts. They professed to base voting decisions on issues, rather than personal qualities, yet they overwhelmingly preferred "presidential" attributes such as leadership and honesty to policy positions. And since these preferences affect voting behavior, choices were closely divided.

On Election Day, the conflict between issues and character drove much of the vote. A strong 62-percent majority of voters said that issues were more important to their vote than personal qualities, and, as table 4.8 demonstrates, these voters supported Gore by a 55-percent-to-40-percent margin. Thirty-five percent of voters said that personal qualities were paramount in their vote, and among these voters Bush had a 27-point advantage.

While most voters ranked issues as more important than personal qualities, the relative cohesiveness of those who prized personal qualities resulted in the close electoral outcome. In the Election Day exit poll, no single issue dominated voters' choices, but one personal quality did: honesty. When asked which issue mattered most to them, voters named a variety of issues, none of which was

Table 4.9 The Country's Moral Direction and the President's Role

Q: Considering just the moral climate of the country today, do you think things are generally going in the right direction, or seriously off on the wrong track? Which is more important in a president— his ability to manage the government or his ability to provide moral leadership?

President's Priority	Right Direction	Wrong Track
To be a good manager	75%	50%
To be a moral leader	22	44

Source: CBS News exit poll, 7 November 2000.

mentioned by more than a fifth: 18 percent chose the economy, 15 percent chose education, 14 percent each chose taxes and Social Security, and 12 percent said world affairs. In contrast, when asked which candidate *quality* was most important to their vote, a full quarter of voters agreed that they wanted a candidate who was honest and trustworthy, and 80 percent of these voters chose Bush. The second most important quality — experience — trailed at 15 percent.

Morality in Government. Voters were also divided about the role of morality in government, and Bush had consistently emphasized in his campaign that he would "restore honor and dignity to the White House." But while voters were concerned about the moral state of the nation, they did not necessarily believe that it was the president's job to correct it.

Nearly six out of every ten voters said on Election Day that they thought the moral climate of the country was "seriously off on the wrong track." And these voters were Bush supporters — 62 percent voted for Bush. The 39 percent who said they thought the country was morally on the right track supported Gore by 70–27 percent.

But voters also had reservations about how important it is for a president to exhibit moral leadership: only 35 percent thought that was a more important quality than job performance. Sixty percent of voters said that it was more important for the president to be a good manager than it was for him to be a moral leader. These reservations extended even to those who claimed to be concerned about the country's moral climate: as table 4.9 demonstrates, half of those disapproving of the moral direction of the country also said that they thought it was more important for the president to be a good manager than to be a moral leader. And these conflicted voters divided evenly between Gore and Bush — 48 percent to 46 percent respectively.

The Size and Role of Government. Voters' ambivalence about the role and size of the federal government carried over to Election Day. Just over half — 52 percent — said in exit polls that the government was doing too many things better left to businesses and individuals, while 43 percent thought the government should do more to solve problems. But when it came to specific problems, such as

Table 4.10 Smaller Government but More Government Programs

Q: Which comes closer to your view: Government should do more to solve problems or government is doing too many things better left to businesses and individuals. When a public school is failing, the federal government's priority should be to: Fix that school's problems or help parents pay for private school? Which of these would be the best way for the federal government to help senior citizens pay for prescription drugs—increase funds for Medicare or provide funds for private insurance plans? Do you support or oppose stricter gun-control legislation?

Favor	All Voters	Voters Favoring Smaller Government
Fixing schools instead of giving vouchers	78%	66%
Increase Medicare funding to cover prescription drugs	57	48
Support stricter gun-control laws	60	41

Source: CBS News exit poll, 7 November 2000.

education, Medicare, and gun control, even those who said the government was already doing too much expressed a preference for the government to do more.

Overall, voters supported government (rather than private) solutions to the problems currently facing education, Medicare prescription drug coverage, and gun control. On Election Day, voters expressed strong support for public (rather than private) education: 78 percent of voters said that when public schools are failing, the government's priority should be to fix the problems rather than to use tools like vouchers to help parents pay for private schools. In addition, 57 percent of voters thought that the best way the federal government could help seniors pay for prescription drugs would be by increasing funds for Medicare, rather than by providing funds to encourage private plans to cover prescription drugs. And finally, 60 percent of voters said they supported stricter gun-control legislation, while only 36 percent opposed such legislation.

Many voters who expressed a preference for having government do less in general still supported its doing more in these areas. Specifically, 78 percent of voters who supported leaving more things to business and individuals also said they supported at least one government solution for education, Medicare, or gun control. Sixty-six percent said they thought government's priority should be to fix schools, rather than to offer vouchers; 48 percent expressed support for expanding Medicare to cover prescription drugs; and 41 percent said they supported stricter gun laws (see table 4.10).

These divided views on the role of government helped to make the election close. Not surprisingly, voters who favored a limited government were Bush supporters, while those who favored having the government solve more problems mostly voted for Gore. Among those who said they wanted government to leave more of its responsibilities to the private sector, 71 percent voted for Bush. But among those who thought the government should be doing more, 74 percent chose Gore. Similarly, those who favored expanded government roles in the areas of education, Medicare, and gun control also favored Gore by large margins, but among those with conflicted views, Bush had an edge.

Voter Division

The lack of a clear, defining agenda must surely have contributed to what turned out to be one of the closest elections in U.S. history. Because voters could not resolve issue conflicts in their own minds, their candidate support was muddled. The candidates had similar strengths and weaknesses, and although the choices satisfied most voters, many of them ended up on Election Day with qualms about their vote.

Swing voters, who typically decide an election, were the most uncertain. As Nie, Verba, and Petrocik found, voters who are cross-pressured by issues, or by party and issues, tend to be moderate, or swing, voters and support the candidate they see as the most moderate. This year, that distinction was not clear.[3]

While a majority of voters supported their candidate without reservations, more than four out of every ten voters said they had reservations about their choice. Specifically, 45 percent of Gore voters and 42 percent of Bush voters had reservations about their vote.

Voters who held conflicting views about the role of government were especially likely to have reservations about their vote choice. Among those who indicated a preference for smaller government but then also expressed specific support for an increased government role in education or Medicare, half had reservations about their candidate. In contrast, among those with consistent views — such as a preference for smaller government *and* opposition to expanding specific government programs — upwards of 60 percent said they supported their candidate with no reservations.

For example, 59 percent of Independents had reservations about their vote choice, compared with only 38 percent of Democrats and 37 percent of Republicans. In addition, half of moderates had reservations about their candidate, and Midwesterners — considered the key to this election — were the most leery of voters in any region.

The Election Day confusion and the indeterminate outcome mobilized partisans and hardened the positions of each candidate's true believers. In national polls conducted in November and December, after the official Election Day, both Bush and Gore supporters expressed concerns about what would happen next. In late November, two-thirds of the public described the Florida vote controversy as a big problem for the country. Less than half thought the outcome would be the "fair and accurate" vote count each side said it wanted.[4]

But each candidate's supporters had different views about what should happen next, with Gore's voters wanting more counts, and Bush's voters wanting them to stop. Overall evaluations of Al Gore, which had improved in August, dropped to the low levels of the spring. And questions of the legitimacy of any victory dogged both candidates. In early December, before the Supreme Court ruling that effectively ended the election, only a quarter of Bush voters believed a Gore victory would be a legitimate win, and just a third of Gore voters believed a Bush victory would be legitimate. Immediately after the Supreme Court decision, only 11 percent of Gore's voters said the outcome (the Bush victory) was a legitimate win.

The rancor and divisiveness engendered by the postelection counting overshadowed the very different picture presented by the voters on Election Day, however. Rather than being harshly divided, the electorate on 7 November was complacent about the state of the nation and ambivalent in its preferences for the future. The result — a 500,000-vote popular victory for one candidate and an electoral college victory and the presidency for the other — was the product of those attitudes. In sum, the voters got what they wanted.

NOTES

1. According to CBS News polls, various dates.
2. For a discussion of the forecasting models that were being applied in 2000, see Robert G. Kaiser, "Is This Any Way to Pick a Winner? To Researchers It's All Over But the Voting," *Washington Post*, 26 May 2000, A1.
3. Norman H. Nie, Sidney Verba, and John R. Petrocik, *The Changing American Voter* (Cambridge, Mass.: Harvard University Press, 1979).
4. The 87-page CBS News report of what happened on election night can be downloaded from http://cbsnews.com/htdocs/c2k/pdf/REPFINAL.pdf

CHAPTER 5

Financing the 2000 Elections

Anthony Corrado

> *Ford:*   *They say, if money go before, all ways do lie open.*
> *Falstaff:*   *Money is a good soldier, sir, and will on.*
> —Merry Wives of Windsor (II, 2)

THE 2000 ELECTIONS were characterized by an insatiable demand for campaign money. With a close race for the White House and majority control of Congress at stake, candidates, party committees, and political groups raised funds at a frenetic pace throughout the election cycle, amassing war chests that greatly exceeded those of previous elections. By Labor Day, federal candidates and political organizations had already spent close to $2 billion, or as much as was spent in all of 1996. By Election Day, many analysts predicted that total spending in connection with federal races would be close to $3 billion, or almost 50 percent more than four years earlier.[1]

Every high-water mark established in previous elections was surpassed, in most instances by sizable margins. George W. Bush, for example, became the first major-party presidential candidate to refuse public matching funds and win the nomination since the adoption of public financing in 1974. Bush raised over $100 million in private contributions, more than double the $50.7 million in private funding received by Republican presidential nominee Bob Dole in 1996. In the Senate contests, Democratic challenger Jon Corzine spent over $60 million of his own money in his successful effort to capture New Jersey's open seat, more than twice as much as the sum spent by Michael Huffington in his unsuccessful 1994 bid for a Senate seat in California. In the high-profile New York contest between First Lady Hillary Rodham Clinton and Representative Rick Lazio, the candidates and party committees spent well over $80 million, making it the most expensive race yet for a seat in that chamber. A new benchmark for House races also was established, as incumbent Representative James Rogan (R-Calif.) and his challenger, Democrat Adam Schiff, raised a combined $10 million in their contest, surpassing the previous high mark of $8.9 million set in 1996 in the race between then Speaker of the House Newt Gingrich and his opponent, Democrat Michael Coles.[2]

The total amount of money raised in connection with the 2000 elections was not simply a result of a number of extraordinarily expensive contests. At every level of election, candidates, party committees, and independent groups raised substantially more than they had in 1996. This emphasis on fund-raising was due in part to the closeness of the contests: the prospects of a toss-up presidential race and a hard-fought partisan battle for control of Congress spurred fund-raising efforts from the very beginning of the election cycle. Candidates and party committees sought to ensure that they would have the funds needed to win in key battleground states and targeted congressional contests. With so much at stake, party leaders and congressional incumbents sought to preserve their power and status or, in the case of Democrats, to enhance them, by raising money for other candidates as well as for their own campaigns. The party committees also did their part, funneling tens of millions of dollars into marginal states and races throughout the country.

While the competitiveness of races was important, the jump in fund-raising was primarily due to a surge in the amount of unregulated funding that flowed through the system. The continuing breakdown of the rules that govern campaign finance encouraged politicians and political committees to seek contributions far in excess of those allowed under the Federal Election Campaign Act (FECA). The major beneficiaries of this largesse were the national party committees, which took in unprecedented amounts of soft money, which is not subject to the limits of federal law, and used these funds to pay for advertising, voter mobilization efforts, and other activities designed to benefit their candidates. As a result, the party committees played a greater role in campaign funding than they had in prior elections under the FECA. Independent political groups and tax-exempt organizations also exploited the gaps in the law, spending tens of millions of dollars on candidate-specific issue advertising and other political activities designed to help their favored candidates.

The predominant feature of the 2000 elections with respect to financial activity was thus the on-going disintegration of the regulatory structure that had been erected after the Watergate scandal to control campaign funding. While most of the monies spent in connection with federal races still came from sources regulated under the FECA, the growth in unregulated funding was noteworthy, evidencing the further erosion of the impact of the law. This erosion has been taking place for more than a decade, but the system essentially collapsed in 2000 under the weight of precedents that gave political actors a greater incentive to rely on unregulated funds. The use of these monies became more formalized and extensive, and greater and greater sums that were beyond the reach of effective public disclosure flowed into coffers established by candidates and political organizations. The result was a new model of campaign financing with new tactics, a model unanticipated by the regulatory reforms of the 1970s and one that brought into high relief the need for a major overhaul of the nation's campaign finance system.

THE COLLAPSE OF THE FECA

The FECA was adopted in 1974 to prevent the corruption and abuses that can accompany an unchecked system of campaign funding. To accomplish this end, the law placed limits on the size and sources of campaign contributions and required full public disclosure of all financial transactions made by candidates and political committees. The law also created a voluntary system of public funding for presidential candidates, who had to agree to spending limits and some restrictions on fund-raising as a condition of public funding. But these rules exerted little control over campaign financing in the 2000 cycle, due to a failure to address innovative methods of circumventing the law that began in the 1996 election.

Under the provisions of the FECA, individual donors are limited to $25,000 in aggregate contributions to federal candidates, political action committees (PACs), and party committees. Candidates are supposed to receive no more than $1,000 per election from an individual donor and no more than $5,000 from a PAC. Party committees are limited to individual contributions of no more than $20,000 per year and PAC contributions no greater than $15,000 per year. In addition, national party committees are allowed to spend a limited amount of money in coordination with a candidate to assist that candidate's campaign. In 2000 the amount a party could spend on behalf of a presidential general election candidate was $13.7 million. The amount that could be spent in Senate races ranged from a low of $135,120 in Delaware to a high of more than $3.2 million in California. In a House race, the ceiling was $33,780, except in states with a single congressional district, where the limit was $67,560.[3] The funds raised and spent in accordance with these federal restrictions are known as *hard money*. Parties can also raise and spend funds for party-building efforts and activities that are not defined as "campaign expenditures" under the law. These funds are known as *soft money* and are not subject to FECA rules governing the size or source of contributions.

Presidential candidates who accept public funding are subject to additional restraints. Besides the contribution limits, these candidates are required to abide by spending ceilings and can spend no more than $50,000 of their own money on the campaign. During the 2000 nomination campaign, the maximum amount a publicly funded presidential challenger could spend was $45.6 million, which included $40.5 million for operating and fund-raising costs and an additional $5.1 million for legal and accounting expenses incurred to comply with the law. These challengers were also subject to state spending ceilings, which ranged from $675,000 in New Hampshire to $13.1 million in California. But the rules governing the state-by-state allocation of expenditures have become so riddled with loopholes that these ceilings have proven to be less important than the overall ceiling. The maximum amount a publicly funded candidate could spend in the general election was $67.6 million, exclusive of legal and accounting costs. These costs could be financed separately through private monies raised for this purpose from contributions subject to the contribution limits.[4]

In practice, the financing of the 2000 elections bore a greater resemblance to campaign funding prior to the passage of the FECA than to the patterns that were supposed to prevail after it. Although the law remained in place and candidates had to be aware of the contribution and expenditure limits imposed on their campaigns, the rules had little impact on the amounts of money raised and spent in connection with federal contests. Any donor who wanted to make contributions in excess of the amounts permitted by federal law could do so easily. Any political group that wanted to spend unregulated monies to influence the outcome of an election could do so easily. The major effect of the law was less to stem the amount of money in campaigns than to direct the flow of money, channeling large amounts into forms of financial activity that allowed circumvention of the law.

Some of the means used to evade the law were well-established and, in most cases, had become a common component of federal campaigns. These included the parties' ability to raise and spend soft money; the ability of candidates to use alternative political organizations, especially PACs and tax-exempt organizations, as surrogate campaign committees, and the use of candidate-specific issue advertising campaigns by political groups. Others, however, were new or could be considered new, since they were used much more extensively and effectively than in any previous presidential election year. These latter innovations were largely a result of adaptations that occurred in response to the shifting regulatory environment that emerged in the aftermath of the 1996 election.

In 1996 the Democratic Party and then the Republican Party supplemented the finances of their presidential nominees by spending millions of dollars on issue advertisements, which they claimed were not campaign expenditures subject to FECA restrictions because they did not use the "magic words," such as *vote for* or *vote against,* that most previous court decisions had deemed necessary for the application of federal limits. The committees therefore paid for the advertising campaigns with a mixture of hard money and soft money—but mostly soft money—eventually spending a combined total of more than $65 million.[5]

These advertising campaigns pushed the borders of federal law and directly challenged the ability of federal regulators to control spending in presidential campaigns. If such actions were allowable, then the regulations were basically meaningless, since candidates could rely on party monies or other outside funding to assist them in their campaigns, regardless of any spending limits. Moreover, party committees could work with candidates to raise soft money that could be used to finance activities designed to benefit their campaigns. But whether such efforts were permissible under the provisions of the FECA was uncertain in 1996. While party lawyers claimed that these methods of subverting the rules were legal, they were based on gray areas in the law that needed further regulatory decisions.

Prior to the 2000 elections, the Federal Election Commission (FEC) took no action to prohibit or even deter the financial schemes that were used in 1996. Various recommendations were made for penalizing the Clinton and Dole campaigns for receiving "excessive contributions" from the party committees and exceeding the spending limits,[6] for censuring the Democratic Party for improperly coordinating its ads with the Clinton campaign,[7] or for punishing the AFL-CIO for aligning its activities too closely with Democratic campaigns, but the Commission deadlocked, closed its investigations, and failed to rule as to whether these practices were legal or illegal.[8] It simply left the law in limbo, albeit in a lighter shade of gray, since in this case not to decide was to decide with respect to future election activity.

Congress and the Department of Justice also investigated the financial activities associated with the funding of the 1996 presidential campaign, but neither took actions that would prevent similar efforts in the future. The FEC considered new rulemakings on soft-money coordination, but discussions in both 1998 and 2000 failed to produce any new guidelines or restrictions.[9] These regulatory failures emboldened party leaders and candidates alike in advance of the 2000 campaign. In 1998 they further extended and refined the tactics used in 1996, expending millions of dollars in soft money on issue ads and voter mobilization efforts to assist congressional candidates during the midterm elections.[10]

As a result, a new model of campaign funding emerged, one that relied on soft-money advertising by parties to supplement the resources raised by the candidates themselves. This new model placed a premium on soft money and encouraged party candidates to seek such contributions more aggressively. It also produced a more dynamic calculus for campaign finance, since the regulatory actions following the 1996 election also did nothing to prevent ad hoc political committees and organized political groups from spending money on issue ads to influence federal races. Candidates therefore had to worry about the outside money that might flood into the districts from the parties or other sources, as well as the monies raised by their opponents, in planning their own fund-raising efforts. This encouraged candidates, particularly those in marginal races, to raise as much as they could in anticipation of the 2000 contests, and led them to look to the parties for assistance more than they had in the recent past.

Given the premium on fund-raising in such an environment, it is not surprising that some party leaders and political groups soon found an innovative solution to their strategic concerns: the formation of political committees under Section 527 of the Internal Revenue Code, which exempts "political organizations" from income taxes. So long as a Section 527 organization does not "expressly advocate" the election or defeat of federal candidates, it can engage in activities that seek to "influence the outcome of federal elections" without being subject to FECA restrictions or disclosure requirements. Moreover, because these organizations are exempt from federal taxation, they can receive gifts of more than $10,000 without being subject to the federal gift tax.[11]

Established before issue advocacy advertising became a popular campaign strategy, Section 527 did not require the disclosure of an organization's contributors, because Congress assumed that they would already be reported to the FEC or the appropriate state agency. This gap between the FECA and the Internal Revenue Code, a gap largely created by the gray area of "issue advocacy," provided political groups with a loophole that they rapidly began to exploit in anticipation of the 2000 election. Specifically, groups began to form under Section 527 for the express purpose of raising and spending unlimited sums on issue advocacy.[12] This tactic allowed them to avoid federal campaign finance regulations and federal taxation, thus providing them with a secret and unrestricted ability to participate in election campaigns.

Congress swiftly reacted to this development and passed legislation in July 2000 that placed a minimal reporting requirement on these organizations,[13] but it did not impose any limits on funding or prohibit any issue advocacy activities. This new legislation, the first major change in federal campaign finance rules since 1979, therefore did little to discourage the use of these organizations in connection with federal elections. It did, however, offer candidates and political groups yet another means of funding campaign activities without significant restrictions.

PRESIDENTIAL PRENOMINATION CAMPAIGNS
The dramatic growth in campaign resources began with the race for the White House. Overall, the eighteen major candidates who sought the party nominations raised a total of $343 million, or $100 million more than the amount raised by the seventeen major candidates who had sought the party standards in 1996. This rise was largely due to the lopsided financial battle led by two Republican candidates, George W. Bush and Steve Forbes, who chose to forego public monies and operate their campaigns free of spending limits. The Democratic contest was waged between two candidates, Al Gore and Bill Bradley, who did accept public funding and spent relatively equal sums on their campaigns.

Public money played an important role in the financial strategies of a few candidates, particularly Democrats Gore and Bradley and Republican John McCain. But the percentage of total funding provided by public matching funds, which are provided to qualified candidates on a dollar-for-dollar basis on individual contributions up to $250, was only about 17 percent, the smallest share since the program was adopted (the normal share is around 30 percent). This reduced public funding rate was primarily due to the fact that two of the best financed contenders, Bush and Forbes, did not participate in the program, while five other Republican hopefuls either failed to qualify for the subsidy or refused to accept it (Orrin Hatch). Another reason for the low proportion of matching funds was that all candidates concentrated on large gifts in an effort to raise money more quickly and efficiently. For example, by the third quarter of 1999, Gore and Bradley were raising over 70 percent of their total receipts from $1,000 donors, and McCain was accruing almost half of his receipts from this source.[14]

Another factor that spurred campaign fund-raising in the race for the Oval Office was the compressed delegate selection calendar, which significantly increased the revenue demands of the process, since it required candidates to campaign in at least eighteen states during the first month of the selection process (see chapter 2). Candidates therefore had to raise more money early in the election cycle than was the case in previous elections if they hoped to build the war chests needed to wage viable campaigns in key contests. This need for early money was exacerbated in the Republican race by the decisions of Bush and Forbes to opt out of the public funding scheme, since it meant that any candidate who hoped to compete financially would have to amass substantial resources to contend against these opponents capable of spending unlimited sums.

Candidates also had to accommodate the operational disparity between campaign spending limits and contribution limits. Because the spending limits are indexed to inflation and because the FEC made some changes in the rules regarding legal and accounting costs, candidates who accepted public funding were able to spend up to $45.6 million in 2000, as opposed to $37.1 million in 1996. The contribution limits, however, are not indexed, so candidates had to raise a significantly greater number of contributions than they had four years earlier if they were going to spend the total amount allowed by the law.

One solution to the strategic problem of balancing massive fund-raising efforts against tight spending limits is to forego public money and thereby avoid the spending limits, but no major party nominee had ever successfully adopted this approach. That changed in 2000, when George W. Bush demonstrated that it was possible to wage an entirely privately financed campaign and capture the party's presidential mantle. In all, Bush raised more than $94 million during the primary season — $91 million in individual contributions — or about $25 million more than the total individual receipts of his ten opponents combined. His leading challengers, Forbes and McCain, each raised about half the amount that Bush did, but Bush's war chest dwarfed the resources of the other Republican challengers, leaving them financially uncompetitive (see table 5.1).

Bush could do without public funding because he entered the race with a fund-raising base comparable to that of an incumbent president. In January 1998, more than a year before the first check was sent to his presidential exploratory committee, Bush had begun meeting in Texas with some of the Republican Party's most influential fund-raisers and several governors who promised to assist his campaign for the nomination.[15] This base of supporters built upon a broad

Table 5.1   Financial Activity of 2000 Presidential Prenomination Campaigns

Candidate	Adjusted Receipts ($)	Individual Contributions ($)	Public Matching Funds ($)	Political Committee Contributions ($)	Other Receipts ($)	Total Expenditures ($)
Democrats						
Gore	49,202,745	33,871,206	15,317,872	0	13,667	42,478,461
Bradley	42,142,565	29,270,589	12,462,045	0	409,931	41,088,547
LaRouche	4,505,658	3,319,038	1,184,372	590	1,658	4,481,792
Republicans						
Bush	94,466,341	91,331,951	0	1,960,060	1,174,330	89,135,337
Alexander	3,085,631	2,301,747	0	80,383	703,501	3,085,632
Bauer	12,136,548	7,553,317	4,632,803	6,000	(55,572)	11,761,561
Dole	5,127,832	5,001,635	0	118,292	7,905	5,122,723
Forbes	48,144,976	5,752,150	0	0	42,392,826	47,846,044
Hatch	2,552,723	2,124,707	0	173,016	255,000	2,509,154
Kasich	3,191,083	1,702,668	0	77,224	1,411,191	2,335,793
Keyes	10,999,752	7,663,253	3,325,340	10,100	1,057	10,575,767
McCain	45,047,937	28,143,613	14,467,788	405,599	2,030,937	44,614,846
Quayle	6,317,695	4,083,201	2,087,748	43,200	103,546	5,922,577
Smith	1,614,198	1,522,128	0	17,070	75,000	1,795,231
Other Parties						
Buchanan	10,536,435	6,651,221	3,852,247	1,000	31,967	10,625,582
Hagelin	1,179,980	755,319	314,135	0	110,526	770,257
Nader	1,463,567	1,319,434	100,000	0	44,133	993,506
Browne	1,248,198	1,217,198	0	0	31,000	1,254,213
Subtotals						
Democrats	95,850,968	66,460,833	28,964,289	590	425,256	88,048,800
Republicans	232,684,716	157,180,370	24,513,679	2,890,944	48,099,723	224,704,665
Others	14,428,180	9,943,172	4,266,382	1,000	217,626	13,647,616
Grand total	342,963,864	233,584,375	57,744,350	2,892,534	48,742,605	326,401,081

Source: Federal Election Commission, as of 31 July 2000.

Note: The totals for "other receipts" include candidate contributions, all loans, and transfers from other committees. The totals for expenditures include operating expenses, fund-raising costs, and legal and compliance funds.

preestablished fund-raising base: in his two winning gubernatorial campaigns in Texas, Bush had generated $41 million, so his home state promised to provide a solid foundation for financial success.[16] Bush also could rely on the fund-raising network that his father, former President George H. W. Bush had built over the years. (The Bush family Christmas card list alone consisted of 35,000 people, and his father's network included an estimated 50,000 donors.[17]) More important, Bush recruited a broad group of campaign fund-raisers, the Pioneers, who each agreed to be responsible for raising $100,000 by identifying ten individuals who would each give $1,000 and then in turn find ten others to do the same.[18] By

March of 2000 the campaign had more than 180 Pioneers, who had raised more than $18 million.[19]

What was truly remarkable, however, was the success of this operation, which went far beyond the Bush campaign's own expectations and clearly established Bush, not just as the front-runner in the race, but as the prospective nominee long before a single vote was cast. Within a month of announcing the formation of a presidential exploratory committee, Bush had collected $7.6 million, including 500 donations of the maximum $1,000.[20] This sum was more than twice the amount collected by any of his competitors and was only the beginning of an astonishing fund-raising effort. By September 1999, he had generated $57 million, including more than $12 million from Texas donors.[21] In contrast, Forbes, his closest competitor, had raised only $21 million by this time, and McCain less than $9 million. By the end of the year, Bush's lead was even greater, as he garnered another $10 million in the fourth quarter alone, for a 1999 total of $67 million, more than three times his original goal of $20 million for the year and more than twice as much as any presidential candidate had ever before raised in a preelection year.[22]

Bush's financial momentum built steadily, as donors looking to follow a winner concentrated their giving on his campaign. By the end of the year, his campaign claimed 171,000 donors, and a senior adviser noted that "for every dollar we went out and raised, another $2 came in, unexpected, over the transom."[23] Forbes tried to stay competitive, spending more than $28 million from his own wallet, but he still managed to reach only about half of Bush's total. McCain remained a distant third with close to $16 million, including $2 million transferred from his Senate campaign fund to his presidential committee.[24]

Bush's financial superiority had a number of effects on the dynamics of the Republican contest. First, it played a principal role in establishing Bush as the candidate to beat and the likely nominee. Having won the money race hands down, he built an unparalleled national campaign infrastructure and spent large sums on media and voter outreach during the crucial period leading up to the Iowa caucuses and New Hampshire primary. By the end of January, his campaign had thirty-four offices spread from Anchorage to Atlanta and 174 paid staff persons. McCain, in contrast, had only ten offices nationwide and a staff of 80.[25] In the last three months of 1999 Bush spent $17 million in total, which was more than McCain had raised during the entire year. In February 2000 Bush spent $13 million, or about $400,000 a day, with almost half of this total devoted to television and radio advertising in 7 March primary states and other important contests.[26]

Second, Bush's money, combined with his commanding lead in preelection year polls, which was in part a reflection of his money, made it extremely difficult for most other Republican hopefuls to get their own campaigns off the ground. The scope of his financing created a sense of inevitability that undermined the

fund-raising efforts of other challengers, leaving most of them in a financial position so weak that it was unlikely that they would last through the first events in
the process. The winnowing of the field thus began well before the voting in Iowa
and New Hampshire, where a significant paring of the field usually occurs. By
October 1999 six Republicans had opted out of the party nomination contest.[27]

One candidate who did not fall easily before the Bush juggernaut was
McCain, who made the most of his resources by deciding to avoid the Iowa caucuses and stake his fortunes on the outcome of the New Hampshire primary. He
sent 50,000 biographical videos to New Hampshire residents in July 1999 and
embarked on an aggressive travel schedule, making forty-nine trips to the state
between March 1999 and the first week of 2000, which was more than twice
the number of visits by Bush during the same period.[28] By July 1999 he had
moved ahead of Forbes to become Bush's main challenger in New Hampshire,
even though Forbes already had spent more than $8 million in the state and had
aired about $2.7 million in advertising in New Hampshire and other states.[29]

As a result of the front-loaded primary schedule, the advertising campaigns
began early in Iowa and New Hampshire. McCain had the monies needed to
compete over the airwaves, which was one of the keys to his surprisingly strong
New Hampshire victory. From the beginning of November until the week before
Christmas, McCain spent more than $650,000 on advertising in the Manchester,
New Hampshire, and Boston media markets — only about half the $1.1 million
spent by Bush, but enough to maintain a viable presence and allow McCain to
spread his pro-reform message, thereby reinforcing the basic themes he was artic-
ulating in dozens of small town-hall meetings throughout the state.[30] As of the
week before the primary, a Bush campaign official reported total media spending
in New Hampshire of $3.3 million, as opposed to $2.1 million for McCain.[31]

In recent presidential elections, unexpected winners in New Hampshire,
such as Democrat Paul Tsongas in 1992, or even those who finished better than
expected, found it difficult to build on any momentum that might come from
a strong performance in the nation's first primary because they did not have the
time to refill their depleted coffers before they had to begin spending money on
the next round of selection contests. In 2000, however, McCain was able to solve
this strategic problem and capitalize on his victory in New Hampshire as a result
of the advent of the Internet as a means of campaign fund-raising.

Although the Internet played little role in the 1996 election, in 2000 most of
the major presidential candidates used it both to distribute information through
campaign web sites and to raise money and recruit volunteers. McCain was one
candidate who recognized the potential of the Internet as a vehicle for building
support from very early on in the campaign, using it to raise campaign contributions throughout 1999. By the end of September, he had raised at least $260,000
online, second only to Democrat Bill Bradley, who had raised $650,000 via the
web by this point.[32] On the morning after his Granite State win, McCain re-

ceived more than $162,000 in credit card donations via his web site. At one point, contributions were pouring in at the rate of about $18,000 an hour. By the end of the week, more than $1.4 million had come in — nearly as much as he had raised over the Internet in the previous nine months. Most of the contributions were small gifts, averaging about $119 apiece, but with the matching funds these contributions drew, the total take was more than $2 million.[33] Two weeks later, the sum from Internet donations in February had reached $3.7 million, and the campaign's overall Internet revenues had reached $5 million.[34]

This influx of cash provided McCain with the resources needed to run aggressively in the post-New Hampshire primaries. In the next critical contest, South Carolina, he devoted $2.8 million to advertising, as compared to $3.3 million for Bush.[35] But Bush was able to slow McCain's momentum there largely because of the assistance he received from his political allies and organized interests.

The open-seat race for the presidency and the deep partisan divisions fueled by the scandals and investigations of the Clinton administration created a fruitful environment for issue advocacy efforts during the presidential primaries. Dozens of groups on both sides of the political aisle — many of them organized under Section 527 — engaged in advertising campaigns and voter turnout efforts to influence the outcome of the primaries. Most of these activities, about 62 percent, were devoted to supporting or opposing a particular candidate.[36] Organized interests that were particularly prominent included labor unions, pro-choice groups, environmental organizations, health care associations, and conservative groups such as the Christian Coalition, the National Tax Limitation Committee, and the Republican Leadership Council.

A major study of issue advocacy electioneering in the presidential primaries found that interest groups were very active in the contests leading up to the mid-March Super Tuesday primaries. At least fifty-five groups mounted issue advocacy campaigns on the Republican side, while forty-nine were active on the Democratic side. This electioneering, which was especially intense in the Republican race, began as early as March 1999, and the first target was George W. Bush, who faced television ads financed by the National Abortion Rights Action League (NARAL) that cast Bush as hostile to abortion rights. The Sierra Club also advertised against Bush's environmental record, spending about $60,000, with radio and television advertising beginning in New Hampshire in November 1999.[37] These efforts, however, were largely geared toward weakening Bush's prospects in the general election campaign rather than the presidential primaries, and were more than counterbalanced by the support Bush received from conservative groups throughout the primaries, including substantial expenditures by pro-life groups, the Christian Coalition, and the National Tax Limitation Committee, among others.[38]

The principal target of these issue advocacy efforts, however, was McCain, whose positions on campaign finance reform, tobacco taxation, federal budget reductions, and other issues established him as a maverick and drew strong opposition from conservative groups. After New Hampshire, the attacks on him intensified and groups concentrated their efforts on the South Carolina primary, which had become a must-win state for Bush. National and state pro-life groups worked together to send mailings to about 80,000 households in the state.[39] The Christian Coalition reportedly targeted mailings to 140,000 voters in the state,[40] and its head, the Reverend Pat Robertson, recorded 45,000 to 50,000 get-out-the-vote telephone calls.[41] The National Smokers Alliance spent $25,000 on radio and television advertising to remind voters of McCain's support of a $500 billion increase in taxes on tobacco, South Carolina's No. 1 cash crop.[42] These and other such efforts helped Bush to a 13-point victory in the state.

McCain's fund-raising success after New Hampshire left him in the best financial position that he was to experience throughout the entire campaign. Bush's profligate spending in the months leading up to South Carolina had left him with only about $10 million in cash by the end of February, while McCain had over $8 million to spend.[43] But this was not enough to overcome Bush's substantial aggregate advantage in money and organizational strength, which was compounded by the electioneering of outside groups. On 7 March McCain failed to achieve the victories he needed to continue his quest, but even if he had managed enough victories, he would have had trouble capturing the nomination. Before the end of March, he had already essentially reached the spending limit imposed on publicly funded candidates. The story of his campaign thus highlighted many of the problems of the current campaign finance system, demonstrating the need for further regulation of unrestricted funds, while at the same time exposing the inadequacy of the limits that now exist.

The Democratic race differed greatly from the Republican race in that it featured a contest between two major candidates, Vice President Al Gore and former U.S. Senator Bill Bradley, with relatively equal resources. Gore differed from Bush in that he accepted public funding and agreed to abide by spending limits. But his basic strategy was essentially the same: to capitalize on his fund-raising abilities and amass an insurmountable financial advantage that would allow him to outspend his opponents by substantial amounts in the key early contests. His campaign spoke of a $55 million fund-raising goal — the amount they thought could be raised and spent legally under the FECA limits if every loophole was exploited.[44] Gore ended up raising $49.2 million, and actually exceeded his goal, because the $55 million included $8 million the campaign hoped to raise for general election compliance funding that was not raised until after he secured the nomination due to a change in FEC rules.

Bradley, however, proved to be a candidate with financial muscle of his own, and he presented a greater challenge to Gore than most assumed at the beginning of the election cycle. Although he was no longer a member of the Senate, he retained a strong network of supporters from his years in office and offered the option of a party standard-bearer who would not be tainted by the scandals that beleaguered the Clinton administration. By the middle of 1999, Bradley was on track to raise more than $20 million in the preelection year, which most experts considered to be the sum needed to finance a viable effort in the front-loaded selection process. More important, his lower rate of spending and comparable amount of cash on hand suggested that he would be able to compete financially with the vice president and established his credibility as a candidate.[45]

In the third quarter of 1999 Bradley's fund-raising was gaining momentum, as he generated more money than Gore in three key Democratic money states — California, New York, and Illinois — and, like Gore, had great success with large donors, receiving about 80 percent of his funds from $1,000 givers.[46] By early October, his fund-raising total had reached $18.4 million, or about $6 million less than the vice president. But Bradley's relatively small and efficient operation had spent less than $9 million, as compared to the Gore campaign's $14 million.[47] As a result, the campaigns were basically equal in available cash ($10 million), and Bradley had gained a sizable advantage in terms of potential spending, since under the spending limit he would be able to spend $5 million more than the vice president during the actual selection phase of the process.

Gore's greater rate of spending was largely due to the higher overhead costs he incurred as a result of his large campaign organization and costly downtown Washington office location. Recognizing that this spending pace could not continue without ceding a major financial advantage to his opponent, Gore took action in October, substantially reducing his campaign budget in an effort to conserve resources for the Iowa and New Hampshire contests. The most dramatic change was to move the campaign headquarters to Nashville, Tennessee, where rent and other overhead expenses would be much cheaper, but the campaign also reduced the size of its staff, cut salaries and consulting fees, and streamlined its fund-raising and polling operations.[48]

By the end of January 2000 the two Democrats had reached equity in their campaign funding, at $29.6 million and $29.2 million, respectively.[49] Although he trailed Gore in the polls, Bradley thus had the resources available to compete financially in Iowa and New Hampshire, and he did. As of mid-January, he had more days in Iowa and New Hampshire than Gore had,[50] and he outspent the vice president on television advertising in both states. By the last week of January, Bradley's total television spending in New Hampshire had reached $2.9 million versus $1.7 million for Gore, and in the week before the New Hampshire primary he outspent Gore by a margin of $735,000 to $499,000.[51]

While Bradley spent more, Gore won more, essentially locking up the nomination by winning in both Iowa and New Hampshire. Bradley continued on, devoting resources to the non-binding primary in Washington State and beginning to advertise in important early March primaries. By the middle of February, he had outspent Gore on television in upcoming primaries by a margin of 2 to 1.[52]

But these efforts were not enough to overcome Gore's strengths, which included his campaign's organizational advantage in key states, his performance in the candidate debates, and the momentum he gained from his early victories. Nor were they enough to overcome the support Gore received from organized groups, especially labor unions, during the early stages of the selection process (see chapter 2). As in the Republican contest, organized groups spent substantial sums on electioneering campaigns that benefited the front-runner. The vast majority of these efforts centered on Gore and were based on pro-Gore messages that sought to reinforce the campaign's message and broaden his base of support. According to one analysis, about 70 percent of the interest group electioneering on the Democratic side focused on supporting Gore.[53]

With both party nominations wrapped up before the end of March, the presidential general election contest would begin well before the national nominating conventions. In mid-March, the two presumptive nominees, Bush and Gore, had relatively equal amounts of money, as Bush had $10 million remaining from his $70 million war chest, and Gore had $3.7 million plus an additional $7.3 million in accrued matching funds.[54] Bush would go on to raise an additional $20 million before his primary campaign was over, while Gore faced the constraint imposed by the public funding limit. But, in the end, these monies would represent a relatively small portion of the monies expended on the general election campaign, as party committees and organized groups joined the candidates in spending record sums in the race to gain the Oval Office.

PRESIDENTIAL GENERAL ELECTION

Bush and Gore both accepted the general election subsidy provided by the public financing program. Each received $67.6 million in public money after being declared the nominee at his respective party nominating convention. In addition, these candidates were allowed to raise private contributions, subject to federal contribution limits, to pay for the legal and accounting costs incurred to comply with the spending limits and other requirements of the law. Both candidates began to raise these funds, known as General Election Legal and Accounting Compliance (GELAC) funds, early in the general election campaign. By the end of November, Bush had raised $6.8 million for this purpose, while Gore had raised $8.2 million (see table 5.2, p. 106). Each of the major-party candidates therefore had about $75 million available to his campaign committee in monies subject to FECA regulations.

Two other candidates, both running as nominees of minor parties, also raised significant amounts for the general election campaign. Ralph Nader, the Green Party nominee, was not eligible for general election public funding because his party had not received the requisite 5 percent of the vote in the previous presidential election to qualify for a share of the total subsidy, so he was allowed to raise private contributions subject to federal limits with no cap on spending. Nader formed a

Table 5.2 Presidential Candidates' General Election Funding (in millions)

Source	Total	Bush	Gore	Buchanan	Nader
Public Funding	$147.8	$67.6	$67.6	$12.6	0.0
Private Contributions	3.9	0.0	0.0	0.6	3.3
GELAC Funds	15.0	6.8	8.2	0.0	0.0
Total	$166.7	$74.4	$75.8	$13.2	$3.3

Source: Federal Election Commission, as of 30 November 2000 filings.

campaign committee before the general election, which solicited close to $1 million, most of it in the form of small contributions received through solicitations at campaign events, concerts, and other party fund-raising activities. The committee also qualified for public matching funds, although it had been awarded only $44,000 by end of the campaign. Nader's general election fund-raising effort was more successful, as his outsider image and appeal as a reformer led to a modicum of support that netted him about $3.3 million in individual donations.

More substantial funding was available to the Reform Party nominee, who qualified for $12.6 million in public money by virtue of the 8.4 percent of the vote Ross Perot had received as the Reform Party candidate in 1996.[55] This financial award enhanced the desirability of the party's nomination significantly and led to a dispute over which candidate should receive this money. Because of the split that occurred at the Reform Party convention during the summer, the conservative former Republican Patrick Buchanan and the Natural Law Party's presidential nominee in 1992 and 1996, John Hagelin, were both claiming the Reform Party mantle. For the first time, the FEC was forced to resolve a dispute over the certification for general election funding and determine which of the two was entitled to receive the public funds.

In mid-September the FEC decided to grant the federal monies to Buchanan, simply resolving the funding dispute by relying on its rules regarding ballot status. These rules require that a minor-party candidate be on the general election ballot in at least ten states in order to receive a party's financial entitlement. The Commission determined that Buchanan was officially listed as a Reform Party candidate in twelve states, while Hagelin was only listed in three. It therefore ruled that Buchanan should receive the entitlement. The Commission did not try to resolve the contentious issue of which candidate was the "legitimate" party nominee, nor did it establish guidelines for the future as to how to proceed in an instance where two competing candidates met the minimum qualification.[56]

Under the law, Buchanan was allowed to raise private contributions up to the $67.6 million total that was permitted for presidential candidates. But he managed to raise only about $600,000, for total funding of $13.2 million. That sum allowed Buchanan to mount a campaign and even buy television advertising, but his effort produced little support, and the major effect of his poor showing in the general election was to render the Reform Party ineligible for preelection public funding in 2004.

While the public funding available to the major-party candidates continued to be important, the most noteworthy phenomenon in the general election was the tens of millions of dollars poured into the contest from parties and organized groups, beginning in the summer and continuing throughout the general election campaign. Indeed, for the first time since the FECA was adopted, the party committees spent more on political advertising than did the presidential candidates themselves. This change in financial patterns documented the changes taking place in the campaign finance system and demonstrated, once and for all, the minimal effect of the candidate spending ceilings.

Party committees followed the model established in 1996, devoting substantial resources to issue advocacy advertisements that featured their respective nominees. This tactic allowed them to spend much more in connection with the presidential contest than was permitted under the coordinated spending provisions of the FECA, under which each national party was allowed to spend up to $13.7 million in support of the presidential ticket, all of it derived from hard-money funds. The parties did make coordinated expenditures in the presidential race, but this spending was not their major emphasis. According to FEC filings as of 18 October, the Republicans had spent $11.7 million on behalf of Bush, but the Democrats had only spent $5.4 million in support of Gore, less than half the permissible amount, with only three weeks left in the election. Additional spending in the final days may have increased these totals and perhaps even reached the legal maximum. Even so, these amounts were dwarfed by the amounts of money spent on issue advertising.

Altogether, candidates, parties, and organized groups combined for more than $163 million in presidential general election television advertising.[57] The national party committees together spent $79.1 million on television advertising in the presidential campaign, as compared to $67.1 million spent by the candidate committees. According to an analysis by the Brennan Center for Justice of the top seventy-five media markets during the period from 1 June to 7 November, the Bush campaign devoted $39.2 million to television advertising, or about 58 percent of its public funding, while the Republican National Committee spent $44.7 million. On the Democratic side, the Gore campaign spent $27.9 million on television advertising, or just over 40 percent of its public money, while the Democratic National Committee expended $35.1 million. In addition, organized political groups spent $16.1 million on presidential election ads, $14 million of which was spent in support of the Democratic ticket. In all, the Bush campaign and Republican Party spent a combined $84 million on television ads, as compared to an estimated $48 million in Republican spending four years earlier. Gore and the Democratic Party spent a combined $63 million, which was slightly more than the $61 million spent by the Democrats in 1996.[58]

The Democrats were the first to resort to issue advocacy spending, airing their first ad in early June, despite the fact that Gore had earlier said that Democrats would not run soft-money-financed advertising unless the Republicans did so first. In announcing the advertising strategy, the Democrats cited what they estimated to be $2 million in anti-Gore advertising by political groups that favored Bush, including a group called Shape the Debate and a missile defense organization called the Coalition to Protect America Now.[59] The Democrats' ad, which touted Gore's commitment to fight for a prescription drug benefit for seniors, ran in fifteen states and was financed with a combination of hard and soft money.[60] Most of the funding was in the form of soft money that the national party transferred to state parties, since parties were able to use a greater percentage of soft money when buying television time if it was purchased by state party committees. This was in accord with FEC rules, which place different allocation requirements on state party committees. Generally, these committees can finance at least two-thirds of their advertising costs with soft money, as opposed to 35 percent for the national committees in a presidential year. In using this tactic, the Democrats were following the approach they had first used in 1996, which had become a basic method of operating by 2000. The Republicans also used this approach in paying for their candidate-specific issue advertisements.

Once the Democrats had begun their assault, the Republicans were quick to follow. Only a few days after the Democrats launched their ads, the Republicans announced a campaign of their own. On 10 June, the Republican National Committee unveiled a $2 million ad campaign targeted mainly in the same presidential battlegrounds as the Democratic television buy. The only difference was that the Republicans also purchased time in Maine and Arkansas. This first commercial presented Bush's proposal to allow workers to invest part of their Social Security payroll taxes in the stock market.[61]

The key electoral battleground states received the heaviest concentrations of advertising dollars. Other than California, the only major states in which the Republicans outspent the Democrats in terms of advertising dollars were Florida and Tennessee. In Florida, the state that proved to hold the key to the White House, the combined advertising by candidates, party committees, and political groups gave Bush a significant advantage, with total spending of about $14.5 million, as compared to $10.1 million on the Democratic side. In Tennessee, which Bush won even though it is Gore's home state, the Republican margin was $1.1 million to $869,000. But in most of the other major battlegrounds, including Pennsylvania, Ohio, and Michigan, the Democrats held the lead.[62]

Even more striking was the disparity in issue advertising by political groups, which favored Gore by a margin of 7 to 1. Americans for Job Security, a Section

527 organization supported by Republican Senate Majority Leader Trent Lott, was the only group to spend a substantial sum on behalf of Bush. This committee purchased almost $1.8 million in advertising (mostly in Washington, Oregon, Florida, and Tennessee), which represented 90 percent of the total amount of group advertising in support of Bush aired during the general election.[63]

Groups spent a combined $14 million on television advertising in support of Gore. This included $7.2 million in ads sponsored by Planned Parenthood, which constituted about half of all pro-Gore group advertising in the general election. The AFL-CIO spent $3.1 million, the Sierra Club about $1 million, and Handgun Control, Inc., $1.7 million. As with the advertising done by Americans for Job Security, the television time was mostly bought in media markets in swing states where each group's particular issues were most salient.[64]

What effect all this spending had on the eventual outcome of the race is difficult to assess. What is clear is that candidate financing was only a part of a much broader pattern of funding that, in essence, produced an almost indistinguishable flow of money that came from different sources but was put to similar purposes and delivered reinforcing messages to the electorate. Public money, hard and soft money raised by party organizations, and unregulated group money was all put to work toward common goals in a way that rendered the restrictions of the public funding program wholly ineffective. Indeed, the public money provided to candidates, while still important, played less of a role than in any other recent election, as the incentive to rely on soft money and the finances of independent groups became stronger and stronger.

FINANCING THE CONGRESSIONAL ELECTIONS

Party committees and independent political organizations were also very active in the congressional races. In fact, many groups devoted most of their resources to these contests, since the party in control of the legislative process was likely to have a greater effect on their particular policy interests than the party in control of the White House. As an added incentive, in many cases the resources available to these committees could have a greater effect if concentrated on particular House or Senate races where they could make a difference than if spent on the presidential election. At the very least, they would leave an impression that would gain a member's attention.

Further, party committees and organized interests had mounted substantial issue advocacy campaigns in the 1998 elections. They were therefore familiar with the strategies employed in these races and the influence they could have on particular outcomes, especially in marginal districts or close Senate contests.[65] This experience led parties and interest groups to conclude that in 2000 they should do more of the same. And that they did. In advertising alone, independent groups spent more than $25 million on issue advocacy advertising in support of Republican congressional candidates and about $15 million in support of Democrats.

The party committees also spent heavily, including nearly $23 million worth of advertising in House races by the Democrats and close to $17 million by the Republicans.[66] The national party committees, especially the House and Senate campaign committees on both sides of the aisle, each spent millions more on voter identification programs and get-out-the-vote efforts. Unregulated monies thus played a meaningful role in the congressional contests, just as they did in the presidential race. (For a discussion of the particulars of party and group spending in congressional races, see chapter 7.)

Anticipating that parties and interest groups would commit substantial amounts of money to congressional contests, congressional candidates raised record amounts of money. Incumbents and challengers alike sought to build war chests that would not only allow them to mount viable campaigns but also provide them with the resources needed to counter any outside funding that might be channeled into their races. Legislative candidates therefore had a powerful incentive to raise as much money as possible, as early as possible.

Expectations of a highly competitive congressional election year and of a stronger than usual complement of challengers encouraged legislators to begin raising money very aggressively early in the election cycle. House Republican leaders urged members elected with less than 55 percent of the vote or those who were otherwise vulnerable to try to have $200,000 in the bank by the middle of 1999, while House Democratic leaders urged their vulnerable members, including all freshmen, to set a goal of $150,000 in the bank by that time.[67]

Incumbents were not the only contenders to focus on fund-raising early: challengers were also getting a head start on fund-raising, especially in those districts likely to be competitive. Many of the candidates in these districts were encouraged to start early by party leaders or professionals at the congressional campaign committees, so that they would have the time needed to build a strong fund-raising base and garner the sums needed to contest these seats. Consequently, by the middle of 1999, sixteen Democratic candidates planning to run in marginal districts or seek open seats had already received over $100,000, as compared to three who reached that level at the same point in 1997. Among Republicans, at least eighteen nonincumbents had reached $100,000, and five had surpassed the $200,000 mark.

Given this early start, it is not surprising that congressional candidates raised a record amount of money. In all, candidates in the congressional general elections had solicited $800.7 million with three weeks to go before Election Day, an increase of 39 percent over the 1998 total. Spending had reached $683.1 million, a 42-percent increase over the amount disbursed two years earlier. The rise in financial activity was significant both in the House races, which saw increases of 31 percent in receipts and 35 percent in spending over the previous two-year period, and in the Senate races, where increases of 52 percent and 53 percent, respectively, were recorded (see tables 5.3 and 5.4).

Table 5.3 Financial Activity of 2000 House General Election Campaigns

	Number of Candidates	Receipts ($)	Individual Contributions ($)	Political Committee Contributions ($)	Candidate Loans and Contributions ($)	Other Loans ($)	Total Expenditures ($)
House	804	473,433,610	254,715,666	167,972,748	29,236,800	316,448	384,582,640
Democrats	371	235,308,296	120,236,307	86,854,101	17,519,424	251,142	192,163,049
Incumbents	204	150,534,048	73,398,961	68,128,756	568,371	35,035	117,628,695
Challengers	135	55,775,048	32,703,582	11,379,913	10,081,910	215,994	48,783,663
Open Seats	32	28,999,200	14,133,764	7,345,432	6,869,143	113	25,750,691
Republicans	359	234,529,537	132,523,866	80,675,713	10,728,422	50,629	189,561,716
Incumbents	196	168,269,518	92,953,241	65,574,734	1,765,870	32,000	132,230,711
Challengers	132	32,594,248	21,624,568	5,233,135	3,801,871	17,629	28,542,530
Open Seats	31	33,665,771	17,946,057	9,867,844	5,160,681	1,000	28,788,475
Other Party	74	3,595,777	1,955,493	442,934	988,954	14,677	2,857,875
Incumbents	3	1,847,599	1,385,103	399,485	0	0	1,478,193
Challengers	62	1,129,438	497,171	22,899	558,657	13,003	992,389
Open Seats	9	618,740	73,219	20,550	430,297	1,674	387,293
Totals							
Incumbents	403	320,651,175	167,737,305	134,102,975	2,334,241	67,035	251,337,599
Challengers	329	89,498,734	54,825,321	16,535,947	14,442,438	246,626	78,318,582
Open Seats	72	63,283,711	32,153,040	17,233,826	12,460,121	2,787	54,926,459

Source: Federal Election Commission, as of 18 October 2000 filings.

In the House races, Democrats and Republicans raised relatively equal amounts, with the Democrats holding a slight lead, taking in $235.3 million to the Republicans' $234.5 million. As is always the case in House races, the incumbents raised the largest portion of these sums and enjoyed a commanding advantage over those who sought to unseat them. Overall, incumbents raised more than three times as much as their opponents raised and spent. Republican incumbents raised about three times as much as was received by their Democratic challengers, while Democratic members raised more than four times as much as was brought in by their Republican challengers. The monies raised in open-seat contests slightly favored the Republicans, who raised about 15 percent more than their Democratic counterparts.

With more money available to spend, candidates disbursed more than ever, driving up the cost of a winning campaign for the House.[68] On average, the winners in House races had taken in about $825,000 by mid-October, which represented an increase of 26 percent from the average in 1998 and nearly twice as much as the level set in the period from 1990 to 1994. The cost of victory, however, was significantly higher in open-seat races. Incumbents raised an average of $630,500, almost twice the average of $326,400 received by their opponents, but

Table 5.4 Financial Activity of 2000 Senate General Election Campaigns

	Number of Candidates	Receipts ($)	Individual Contributions ($)	Political Committee Contributions ($)	Candidate Loans and Contributions ($)	Other Loans ($)	Total Expenditures ($)
Senate	108	327,220,360	186,489,306	45,397,696	75,768,118	515,068	298,558,105
Democrats	32	178,138,888	76,782,093	16,959,506	74,615,695	300,000	161,266,389
Incumbents	11	39,618,416	24,433,377	9,025,344	4,084,276	0	28,904,018
Challengers	16	45,613,784	21,407,800	4,606,616	16,848,748	300,000	43,150,294
Open Seats	5	92,906,688	30,940,916	3,327,546	53,682,671	0	89,212,077
Republicans	33	146,837,255	108,010,607	28,415,188	659,535	215,000	135,231,307
Incumbents	18	78,803,908	50,886,957	20,611,111	300,100	0	71,984,213
Challengers	10	16,940,467	13,092,423	1,551,787	307,135	215,000	14,267,814
Open Seats	5	51,092,880	44,031,227	6,252,290	52,300	0	48,979,280
Other Party	43	2,244,217	1,696,606	23,002	492,888	68	2,060,409
Challengers	29	1,669,882	1,270,036	7,678	370,179	18	1,520,205
Open Seats	14	574,335	426,570	15,324	122,709	50	540,204
Totals							
Incumbents	29	118,422,324	75,320,334	29,636,455	4,384,376	0	100,888,231
Challengers	55	64,224,133	35,770,259	6,166,081	17,526,062	515,018	58,938,313
Open Seats	24	144,573,903	75,398,713	9,595,160	53,857,680	50	138,731,561

Source: Federal Election Commission, as of 18 October 2000 filings.

in the open-seat races, the average was over $1 million, as opposed to $636,300 for open-seat contenders in 1998.

The sizable financial difference between candidates in safe seats and candidates in close contests is best discerned by considering their finances in light of the final results. House incumbents who won with 60 percent of the vote or more averaged $684,700 with three weeks to go in the election. Those who won in close races with less than 60 percent of the vote, averaged more than $1.2 million. Open-seat candidates who received at least 60 percent of the vote averaged $960,400, while their counterparts who won in close contests averaged almost $1.3 million.

But money was not the whole story. As in every election since 1976, a winning challenger did not have to outspend an incumbent opponent in order to gain victory. Instead, what was needed was enough money to be able to mount a viable campaign and get one's message heard by the voters. Given the role of party and group spending in close contests, this took more money in 2000 than it had in the past, but it did not require that challengers match their more established opponents dollar-for-dollar. In races where incumbents were defeated, the incumbent's receipts averaged $2.2 million, or about one-third more than the $1.7 million received by the challenger. If the extraordinarily expensive race between Rogan and Schiff in California is excluded, the average amount raised by defeated incumbents drops to $1.4 million, which was still about a third more than the $1.1 million raised by their challengers.

In the Senate general election contests, Democrats raised more ($178.1 million) than did the Republicans ($146.8 million), even though there were eighteen Republican incumbents and only eleven incumbent Democrats The difference was largely due to the difference in open-seat races, and there the Democratic margin can be attributed wholly to the lavish spending of Jon Corzine, the Democratic challenger in the New Jersey open-seat race, who had raised $55.7 million as of 18 October, including $52.7 million out of his own pocket. His Republican opponent, Representative Robert Franks, received only $5 million, less than a tenth of Corzine's total.

Senate incumbents outraised their challengers by a margin of almost 2 to 1, but this advantage was not as great as that enjoyed by their House counterparts. Because the challengers in Senate races tend to be more established candidates with broad bases of support, they tend to fare better than challengers in House contests, who tend to be less experienced and less well-known to the electorate. The eighteen Republican incumbents solicited $78.8 million, as compared to $45.6 million for the sixteen Democratic challengers. The eleven Democratic incumbents had an even greater advantage, receiving a total of $39.6 million, or more than twice the $16.9 million received by the ten Republican challengers.

As of 18 October, the cost of winning a Senate seat was up significantly.[69] Overall, winning candidates raised an average of $6.3 million, substantially more than the $3.8 million average in 1994, which was the corresponding election year for the states holding Senate races in 2000. Winning incumbents, however, raised an average of $4.1 million, which was only slightly more than the average in 1994. The greatest change was in the open-seat races, largely due to the expensive contests in New York and New Jersey. On average, open-seat candidates raised $14.4 million, almost six times more than the $2.6 million averaged in 1994.

As in the House races, the cost of winning was greatest in close contests. Incumbents who won with 60 percent of the vote or more raised an average of $3.3 million, while those who won with less than 60 percent averaged $4.4 million. These amounts also were relatively equal to the comparable amounts in 1994, when incumbents in close contests averaged $4.3 million and those in safe seats averaged $3.6 million. But unlike the case in the House, challengers who defeated incumbents did surpass their opponents, although not by wide margins. Winning challengers averaged $7 million, as opposed to the $6.7 million raised by the incumbents they defeated.

Besides the growth in candidate fund-raising, the 2000 congressional elections were notable for the innovative fund-raising devices used to build candidate coffers or supplement the monies raised by candidate campaign committees. Some of these financial tactics fell completely within the limits of the FECA, but others relied on legalisms that allowed candidates to circumvent the FECA and raise funds that were not reported to the FEC as part of the candidates' campaign financing.

The most innovative tactic was the creation of the joint fund-raising committee, established between a candidate and a party organization or between two or more party organizations to raise money for both of the participants. The committee conducts one fund-raising operation and then splits the proceeds in some way or simply spends the money. Prior to 2000 most joint fund-raising committees were related to party fund-raising efforts, wherein a national party committee and state party committee(s) would form a separate committee to raise monies that would then be divided between the participating party organizations. The 2000 cycle, however, produced a new twist on this old technique: the establishment of joint fund-raising committees between specific federal candidates and party committees.

Joint candidate-party fund-raising committees began to be set up deliberately early in 2000, especially in connection with competitive Senate races. Most of the committees were created between the party's Senate contender and the party's Senate campaign committee, either the Democratic Senate Campaign Committee (DSCC) or the National Republican Senatorial Committee (NRSC). In New York, the Democrats established a committee called New York Democratic Victory 2000 that linked Hillary Rodham Clinton's campaign committee and the Democratic National Committee, as well as a committee called New York Senate 2000 that linked the DSCC and the New York State Democratic Committee. Democratic committees were also formed in conjunction with senators or Senate candidates in California, Delaware, Florida, Indiana, Massachusetts, Michigan, Missouri, New Mexico, and Pennsylvania. On the Republican side, committees were established in California, Missouri, Pennsylvania, and Washington.

These joint committees allowed candidate and party organizations to mine candidate donor bases for contributions that candidate campaign committees could not accept under FECA rules. Candidates could solicit additional monies from donors who had given the maximum $1,000 to their campaigns or from PACs that had given the maximum $5,000 by asking them to make an additional contribution to the joint committee. It also provided a means by which soft money contributions from individuals, corporations, and labor unions could be solicited. The funds received could not be used to expressly advocate the election or defeat of a particular Senate hopeful, but they could be used to finance party activities that would benefit that candidate — such as issue advocacy advertising or voter turnout efforts in a particular state. This innovation thus blurred the line between hard-money and soft-money funding in federal races and provided a way for candidates to solicit soft-money donations that would be earmarked for use in connection with their own individual races.

By June 2000 at least eighteen joint fund-raising committees established in association with federal candidates had already received about $13 million. Most of this money, about $10 million, had been raised by the thirteen committees established by the Democrats; the other $3 million was received by the five committees established by Republicans.[70] In most instances, the funds generated were divided in complicated ways. Generally, the candidate's campaign committee received the first $2,000 given by a donor, which represented the maximum contribution of $1,000 for the primary and $1,000 for the general election. The remainder of any hard-dollar contributions were taken by the party, up to the federal maximum of $20,000. Any additional funds from a donor or any monies from sources not allowed to make hard-dollar donations were categorized as soft-money gifts to the party. The tactic thus broke down the walls on candidate contribution limits, since it allowed candidates to solicit gifts that exceeded contribution limits.

Congressional incumbents also devoted a substantial amount of time to raising money from their donors for other candidates or party committees. While members have been making contributions to other members or challengers from their own campaign funds for some time, and have solicited funds for the party for some time, none of the previous efforts were as extensive or aggressive as those in 2000. The leadership in both parties urged members in safe districts to help the party's candidates in marginal districts by raising money on their behalf and raising hard money for the party that could be used to finance the hard-dollar share of party issue advertising campaigns and get-out-the-vote programs.

The most ambitious effort in this regard was launched by the House Republicans in a new program known as Battleground 2000, which was designed to raise money for the party's congressional campaign committee by imposing party fund-raising quotas on Republican members of Congress. The quotas varied depending on the status of the individual member, with higher amounts imposed on leaders and committee chairs and those members who were running in safe districts. Some senior members in safe districts were asked to raise as much as $700,000 for the party, with the overall goal of raising $16 million from 222 House Republicans. The funds were to be used by the party to win the "ground war" in thirty-five tightly fought congressional districts.[71]

In mid-October, the Republicans announced that they had met their Battleground 2000 goal: 204 House Republicans, 94 percent of the party's delegation, had raised a total of $17.5 million, including $1.7 million in soft money. The largest funders included Speaker Dennis Hastert, who had given $850,000; Majority Leader Dick Armey and Majority Whip Tom DeLay, who each contributed about $800,000; and National Republican Congressional Campaign Committee chair Tom Davis, who donated $700,000.[72] All of this money did not come from the candidates' own campaign receipts: in many instances, candidates asked donors to give money directly to the party on their behalf, or they contributed funds from their leadership PACs or other political committees with which they were associated. But the effort was impressive nonetheless, and is likely to stand as a new model for congressional party fund-raising efforts in 2002 and beyond.

In 2000, 317 incumbents who won with 60 percent of the vote or more contributed about $22 million, or 10 percent of their total receipts, to other candidates or party committees.[73] This amount included $4.6 million donated to other candidates — almost twice as much as had been contributed to others in 1992 — and $17.3 million given to party committees. This last figure represented a steep increase over previous presidential election years, and a dramatic change from the practices of less than a decade earlier. In 1992, safe incumbents gave only $400,000 to party committees; in 1996, they gave $5.5 million. Safe incumbents raised record sums in 2000 because they were concerned not only about their own reelection prospects but also about the reelection prospects of others. The assistance they provided did, however, serve their own interests, since their status in the next Congress, especially any prospective leadership positions, would depend on the outcome of the battle for majority control.

POLITICAL PARTY FINANCING

Given the emphasis on party fund-raising throughout the election cycle, it is not surprising that both national parties shattered their previous fund-raising records. The parties raised $877 million by mid-October, almost half of which, roughly $410 million, came from soft-money contributions. This soft-money total was almost double the $262 million that the parties took in during the entire 1996 cycle. This fact alone demonstrates the extent to which party committees have come to rely on unrestricted monies in conducting their election campaigns.

Although party hard-money and soft-money receipts both grew in 2000, the hard-money contributions increased at a much lower rate. This was due in part to the federal contribution limits, which restricted the amounts a donor could give to federal party accounts. As in every election since the FECA was adopted, the Republican Party enjoyed a significant advantage in hard-dollar fund-raising. By mid-October, the Republican National Committee (RNC), National Republican Senatorial Committee (NRSC), and National Republican Congressional Committee (NRCC) had solicited $294.9 million in federal contributions, and spent $252 million (see table 5.5), reflecting modest increases of 6 percent in receipts and 7 percent in total spending over the amounts raised and expended at the comparable point in the 1996 election cycle. The Democratic National Committee (DNC), Democratic Senatorial Campaign Committee (DSCC), and Democratic Congressional Campaign Committee (DCCC) took in a combined $172.7 million in federal contributions and spent $153.5 million, representing increases of 24 percent in total receipts and 15 percent in disbursements. Although the Democrats showed greater improvement, they had a longer way to go, and the Republicans still managed to outraise them by more than 70 percent.

Table 5.5   National Party Committee Federal Financial Activity — Hard Money
(in thousands of dollars)

	Receipts	Expenditures	Contributions	Coordinated Expenditures	Independent Expenditures
Democrat					
DNC	103,942	86,255	1	5,432	0
DSCC	34,108	33,887	323	54	0
DCCC	35,107	33,820	564	1,929	77
Total	172,728	153,533	888	7,415	77
Republican					
RNC	177,278	149,684	382	19,537	0
NRSC	43,238	41,268	427	0.2	0.6
NRCC	84,883	71,644	658	2,082	549
Total	294,850	252,048	1,467	21,620	549

Source: Federal Election Commission, as of 18 October 2000 filings.

Note: Totals exclude transfers between committees.

Parties can use their hard money to make contributions to candidates and finance coordinated expenditures made on a candidate's behalf. The Republicans spent three times as much on these activities as the Democrats, devoting a total of $23.6 million to candidate support, including $21.6 million on coordinated expenditures, $1.4 million on direct candidate contributions, and $549,000 on independent expenditures that expressly advocated the election of a specific candidate. About half the amount used for coordinated spending was disbursed in the presidential race to support George W. Bush. The Democratic committees spent only $8.3 million on candidate support, including $7.4 million on coordinated expenditures, $888,000 on direct candidate contributions, and $77,000 on independent expenditures. More than half the amount disbursed for coordinated spending was used to support Al Gore.

The amounts devoted to candidate support by both parties fell far below the permissible amounts allowed by the FECA. The Republicans devoted less hard money to candidate support than they had in 1996. In fact, the sums were comparable to the amounts spent in 1992, when the Republicans made $1.9 million in candidate contributions and $19.7 million in coordinated expenditures and commonly spent the maximum allowed under the law in every key Senate contest; in 2000, they did not even approach the permissible limit in any race. The Democrats also spent significantly less on candidate support than they had at the beginning of the decade. In 1992 the party raised only $85 million in hard money, half the 2000 total, but spent $20.5 million on candidate contributions and coordinated expenditures, or roughly $12 million more than it did in 2000. In Senate races, the amount of coordinated spending dropped from $6.4 million in 1992 to

$53,000 in 2000. In House races, the decline was less significant but still notable, moving from $2.5 million in 1992 to $1.9 million in 2000.[74]

This decline in the financing of candidate support activities made clear the shift in party financial priorities that had been taking place since 1996: instead of devoting precious hard-money resources on federally restricted candidate campaign activities, both parties conserved these resources to use as triggers for spending soft money on issue advocacy advertising and other candidate-specific electioneering efforts. Hard dollars were more valuable when used in connection with soft money for unrestricted activities, because each dollar in federal money could facilitate the expenditure of two dollars in soft money. The parties could therefore make more efficient use of their resources by concentrating on soft-money spending.

Accordingly, both parties tried to raise as much soft money as possible, because they knew that it could be used for advertising in federal elections. As a result, soft-money financing grew at a much faster rate than hard-money financing. The Republican Party again led the way, with total adjusted soft-money receipts of almost $211 million by mid-October (see table 5.6). This represented an increase in receipts of 74 percent over the same period in 1996. Democrats were even more successful on a relative basis, garnering $199 million in soft-money receipts, which represented an increase of 85 percent over 1996. The Republicans therefore raised 42 percent of their total monies from soft-money contributions, while the Democrats raised 53 percent of their resources from this source—for the first time since the FECA was adopted, a national party received most of its money from unregulated sources.

Much of the increase in soft-money fund-raising can be attributed to the soft-money activities of the congressional campaign committees, especially the Democratic Party committees. For the first time, the DSCC and DCCC took in more soft money than did their Republican counterparts. Moreover, each of these committees solicited five times as much soft money as it had four years earlier and more than twenty times more than it had received in 1992. The Democrats' Senate committee had accumulated $52.3 million in soft money with three weeks to go in the election, as opposed to $9.7 million raised in 1996. The House committee brought in $49.3 million, compared to $9.2 million in 1996. The combined total of $102 million far surpassed the 1996 total of about $19 million and dwarfed the $4.6 million the two committees had raised in 1992.

The Republican Hill committees also increased their soft-money resources, but their rate of growth was not as impressive as that achieved by the Democrats. The NRSC raised $37.6 million, almost twice as much as the $19.9 million it had received in 1996. The NRCC raised $41.2 million, more than double the $17.4 million it had brought in four years earlier.

As indicated in table 5.6, both parties transferred large sums of soft money to state party committees in order to take advantage of the allocation rules and

Table 5.6   National Party Committee Nonfederal Financial Activity — Soft Money
(in millions of dollars)

	Receipts	Expenditures	Transferred Amount to State/Local Party	Percentage of Receipts
Democrat				
DNC	106.2	98.2	52.6	49
DSCC	52.3	51.1	30.3	58
DCCC	49.3	40.6	23.6	48
Total	207.8	190.4	106.5	51
Adjusted Total	199.0	181.6	–	
Republican				
RNC	136.3	124.8	75.6	55
NRSC	37.6	37.3	16.6	44
NRCC	41.2	39.8	6.4	15
Total	217.7	203.9	98.6	45
Adjusted Total	210.7	196.8	–	

Source: Federal Election Commission, as of 18 October 2000 filings.

Note: Adjusted totals exclude transfers between committees.

spend larger amounts. The combined total in state party transfers was $205.1 million, more than twice the amount transferred in 1996. The Democrats transferred $106.5 million to state or local parties, which constituted 51 percent of their soft-money revenues. The DNC and DCCC each transferred about half their soft money to states, while the DSCC led all committees, sending 58 percent of its soft money to other committees. The Republicans sent $98.6 million to state committees, which constituted 45 percent of their soft-money funding. The Republican transfers varied more widely than those of the Democrats, with the RNC sending 55 percent of its receipts to state and local committees, the NRSC transferring 44 percent, and the DCCC shifting only 15 percent.

The largest transfers were made to states that were considered presidential battlegrounds and those with key Senate races. For example, Florida received $8.8 million in soft money from Democratic committees and $8.6 million from Republican committees. Michigan was the recipient of $11.3 million in Democratic soft money and $6.6 million in Republican soft funds. Pennsylvania received $9.6 million in soft-money transfers from the Democrats and $7.5 million from the Republicans.

Exactly how these monies were spent is impossible to determine from FEC disclosure reports. The surveys of advertising conducted by the Brennan Center for Justice, which are the basis for the data on issue advertising expenditures in the presidential and congressional races, discovered that tens of millions of soft dollars were used for issue advertising. Tens of millions more undoubtedly were used to finance voter identification efforts, absentee ballot programs, and get-out-the-vote programs. A total accounting, however, can not be completed from FEC disclosure reports, which is another reason why parties shift funds around and prefer soft funding to hard dollars.

CONCLUSION

The 2000 elections evidenced a reinforcement and extension of the practices and patterns seen in other recent previous elections. The amounts of money raised and spent continued to climb at a significant rate. The trend toward early fund-raising continued unabated. Incumbents outspent challengers. Marginal and open-seat races were the most expensive races. And the quantities of unregulated soft money that flooded through the system rose at a remarkable pace.

The election exposed the inefficacy of FECA regulations and clearly demonstrated that little more than a shell remained of the reforms adopted more than twenty years earlier. While the problems with the current law had been evident for some time, in no previous election had they mattered so little or had so limited an effect on the financing of federal campaigns. The FECA, as currently interpreted and enforced, could no longer restrain most of the financial activity that takes place in modern elections. The rise of issue advocacy advertising and soft money, as well as newer innovations such as the use of Section 527 organizations as shadow campaign operations and joint fund-raising committees, had so blurred the lines between candidate funding and party or political group funding, hard-money activities and soft-money activities, election-related spending subject to the law and non-election-related spending exempt from the law, and express advocacy and issue advocacy that it is hard to speak of a "regulatory structure." It is more accurate to describe the 2000 elections as contests that were financed in a post-FECA regime system of funding and to cite 2000 as the year in which the system erected by that law finally collapsed.

The 2000 elections thus offered further evidence of the need for campaign finance reform and new approaches to the financing of political campaigns. And such reform seemed possible, given the events and outcomes of the 2000 campaigns. For the first time since the FECA was adopted, campaign finance reform was a major focus of attention in the presidential race. Many of the major contenders, spurred by the leadership of John McCain and the public response to his pro-reform platform, advocated reform and presented detailed proposals for how to remedy current problems. Even before the voting had begun, Gore and Bradley had joined McCain in offering major reform proposals. George W. Bush also argued for change, calling for the elimination of corporate and labor soft-money contributions and other modifications in the system, but he stopped well short of supporting proposals such as the McCain-Feingold bill. This bill, which called for a ban on soft-money financing and reform of the rules governing issue advocacy, had received the support of a majority of the House and Senate in the two Congresses that met between the 1996 and 2000 elections, only to be defeated by a Senate filibuster on more than one occasion by only a handful of votes.

After the election, McCain declared that he would once again push for reform, promising to seek quick action in Congress in 2001. His prospects for success were improved by his showing in the presidential race, which enhanced his status with the public, and by the election results, which produced a turnover in the Senate that netted four additional votes for reform.[75] By mid-December McCain believed that he had the votes needed to break a filibuster, but Republican leaders were already signaling their resistance to reform, and Bush made no mention of the subject in his first appearance on Capitol Hill as president-elect.[76]

With an equally divided Senate and a narrow margin of majority control in the House, moderates in Congress seemed ready to exert more influence in the legislature than had been the case in the past two sessions and to forge a proposal for campaign finance reform that could be passed. The dynamics of the 2000 elections also seemed likely to help the prospects for reform, perhaps encouraging some members to change the system rather than to have to be concerned about an onslaught of unrestricted party and group spending in a future race. This prospect, however, would be counterbalanced by the recognition that the new model of campaign finance was of great benefit to incumbents, since they formed the basis of the party elite that could raise the monies needed to compete successfully in a post-FECA system.

If reform legislation were not to be adopted or if Congress should choose to pass a bill containing only minor adjustments to current law, the patterns and practices that characterized the 2000 race would only be reinforced. Creative tactics and other innovations would produce additional means of circumventing the law, and the role of unrestricted monies would continue to grow, increasing the possibility of corruption in the political process.

NOTES

1. Jonathan D. Salant, "A Record-Setting Year for Campaign Spending," Associated Press press release, 6 November 2000, 1.
2. Ibid.; Alan C. Miller and T. Christian Miller, "Election Was Decisive in Arena of High Spending: Ever-Higher Sums," *Los Angeles Times,* 8 December 2000, A1; and Ruth Marcus, "Costliest Race in U.S. History Nears End," *Washington Post,* 6 November 2000, A1.
3. Federal Election Commission, "FEC Announces 2000 Presidential Spending Limits," press release, 1 March 2000, 1; and "FEC Announces 2000 Party Spending Limits," press release, 1 March 2000, 1.
4. Federal Election Commission, "FEC Announces 2000 Presidential Spending Limits."
5. For a discussion of these party advertisements, see Anthony Corrado, "Financing the 1996 Elections," in Gerald Pomper et al., *The Election of 1996* (Chatham, N.J.: Chatham House, 1997), 145–50.
6. See Federal Election Commission, *Report of the Audit Division on Clinton/Gore '96 Primary Committee, Inc.,* 19 November 1998, and *Report of the Audit Division on the Dole for President Committee, Inc.,* 19 November 1998.
7. Federal Election Commission, "Proposed Audit Report on the Clinton/Gore '96 Primary

Committee, Inc. — Media Advertisements Paid for by the Democratic National Committee," Memorandum to Robert J. Costa from Lawrence M. Noble et al., 27 October 1998.

8. Kenneth P. Doyle, "Fulani Filing Reveals FEC Rejected Staff Bid to Pursue Charges against Clinton Issue Ads," *BNA Money and Politics Report,* 25 May 2000, 1; and Kenneth P. Doyle, "FEC Votes to Drop 'Coordination' Case against AFL-CIO and Democratic Party," *BNA Money and Politics Report,* 6 September 2000, 1.

9. Kenneth P. Doyle, "Chairman Says FEC Will Again Consider Rulemakings on 'Soft Money' Coordination," *BNA Money and Politics Report,* 22 September 2000, 1.

10. For a discussion of party soft-money activities in association with the 1998 congressional elections, see *Outside Money: Soft Money and Issue Advocacy in the 1998 Congressional Elections,* ed. David B. Magleby (Lanham, Md.: Rowman & Littlefield, 2000); and Paul S. Herrnson, *Congressional Elections,* 3d ed. (Washington, D.C.: Congressional Quarterly, 2000), 84–119.

11. For background on Section 527 and its development, see Milton Cerny and Frances R. Hill, "Political Organizations," *Tax Notes,* 29 April 1996, 651; and Frances R. Hill, "Probing the Limits of Section 527 to Design a New Campaign Finance Vehicle," *Tax Notes,* 17 January 2000, 387.

12. Common Cause, *Under the Radar: The Attack of "Stealth PACs" on Our Nation's Elections* (Washington, D.C.: 2000), 7–9.

13. Public Law No. 106–230. This legislation, designated H.R. 4762 in both the House and Senate, was signed into law by President Bill Clinton on 1 July 2000.

14. Center for Responsive Politics, "Bigger Bundles in Third-Quarter Presidential Filings Show Rising Importance of $1,000 Donors to Front-Runners," press release, 4 November 1999, 1.

15. Don Van Natta Jr., "Early Rush of Contributions Opened the Floodgates for Bush," *New York Times,* 30 January 2000, A20.

16. Michael Isikoff, "The Money Machine," *Newsweek,* 24 January 2000, 48.

17. Van Natta, "Early Rush of Contributions."

18. Isikoff, "Money Machine," 48.

19. Elizabeth Shogren, "Campaign 2000: Focus Shifts from Voters to Donors," *Los Angeles Times,* 15 March 2000, A16.

20. Van Natta, "Early Rush of Contributions."

21. Ibid.

22. Don Van Natta Jr., "Bush Uses Family Ties to Build Up Treasury," *New York Times,* 30 January 2000, A12; and "Bush Adds $10M to His Record Campaign Fund," *Boston Globe,* 31 December 1999, A18.

23. Van Natta, "Bush Uses Family Ties."

24. "Bush Adds $10M to His Record Campaign Fund"; and Susan B. Glasser, "Bush Raised $69 Million, Spent $37 Million in '99," *Washington Post,* 1 February 2000, A4.

25. John Mintz and Ruth Marcus, "Unlimited Spending, Limited Impact for Bush?" *Washington Post,* 26 February 2000, A1.

26. Don Van Natta Jr., "Campaign Briefing: The Republicans: Bush Reports Spending," *New York Times,* 21 March 2000, A20.

27. Sarah Koenig, "Money Narrows Field Before Voters Do," *Concord Monitor,* 22 October 1999, A1.

28. Michael Kranish, "Presidential Hopefuls Vie in N.H. with Varied Spending Tactics," *Boston Globe,* 25 July 1999, A4; and "At the Races," *National Journal,* 8 January 2000, 116.

29. Kranish, "Presidential Hopefuls Vie in N.H."

30. Charles A. Radin, "Political Battle of Airwaves Is Turning Gentle," *Boston Globe,* 4 January 2000, A8.

31. Glasser, "Bush Raised $69 Million."

32. Glenn R. Simpson, "The Internet Begins to Click as a Political Money Web," *Wall Street Journal,* 19 October 1999, A28.

33. Michael Isikoff, "How He's Catching a Cash Wave," *Newsweek,* 14 February 2000, 35; and Don Van Natta Jr., "McCain Gets Big Payoff on Web Site," *New York Times,* 4 February 2000, A20.

34. Kenneth P. Doyle, "McCain Campaign Puts Internet on Map in Fund-Raising, Voter-Registration, GOTV," *BNA Money and Politics Report,* 25 February 2000, 1.

35. Don Van Natta Jr. and John M. Broder, "With a Still-Ample Treasury, Bush Builds a Green 'Fire Wall' Against McCain," *New York Times,* 21 February 2000.

36. David B. Magleby, "Issue Advocacy in the 2000 Presidential Primaries," in *Getting Inside the Outside Campaign,* ed. David B. Magleby (Brigham Young University, Center for the Study of Elections and Democracy, 2000), 9.

37. Ibid., 11–12.

38. Ibid., 12.

39. Bill Moore and Danielle Vinson, "The South Carolina Republican Primary," in *Getting Inside the Outside Campaign,* 44.

40. Ibid.

41. Magleby, "Issue Advocacy in the 2000 Presidential Primaries," 13.

42. Moore and Vinson, "South Carolina Republican Primary," 45.

43. Don Van Natta Jr., "A Daunting Edge in Campaign Cash Narrows for Bush," *New York Times,* 25 February 2000, A1.

44. Ceci Connolly, "The $55 Million Man," *Washington Post National Weekly Edition,* 12 April 1999, 8.

45. Don Van Natta Jr. and John M. Broder, "Advisers to Gore Are Concerned over Rapid Campaign Spending," *New York Times,* 24 September 1999, A18.

46. Susan B. Glasser, "Bradley Reaches Out to Atypical Donors," *Washington Post,* 25 October 1999, A1.

47. John M. Broder, "Bradley Pulls Ahead of Gore in Latest Fund-Raising Lap," *New York Times,* 1 October 1999, A20.

48. Van Natta and Broder, "Advisers to Gore Are Concerned over Rapid Campaign Spending"; Katharine Q. Seelye, "Gore Heads Home in Move to Revamp Lagging Campaign," *New York Times,* 30 September 1999, A1; and Jeanne Cummings, "Gore, Likely Saving Money, to Move Campaign Headquarters to Tennessee," *Wall Street Journal,* 30 September 1999, A28.

49. Ruth Marcus and John Mintz, "Bush Spending Spree Shrinks GOP Cash Gap," *Washington Post,* 21 February 2000, A7.

50. Mike Allen and Ceci Connolly, "Bradley Divides His Time," *Washington Post,* 20 January 2000, A6.

51. Charles A. Radin, "Bradley Doubles His TV Presence in Final Week," *Boston Globe,* 29 January 2000, A11.

52. "Bradley Fills TV Airwaves; Gore Lies Low," *Central Maine Morning Sentinel* (Associated Press release), 26 February 2000, A5.

53. Magleby, "Issue Advocacy in the 2000 Presidential Primaries," 11.

54. Shogren, "Campaign 2000: Focus Shifts from Voters to Donors."

55. Minor-party candidates can qualify for a proportionate share of the general election subsidy on the basis of their share of the vote in the previous presidential election as compared to the average vote received by the major-party candidates. New parties and minor parties also can qualify for postelection subsidies on the same proportional basis, so long as they receive at least 5 percent of the vote.

56. Federal Election Commission, "FEC Certifies General Election Public Funds for Buchanan-Foster Ticket," press release, 14 September 2000; and Kenneth P. Doyle, "FEC Staff Says Buchanan's Ballot Status Entitles Him to Reform Party's $12.6 Million," *BNA Money and Politics Report,* 11 September 2000, 1.

57. See table 5A, "Television Advertising in the 2000 Presidential General Election," at www.chathamhouse.com/pomper2000

58. Brennan Center for Justice, "2000 Presidential Race First in Modern History Where Political Parties Spend More on TV Ads than Candidates," press release, 11 December 2000, 1.

59. Kenneth P. Doyle, "Democrats Justify Issue Ad Campaign Despite Gore's March Challenge to Bush," *BNA Money and Politics Report,* 7 June 2000, 1.

60. Kenneth P. Doyle, "First DNC 'Issue Ad' of 2000 Campaign Shows Gore Fighting for Drug Benefits," *BNA Money and Politics Report,* 8 June 2000, 1.

61. Kenneth P. Doyle, "GOP Responds to Democratic Ads with Ad on Bush Social Security Plan," *BNA Money and Politics Report,* 13 June 2000, 2.

62. Brennan Center for Justice, "2000 Presidential Race First in Modern History Where Political Parties Spend More."

63. Ibid.

64. Ibid.

65. For a discussion of issue advocacy in the 1998 congressional elections, see Magleby, *Outside Money.*

66. Brennan Center for Justice, "2000 Presidential Race First in Modern History Where Political Parties Spend More."

67. Alison Mitchell, "Congress Chasing Campaign Donors Early and Often," *New York Times,* 14 June 1999.

68. The data on average candidate fund-raising is based on an analysis of FEC data as of 18 October 2000, which was conducted by the Campaign Finance Institute. See Campaign Finance Institute, "Some Campaign Finance Facts about the 2000 Congressional Elections," press release, 13 November 2000.

69. Ibid.

70. Marianne Holt, "Joint Fund-Raising Committees: One-Stop Shopping for Donors," *The Public I,* 22 June 2000. This report is available online at www.public-i.org/adwatch_01_062200 .htm

71. Kenneth P. Doyle and Cheryl Bolen, "Hastert Launches 'Battleground 2000' Effort; Seeks Member Funding to Hold GOP Majority," *BNA Money and Politics Report,* 15 June 2000, 2–3; and Mike Allen, "House GOP Goes Within For Money," *Washington Post,* 14 June 2000, A1.

72. Rachel Van Dongen, "NRCC Expands Targets," *Roll Call,* 26 October 2000, 1, 16.

73. See table 5B, "Contributions by Safe Incumbents," at www.chathamhouse.com/pomper2000

74. This discussion is based on the figures found in the tables on national party financial activity found in Federal Election Commission, "Party Fundraising Escalates," press release, 3 November 2000.

75. Kenneth P. Doyle, "McCain-Feingold Supporters Need Only One or Two More Votes to Break Filibuster," *BNA Money and Politics Report,* 21 November 2000, 1.

76. Kenneth P. Doyle and Cheryl Bolen, "McCain Says He Has 60 Votes for Bill as Hagel Indicates He May Back Cloture," *BNA Money and Politics Report,* 18 December 2000, 1; and Cheryl Bolen, "Bush Administration, GOP Leaders Signal Resistance to Push for Reform," *BNA Money and Politics Report,* 20 December 2000, 1–2.

CHAPTER 6

The Presidential Election

Gerald M. Pomper

> King Henry VI: *Men may talk of kings, and why not I?*
> Second Keeper: *Ay, but thou talk'st as if thou wert a king.*
> King Henry VI: *Why so I am, in mind; and that's enough.*
> Second Keeper: *But if thou be a king, where is thy crown?*
> King Henry VI: *My crown is in my heart, not on my head....*
> —III Henry VI (III, 1)

THE TALE WAS SENSATIONAL, but beyond belief.

In this political illusion, the winning candidate, facing searching questions about his qualifications for office, actually received fewer votes than his opponent. The losing candidate stood for a party boasting the longest period of economic prosperity in American history, peace in the world, and social amity at home. These two candidates, seeking the nation's ideological center, were undermined by minor candidates at the right and left fringes of politics. The election was held on 7 November 2000, but the outcome remained uncertain until the next year. Elaborate academic models and sophisticated polling wrongly predicted the results. The ultimate outcome depended on bungling, dedicated, and even random acts by obscure election officials.

A dramatic but implausible yarn. It also is the true story of the U.S. presidential election of 2000.

The story ended only two weeks before the presidential inauguration, when George W. Bush was certified as the new president before a joint session of Congress chaired by his opponent, Albert E. Gore, the incumbent vice president. In the authoritative vote of the electoral college, Bush won by a margin of 271 to 267, the narrowest victory but one in the course of American popular elections.[1] He fell short in the national popular tally, trailing Gore by an even smaller margin, 540,000 votes—only .5 percent of over 104 million total ballots.

Bush was the first minority U.S. president since 1888, and only the second person in American history to follow his father to the office. His victory recalled the first decades of the United States, when John Quincy Adams won another disputed election to return to his family's former residence in the White House.

THE UNLIKELY STORY

Up to its conclusion, the story was a plot filled with twists, surprises, and improbabilities reminiscent of Dickens or detective fiction. The lightning-fast technology of the twenty-first century proved unreliable in winning the campaign, predicting the election, or even counting the vote. Instead of "the Y2K bug" (the computer breakdown feared at the beginning of the new century), failure came from more familiar sources: survey samples, punchcard machines, and human judgment. The final resolution depended on the nation's eighteenth-century Constitution, the seemingly archaic electoral college, slow procedures in the courts, and old-fashioned hand counting of individual ballots.

On Election Day, all observers and pundits had expected a close race, with most forecasting a Bush victory. When results came in across the nation, these predictions seemed validated, as Gore and Bush garnered ballots from millions of Americans. But the presidential election would be resolved not by these millions, but by hundreds — the 538 persons to be chosen as members of the electoral college. Reflecting the last-minute compromises of the Constitutional Convention of 1787,[2] each state was allocated a number of electors equal to its combined representation in the national House and Senate. By custom and state law, each state's electoral vote would be cast as a bloc for the presidential candidate who won a plurality of its popular vote.[3]

Attention turned to the critical state of Florida. If either Gore or Bush could capture its 25 electoral votes, he would accumulate the necessary majority of 270. Both won. But only one would be president.

The logical impossibility of two winners resulted from the contradictory verdicts rendered by the television projections that had become the unofficial arbiters of American elections. Early in the evening, even before all polls were closed in Florida, Gore was declared the winner on the basis of surveys of voters leaving the election precincts and computer projections. Within two hours, however, the broadcasters withdrew their judgment. Four hours later, with more data in hand, they confidently predicted that Bush would carry the state and be elected.

Although the actual vote was still incomplete, the media's certainty led Gore to telephone Bush to concede defeat. As the vice president traveled to console a gathering of his supporters, new data showed that the Florida election was still in doubt, and Gore again telephoned an incredulous Bush to withdraw his previous (and legally meaningless) concession. By the next day, out of a total of 6 million votes, the difference between the candidates was a Bush lead of 1,784.

And then the plot thickened. For five weeks, the election became a drama that educated an entranced electorate, delighted reporters and political scientists, paraded lawyers, and exhausted vote counters. Changes in the tally over the next weeks of recounting resembled the overtime period of a close football game, in which the Republicans desperately sought to hold their thin lead against a charging Democratic offense, while multiple referees ruled on conflicting violations, until the clock ran out.

Although other states remained close, Florida would be decisive. Its political significance was heightened by a family connection — the state's governor was Jeb Bush, younger brother of the Republican candidate. There, the sixty-seven county election boards first conducted a recount of the vote as recorded on the various devices used for tabulation — most commonly punchcard machines. The Bush lead shrank to a mere 327 votes.

As this machine recount proceeded, Palm Beach County reported a particularly strange result. In this heavily Democratic area, Reform Party candidate Pat Buchanan apparently received 3,400 votes, quadruple his tally in any other county. Why would this county, with its with large proportions of Jewish and African-American voters, stand out in support of a candidate who opposed programs of particular interest to these voters, such as aid to Israel and civil rights?

The reason for this anomaly was not voter decisions, but voter confusion. The county was using a unique ballot form, called a "butterfly ballot" (shown on the following page), on which candidates' names were arranged in two adjacent columns, rather than the usual single-column list. There was, however, only a single set of "punch holes" between the two columns, confusing voters about the appropriate points at which to record their votes.[4] The Democratic Party label above Gore's name was actually placed closest to Buchanan's "hole," although a printed arrow pointed to the correct spot.

Many would later testify (and Buchanan himself publicly would agree) that they had intended to vote for Gore when they accidentally "punched" Buchanan's name. Even more often a voter, realizing his or her mistake, had tried to correct it by marking two places on the ballot, thus rendering that ballot an invalid "overvote." These "Buchanan" votes alone would have netted Gore 2,000 votes and the state.[5] Adding a proportion of the 19,000 "overvotes" would have given Gore a substantial victory. Similar problems invalidated probably another 10,000 votes for Gore in Jacksonville. There was no legal remedy, however, for these critical errors.

Democrats, who were certainly not ready to accept the microscopic margin in the state, exercised their legal right to ask for a manual recount of the ballots in four South Florida counties where they had strong support. Republicans passed up the chance to reciprocate in their own areas of strength, and Democrats declined the opportunity to seek a statewide recount. In an effort to end the process, Katherine Harris, Florida secretary of state and co-chair of the state Bush campaign, construed state law to require that all votes (other than absentee ballots) be reported within a week of the election. Then, a day after a court ordered her to reconsider that decision, and without waiting for the actual recounts, she

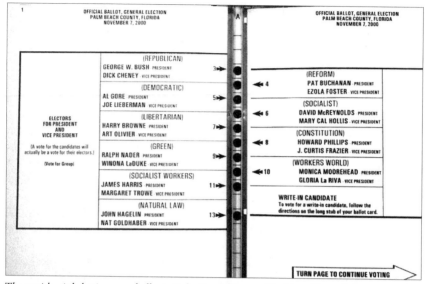

The presidential election 2000 ballot in Palm Beach County, Florida, 7 November 2000. (Corbis)

reaffirmed the deadline. Only one of the four counties could complete its manual tally in this time.

A local court accepted her decision, and Harris waited only for the last absentee ballots before she was to proceed with final certification of a Bush entrance to the White House. Further controversy erupted when nearly 40 percent of these absentee ballots were disqualified for various reasons, including the lack of a required postmark on military ballots. In two counties, moreover, Republicans had gone beyond the technical requirements of the law and added information missing on absentee ballot applications. Still, as counted, the additional ballots — from personnel in the armed forces and other overseas residents — gave Bush a "larger" margin: 930 votes.

Then the Florida Supreme Court intervened, stopping Harris from certifying the official results until a full hearing could be conducted. In a unanimous decision, the seven justices, all appointed by Democratic governors, then reaffirmed an established rule that voter intent should be the guiding principle in election disputes. They cleared the obstacles to manual recounts but set a five-day deadline, including Thanksgiving Day, for final county reporting.

The manual recounts would become a source of contention and comedy. The tabulating machines could only read ballots in which a complete hole had been made by punching through and dislodging a perforated disk, the "chad." The origin of the word was obscure, but it could be traced, strangely, to the seventh century, when Saint Chad had voluntarily resigned his office as archbishop of York after a disputed election.[6] Now, in the third millennium, paper chads were more tenacious, clinging to punchcards at one, two, or three of the corners. In other cases, a voter might make a mark but not penetrate the card, creating a "dimpled" or "pregnant" chad. Deciding the intent of such voters required human judgment, which could be affected by partisan interests.

These decisions were especially important in regard to "undervotes," ballots on which no presidential candidate was clearly selected. It could be that a voter had deliberately skipped this contest, or it might be that his or her vote had simply not registered on the recording device. As the county boards applied ambiguous and differing standards, neither state law nor the courts provided definitive rules. (Ironically, under a Texas law signed by Governor Bush himself, almost all of these ballots would have been counted.)

The county boards labored long and dutifully on these decisions, amid arguments in the counting rooms, continuous court appeals, and intense media coverage.[7] Two of the three remaining counties were able to essentially complete their tallies, although Secretary Harris accepted only one report.[8] But the largest county in Florida, Miami-Dade, having delayed action for days and reversed its position several times, simply quit — its count incomplete — as it met under siege by a threatening audience.

If all ballots had been counted as intended by the voters in Miami, Palm Beach, Jacksonville, and overseas, Gore probably would have won the state and the presidency.[9] But a perfect count was impossible to achieve, "a bit like measuring the lengths of two bacteria with a yardstick."[10] A decision would necessarily be uncertain, given the constraints of the ballot forms, the pressure of time, legal vagueness, partisan distortions, and the inevitable ambiguities of human judgment. In the final official canvass, Bush was declared the winner by the micron-thin margin of 537 votes, less than one hundredth of 1 percent (.00009) of the total turnout. With Florida, he had apparently gained a bare national majority of electoral votes. (The chronology of events is summarized in the list on the following page.)

Still, the story would go on. The Florida Supreme Court ruling that had ordered the hand recounts was reviewed and vacated by the U.S. Supreme Court, sending that ruling back to Tallahassee for further consideration.[11] At the same time, Gore formally contested the official results, first losing in a local trial court, then winning in an appeal to the state supreme court, which restored the votes declined by Secretary Harris and ordered a statewide recount of all "undervotes." The court's action reduced Bush's lead to only 154 votes, creating the prospect of an ultimate Gore victory. (Later counts by newspaper analysts would reduce the Bush margin further, to a mere two dozen votes in one analysis, while others indicated an actual reversal.)[12] On the following day, the U.S. Supreme Court stayed (suspended) this ruling.

The various court actions raised two fundamental constitutional conflicts. The first conflict was that between the Florida courts, particularly the state su-

Chronology of the Florida Vote Count

Date	Event	Plurality
8 November	Completion of Election Day canvass Statutory statewide mechanical recount implemented Democrats request manual recounts in four counties	Bush +1,768
14 November	Mechanical recount completed Manual recount completed in Volusia County	
15 November	Manual recounts incomplete in three counties Secretary Harris refuses additional time	Bush +327
18 November	Count of absentee ballots completed Secretary Harris certifies vote	Bush +930
21 November	Florida Supreme Court orders further hand counts	
26 November	Hand count completed in Broward County Hand count incomplete in Palm Beach County Hand count terminated in Miami-Dade County Additional absentee votes counted Nassau County revises earlier canvass Secretary Harris certifies revised vote	Bush +537
4 December	U.S. Supreme Court remands case to Florida, vacates decision of state supreme court Local Florida court rejects Gore contest of vote	
8 December	Florida Supreme Court reverses local court, restores hand count in Palm Beach County, restores partial count in Miami-Dade County, orders hand counts of "undervotes" in other counties Challenges to absentee votes rejected	Bush +154
12 December	U.S. Supreme Court reverses Florida Supreme Court, ends all recounting	Bush +537
13 December	Gore concedes election to Bush	
18 December	Florida casts 25 electoral votes for Bush	
6 January	Congress officially counts U.S. electoral votes Bush confirmed as winner of electoral vote majority	

preme court, and the state legislature. The legislature, under firm Republican control and supported by Governor Jeb Bush, challenged the authority of the courts to intervene. It based its challenge, first, on Article II of the U.S. Constitution, which provides that a state's electors be chosen "in such Manner as the Legislature thereof may direct." It also invoked a federal statute dating from 1887, which protected electors chosen by 12 December from any challenge in later congressional review. In order to insure a victory for George Bush, the legislators threatened to choose the Florida electors themselves, regardless of the outcome of any court-ordered recounts.

The second constitutional conflict involved federalism, the allocation of power between the state and federal courts. Normally, a state supreme court is the final authority in the interpretation of state law, including election law, but the U.S. Supreme Court can override this authority if it finds a violation of provisions of the national constitution. Bush's lawyers argued that the Florida justices had indeed violated the U.S. Constitution: first, because their recount orders had gone beyond the statute enacted by the legislature; and second, because the tallies were inconsistent and incomplete, denying "equal protection" to those voters whose ballots were not recounted.

Two hours before midnight on 12 December, the deadline for an unchallengeable result, the U.S. Supreme Court made its decision. In a bitter 5–4 division, it ended the recounting, and effectively decided the election contest. In the end, the choice of 104 million Americans depended on the voices of seven Republican and two Democratic lifetime appointees.

The Court ruling, in the appropriately named case of *Bush* v. *Gore*,[13] was neither clear nor eloquent. It appeared to accept the authority of the Florida Supreme Court to interpret the state law, and therefore to validate its authority to order recounts regardless of the objections of the legislature. At the same time, seven members of the Court found that the recount process in operation was too erratic to provide "equal protection" (as required under the Fourteenth Amendment to the U.S. Constitution) to all voters. In this finding, the U.S. justices expanded federal control over state elections in a way that could eventually make national courts the ultimate authority over voting procedures in every precinct.

The equal protection standard had developed as a bulwark of racial minorities. In Florida and other states, however, blacks were more likely to live in counties where outdated voting machines failed to record ballots accurately.[14] Ironically, the Supreme Court decision interpreted "equal protection" in a manner that would count minority votes unequally.

The ultimate issue was the remedy to this problem. The five-person majority refused to allow further efforts, ruling that the deadline was only two hours away, midnight of 12 December, and that the "substantial additional work" needed for a fair recount obviously could not be completed in the time remaining. The dissenters did not accept the 12 December deadline. They would have allowed the Florida authorities to try to set a uniform standard for the recounts and conclude the process before the electors were to meet on 18 December, or before Congress was to count the ballot on 6 January. The dissenters, in the words of Justice Ruth Bader Ginsburg, found the majority decision "a prophecy the Court's own judgment will not allow to be tested."

There was no further appeal. Democrats were angry but impotent. The next day, Gore conceded his loss, and Bush began his effort to heal divisions and to prepare to govern.

The United States could take satisfaction in that it had chosen the most powerful leader in the world in relative calm and by constitutional means. Americans did not choose their president through mass confrontations or a military coup; they talked, watched television, and debated in courts of law. But the nation also had to regret a choice that ultimately resulted from confusing ballots, incompetent election administration, institutional flaws, and irreconcilable partisanship.

The election of 2000 was over. The new chief executive would occupy the White House without a national popular majority, without an electoral plurality, without a mandate, without clear legitimacy — but he would be president.

THE SHAPE OF POLITICS IN 2000
The Geography of the Vote

Not only two candidates, but virtually two nations confronted each other in the election of 2000. While Gore and Bush received essentially identical support in the total popular vote, they drew this support from very different constituencies. The electoral map (figure 6.1) illustrates the cleavage. In carrying the preponderance of states (30), Bush changed the landscape of American politics. He swept the interior of the nation, including great swaths of the nation's territory in the South, Border, Plains, and Mountain areas. Gore won in only 20 states (and the District of Columbia), almost all on the geographical fringes of the nation — bordering the Atlantic Ocean (north of the Potomac), the Pacific Ocean, and the Great Lakes.

Reflecting the sharp geographical divisions, which are detailed in table 6.1 (p. 134), the vote varied considerably among the nation's regions and states. While Gore won as much as two-thirds of the votes in New England, he won fewer than one in three in the Mountain states. These differences among the states were considerably more marked than in recent contests.[15]

The ballots also revealed a rare instance of the conflict between "big states" and "small states" that had been feared by the framers of the Constitution.[16] Gore almost won because he carried six of the nine largest states, an advantage of 165 to 78, while Bush carried thirteen of the nineteen smallest, a 54–23 lead. The Texan's dominance in these small states exactly compensated for his loss of the single largest state, California. Even though he accumulated a million fewer votes than Gore (as well as a smaller plurality) in the combined totals of these states, the inherent tilt of the electoral college toward the smaller states brought a draw in this particular matchup.

The geographical pattern of party support in 2000 was quite similar to that seen in recent elections, a correlation of .94 with the 1996 results.[17] Gore's support among the states was quite similar to that of Clinton — but it was critically smaller across the nation, a median loss of 5 percent. State size aside, the source of Bush's victory was his success in moving eleven states — including Gore's Tennessee and Clinton's Arkansas — that had supported the previous Democratic ticket into the Republican column, adding 112 electoral votes.

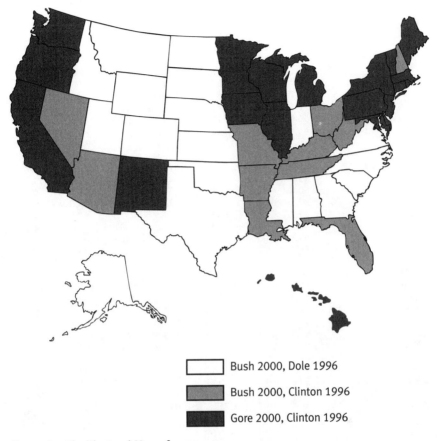

Bush 2000, Dole 1996

Bush 2000, Clinton 1996

Gore 2000, Clinton 1996

Figure 6.1 The Electoral Map of 2000

The close national division was reflected in some of the states. A shift of merely a quarter of 1 percent of state votes — an infinitesimal national total of 17,000 ballots nationally — would have reversed 55 electoral votes from five states (Florida, Iowa, New Mexico, Oregon, and Wisconsin). Only in these close states, particularly Florida, did votes for the minor candidacies of Ralph Nader and Pat Buchanan make a difference — but there they were still an immense influence.

Nader and his Green Party won only 2.7 percent of the national vote, far below the 5 percent required to receive federal financial support in the future (his principal goal), even less than the support won by Ross Perot as a third-party candidate in 1996 (8 percent) and 1992 (19 percent), and vastly less than the extravagant attention Nader had attracted in the press. Buchanan did far worse, gaining less than half a million votes, even though he had over $12 million in federal money, inherited from the Reform Party previously headed by Perot.

Despite their small numbers, Nader's and Buchanan's supporters provided

Table 6.1 The Presidential Vote of 2000

State	Electoral Vote		2-party Vote %		Popular Vote (1,000s)			1996 2-party Vote %	
	Gore	Bush	Gore	Bush	Gore	Bush	Nader	Clinton	Dole
Ala		9	42.4	57.6	692.6	941.2	18.2	45.9	54.1
Alaska		3	32.1	67.9	79.0	167.4	28.7	39.7	60.3
Ariz		8	46.7	53.3	685.3	781.7	45.6	51.5	48.5
Ark		6	47.2	52.8	422.8	472.9	13.4	59.3	40.7
Calif	54		56.2	43.8	5,861.2	4,567.4	418.7	57.6	42.4
Colo		8	45.5	54.5	738.2	883.7	91.4	49.3	50.7
Conn	8		59.3	40.7	816.0	561.1	63.3	59.7	40.3
Del	3		56.7	43.3	180.1	137.3	8.3	58.6	41.4
DC	3		90.5	9.5	171.9	18.1	10.5	90.2	9.8
Fla		25	50.0	50.0	2,912.3	2,912.8	97.5	53.2	46.8
Ga		13	44.0	56.0	1,116.2	1,419.7	0.0[a]	49.3	50.7
Hawaii	4		59.8	40.2	205.3	137.8	21.6	64.3	35.7
Idaho		4	29.1	70.9	138.6	336.9	0.0[a]	39.2	60.8
Ill	22		56.2	43.8	2,589.0	2,019.4	103.8	59.3	40.7
Ind		12	42.0	58.0	902.0	1,245.8	0.0[a]	46.8	53.2
Iowa	7		50.2	49.8	638.5	634.4	27.7	55.6	44.4
Kans		6	39.1	60.9	399.3	622.3	36.1	39.9	60.1
Ky		8	42.3	57.7	638.9	872.5	23.1	50.5	49.5
La		9	46.1	53.9	792.3	927.9	20.4	56.7	43.3
Maine	4		52.8	47.2	320.0	286.6	37.1	62.7	37.3
Md	10		58.4	41.6	1,144.0	813.8	53.8	58.6	41.4
Mass	12		64.8	35.2	1,616.5	878.5	173.6	68.6	31.4
Mich	18		52.6	47.4	2,170.4	1,953.1	84.1	57.4	42.6
Minn	10		51.3	48.7	1,168.3	1,109.7	126.7	59.3	40.7
Miss		7	41.4	58.6	404.6	572.8	8.1	47.0	53.0
Mo		11	48.3	51.7	1,111.1	1,189.9	38.5	53.5	46.5
Mont		3	36.4	63.6	137.2	240.2	24.4	48.3	51.7
Neb		5	34.8	65.2	231.8	433.9	24.5	39.5	60.5
Nev		4	48.1	51.9	280.0	301.6	15.0	50.6	49.4
NH		4	49.3	50.7	266.3	273.6	22.2	55.5	44.5
NJ	15		58.2	41.8	1,788.9	1,284.2	94.6	59.7	40.3
NM	5		50.0	50.0	286.8	286.4	21.3	54.5	45.5
NY	33		63.1	36.9	4,107.7	2,403.4	244.0	65.4	34.6
NC		14	43.5	56.5	1,257.7	1,631.2	0.0[a]	47.5	52.5
ND		3	35.5	64.5	96.3	174.9	9.5	46.1	53.9
Ohio		21	48.2	51.8	2,183.6	2,350.4	117.8	53.5	46.5
Okla		8	38.9	61.1	474.3	744.3	0.0[a]	45.6	54.4
Ore	7		50.2	49.8	720.3	713.6	77.4	56.0	44.0
Pa	23		52.1	47.9	2,486.0	2,281.1	103.4	55.2	44.8
RI	4		65.6	34.4	249.5	130.6	25.1	69.2	30.8
SC		8	41.8	58.2	566.0	786.9	20.3	46.7	53.3
SD		3	38.4	61.6	118.8	190.7	0.0[a]	48.1	51.9
Tenn		11	48.0	52.0	981.7	1,061.9	19.8	51.3	48.7
Texas		32	39.0	61.0	2,433.7	3,800.0	138.0	47.3	52.7
Utah		5	28.3	71.7	203.1	515.1	35.8	38.0	62.0
Vt	3		55.4	44.6	149.0	119.8	20.4	63.4	36.6
Va		13	45.9	54.1	1,217.3	1,437.5	59.4	48.9	51.1
Wash	11		52.9	47.1	1,247.7	1,108.9	103.0	58.4	41.6
WV		5	46.8	53.2	295.5	336.5	10.7	58.3	41.7
Wisc	11		50.1	49.9	1,243.0	1,237.3	94.1	55.9	44.1
Wyo		3	29.0	71.0	60.5	147.9	0.0[a]	42.5	57.5
Totals	267	271	50.3	49.7	50,997.1	50,456.6	2,830.9	54.7	45.3

Sources: *New York Times,* 30 December 2000, A17; *Washington Post,* 21 December 2000, A9; http://washingtonpost.com/wp-srv/onpolitics/elections/2000/results

Notes: The total national vote was 105.4 million, 51.2% of those eligible. The total Buchanan vote was 448,750, or 0.43% of popular vote. Other candidates are omitted.
[a] The Nader vote was not reported in states showing a vote of zero.

the margin of victory for Bush. If Nader were had not been on the ballot, Gore would have carried Florida and all of the other close states easily, giving him a comfortable electoral total of at least 292.[18] If Buchanan were had not been a candidate, the Florida ballot might have been simpler to understand, giving Gore enough votes to win the national election simply by carrying the Sunshine State. Even without Florida, we might speculate — but cannot demonstrate — that an election without Nader would have enabled Gore to campaign in other winnable states (most obviously Tennessee and New Hampshire) and overcome his shortfall of only 3 electoral votes.

Parties and the Vote

The geography of the election reflected a changing pattern of party loyalties. As the nation endured this odd election at the beginning of the new millennium, major changes in the character of its political parties also emerged.

Two major divisions had structured American presidential elections for much of the twentieth century.[19] During the middle of the century, Democrats dominated, building successive victories on economic and welfare issues and on the heritage of Franklin Roosevelt and the New Deal. The major controversies between the parties centered on the role of the national government, particularly its distribution of taxes and benefits — such as jobs, Social Security, and health care — among different groups. Democrats won all but two presidential elections from 1932 to 1964, assembling a winning coalition of lower-income voters, Catholics, union members, blacks, and white southerners.

During the last third of the century, new issues and new coalitions came to the fore. Cleavages on issues of race, morality, and lifestyle developed alongside the previous divisions on economic and welfare policy. The parties differed on such issues as civil rights and affirmative action, abortion, women's role in society, crime, and school prayer. Republicans reversed the previous pattern of presidential elections, winning five of the six contests from 1968 to 1988, assembling a different winning coalition composed of higher-income voters, white Protestants from both the North and the South, religious conservatives, and defecting Catholics and union members. Even when Democrats won — in 1976 and in the two Clinton candidacies — their victories were unconvincing.

The election of 2000 merged or obliterated many of these divisions. During the Clinton years, Democrats overcame their losing reputation on moralistic issues, as Clinton became identified with such stands as harsh treatment of criminals (including support for the death penalty) and welfare reform. The president maintained his popularity even after revelation of his sexual immorality, as seen in the failure of the Republican effort to impeach and remove him from office.

In 2000 Republicans also moved away from previous unattractive positions. On the economic dimension, no longer opposed to all government programs, the party under Governor Bush proposed new policies to improve education, expand health care, and add funds and programs to Social Security and Medicare. Still conservative, the Bush Republicans now modified their ideology by proclaiming a new "compassionate" outlook and reduced their emphasis on moral issues, particularly abortion. Without overt change in his pro-life stance, George Bush gave only fleeting attention to the previously divisive issue, promising no more than a ban on unpopular and rare late-term ("partial birth") abortions.

Differences remained significant, but the election campaign was notable for the similarity of the issues stressed by the candidates and for the disappearance of older conflicts. A generation earlier, in 1972, Republicans had accused Democrats of favoring "acid, amnesty, and abortion"; that bitter campaign would be later remembered for Richard Nixon's efforts to destroy his opponents and subvert the Constitution in the Watergate break-in.

The old controversies were gone or had given way to consensual policies. Drug usage was condemned, and abortion was ignored. Vietnam, the conflict that had defined a generation and its lifestyle, was now a country to be visited by Clinton, once a draft resister and now the U.S. commander-in-chief. Emblematic of the change was that the Democratic Party, once the arena for the greatest anti-war protests, nominated Gore, a volunteer who had actually served briefly in the war zone, while the Republicans nominated Bush, who had found a safe billet in the Texas Air National Guard.

There remained a basic philosophic difference between the parties and their leaders. Republicans' instincts still led them first to seek solutions through private actions or through the marketplace, while Democrats consistently looked for government solutions. That difference was evident in such fundamental questions as allocation of the windfall surpluses in the federal budget: Bush sought a huge across-the-board cut in taxes, while Gore proposed a panoply of new government programs and tax cuts targeted for specific policy purposes.

Similar differences could be seen on other issues emphasized during the campaign. To improve education, Bush relied on state programs and testing, while hinting at his support for government vouchers that parents might use for private-school tuition; Gore proposed new federal programs to recruit teachers and rebuild schools. To provide funds for Social Security, Bush proposed that individuals invest part of their tax payments in private investment accounts, while Gore would transfer other governmental funds into the Social Security trust fund. This philosophical difference could be seen even in the most intimate matters, such as teenage pregnancy, where Republicans relied on individual morality, namely, sexual abstinence by adolescents, while Democrats supported sex education programs, which might include distribution of condoms in public schools.

By 2000 the parties' supporters had become philosophically coherent as well. Fewer than one of every thirteen Republicans considered themselves liberals, and fewer than one in eight Democrats were conservatives. Voters also responded to the ideological difference between the parties: four out of five self-identified liberals voted Democratic, and the same proportion of conservatives voted Republican, often giving greater weight to ideological preference than to traditional party loyalty (see table 6.2, p. 138). The partisan contest of 2000 was also an ideological conflict.

Social Forces and the Vote

In addition to geographical and party differences, the American electorate was polarized along social lines, as detailed in table 6.2.[20] These cleavages can be seen in the difference in the Gore vote between the following paired groups (the first group being more Democratic):

- the poor and the rich, a 14-point difference;
- single and married people, 13 points;
- working women and homemakers, 14 points;
- gays and straights, 23 points;
- nonbelievers and frequent churchgoers, 25 points;
- Catholics and white Protestants, 15 points;
- Jews and white Christians, 40 points;
- other voters and the religious right, 36 points;
- residents of large cities and of rural areas, 34 points;
- high school dropouts and college graduates, 14 points; and
- union members and nonmembers, 18 points.

Only age, of the major social categories, did not show significant differences between groups.[21] In 2000 the United States was not united.

Most prominent, although unfortunately not novel, was the "racial gap" between blacks' support for Gore and whites' for Bush (a 48-percentage-point difference in the vote of the two races). While the white vote for Gore was similar to that for Clinton, African-American support for the Republican candidate was lower than in any election since the 1960s.

Bush had made some efforts to gain more minority votes, giving blacks prominent roles in the party convention and arguing that some of his programs, such as educational testing, would particularly benefit this group. These appeals turned out to be fruitless, however, given the Republican's conservative position on welfare issues and affirmative action. Black groups, such as the N.A.A.C.P., mounted a multimillion-dollar campaign to increase minority turnout, expecting that the mobilized voters would be Democrats. Although the black proportion of the electorate remained essentially unchanged at 10 percent, these efforts probably were decisive in close northern states. It would require more than televised black faces to win black votes for the Republicans.

Table 6.2 Social Groups and the Presidential Vote (in percentages)

Pct. of 2000 Total Vote	Party and Ideology	2000 Gore	2000 Bush	1996 Clinton	1996 Dole	1996 Perot	1992 Clinton	1992 Bush	1992 Perot
2	Liberal Republicans	31	67	44	48	9	17	54	30
14	Moderate Republicans	11	88	20	72	7	15	63	21
19	Conservative Republicans	4	95	6	88	5	5	82	13
5	Liberal Independents	68	17	58	15	18	54	17	30
15	Moderate Independents	48	41	50	30	17	43	28	30
6	Conservative Independents	17	79	19	60	19	17	53	30
13	Liberal Democrats	91	5	89	5	4	86	5	11
20	Moderate Democrats	86	12	84	10	5	76	9	15
5	Conservative Democrats	73	26	69	23	7	61	23	16
	Ethnic Group								
82	White	42	54	43	46	9	39	40	20
10	Black	90	8	84	12	4	83	10	7
4	Hispanic	67	31	72	21	6	61	25	14
2	Asian	54	41	43	48	8	31	55	15
	Sex and Race								
39	White men	36	60	38	49	11	37	40	22
43	White women	48	49	48	43	8	41	41	19
4	Black men	85	12	78	15	5	78	13	9
6	Black women	94	6	89	8	2	87	8	5
	Sex and Marital Status								
32	Married men	38	58	40	48	10	38	42	21
33	Married women	48	49	48	43	7	41	40	19
16	Unmarried men	48	46	49	35	12	48	29	22
19	Unmarried women	63	32	62	28	7	53	31	15
	Age								
17	18–29 years old	48	46	53	34	10	43	34	22
33	30–44 years old	48	49	48	41	9	41	38	21
28	45–59 years old	48	19	48	41	9	41	40	19
22	60 years and older	51	47	48	44	7	50	38	12
	Education								
5	Not a high school graduate	59	39	59	28	11	54	28	18
21	High school graduate	48	49	51	35	13	43	36	21
32	Some college education	45	51	48	40	10	41	37	21
24	College graduate	45	51	44	46	8	39	41	20
18	Post-graduate education	52	44	52	40	5	50	36	14
	Religion								
47	White Protestant	34	63	36	53	10	33	47	21
26	Catholic	49	47	53	37	9	44	35	20
4	Jewish	79	19	76	16	3	80	11	9
	Family Income								
7	Under 15,000	57	37	59	28	11	58	23	19
16	$15,000–$29,999	54	41	53	36	9	45	35	20
24	$30,000–$49,999	49	48	48	40	10	41	38	21
53	Over $50,000	45	52	44	48	7	39	44	17
28	Over $75,000	44	53	41	51	7	36	48	16
15	Over $100,000	43	54	38	54	6	–	–	–
26	**Union Household**	59	37	59	30	9	55	24	21
	Size of place								
9	Population over 500,000	71	26	68	25	6	58	28	13
20	Population 50,000–500,000	57	40	50	39	8	50	33	16
43	Suburbs	47	49	47	42	8	41	39	21
5	Population 10,000–50,000	38	59	48	41	9	39	42	20
23	Rural areas	37	59	44	46	10	39	40	20

Other ethnic minorities also supported the Democrats. Both parties paid special attention to Latinos, knowing that they would soon be the largest non-white group in the population and that they already comprised a significant voting bloc in critical states such as California, Texas, and Florida. Despite Bush's command of Spanish and past Hispanic backing in Texas, the Republican fell short, prevailing only among Cuban Americans in Florida. Two-thirds of Latinos voted for Gore, a proportion similar to that won by Clinton. In a possible portent of the future, Asian Americans, still a small group among voters, changed to a pro-Democratic vote.

In recent elections, much attention has been paid to the differing attitudes and votes of women and men, the vaunted "gender gap." That gap should not be exaggerated, because much of the difference can be explained simply as a re-flection of party loyalties — both sexes overwhelmingly voted for the candidate of their preferred party. Democratic women and men both voted for Gore (by 87 percent and 85 percent), just as Republican women and men both voted for Bush (by 90 percent and 92 percent). Sex differences became significant only among Independents, where Gore led by 12 points among women, offset by Bush's 9-point lead among men.

Still, the gender gap was evident again, but different from the past, in the presidential vote of 2000. While Bush won 53 percent among men, he gained only 43 percent among women. Gore's opposite advantage among women (54 percent to 42 percent) was insufficient to overcome the Texas governor. This "gap" be-tween the sexes was the largest difference in the twenty years since it first became apparent.

The Bush advantage was even greater among whites. White women divided their vote evenly between Bush and Gore, eliminating any net effect on the total vote. White men voted 5–3 in favor of Bush. This Republican strength among white males was the overwhelming gender influence in the election, probably gaining Bush a net advantage of over 4 million votes.[22]

An explanation for this difference is not easy to find. The simplest reason would be issues with particular impact on one sex or another, with abortion the most obvious possibility. But there is almost no difference between men and women on their "pro-choice" or "pro-life" attitudes. Moreover, although attitudes on abortion were mirrored well in the vote, that issue was actually of very little importance in this election campaign.

Issues may have produced the large gender gap in more subtle ways. Gore's policy agenda was a more "female" agenda, in a political rather than biological sense: the vice president focused on questions likely to be of more concern to women because of their social situation. The social reality in the United States is that women bear a greater responsibility for children's education and for health care of their families and parents, and that women constitute a disproportionate number of the aged. This reality was reflected in political concerns, as women saw education, health care, and Medicare as the principal issues of the election.[23] For these reasons, Gore's greater readiness to use government to solve these problems might appeal particularly to women.

A gender gap has two sides, however, and in 2000 it reflected men's preferences even more than women's. Bush's appeal, too, can be found in particular issues. The social reality is that men are more likely to be the principal source of family income and to assume greater responsibility for family finances. This reality was again mirrored in issue emphases, with men making the state of the economy and taxes their leading priorities, with defense and Social Security of lesser importance.

The gender difference in issue focus was the foundation of gender difference in the vote. Gore was favored among voters who emphasized the "female" issues of health care (an advantage of 31 percent), education (8 percent), and Social Security (18 percent) and Medicare (21 percent). But Bush was favored far more strongly on taxes (a huge advantage of 63 percent) and on world affairs and defense (14 percent), as well as on lesser issues that brought male attention, such as the stereotypically gendered issue of gun ownership.

THE CAMPAIGN: WHY GORE LOST

The presidential race should have been a runaway, according to precampaign estimates. In the end, to be sure, the outcome came down to miscounting or manipulation of the last few ballots. Analytically, however, the puzzling question is why Gore did so badly, not why Bush won.

The economy, usually the largest influence on voters, had evidenced the longest period of prosperity in American history, over a period virtually identical with the Democratic administration. A second predictor, the popularity of the incumbent president, also pointed to a Gore victory, for President Clinton was holding to 60-percent approval of his job performance. In elaborate analyses just as the campaign formally began on Labor Day, academic experts unanimously predicted a Gore victory. Their only disagreements came on the size of his expected victory, with predictions of Gore's majority ranging from 51 to 60 percent of the two-party popular vote.[24]

The academic models failed. It is simpler to explain Clinton's inability to transfer his popularity to his selected successor. Vice presidents always labor under a burden of appearing less capable than the sitting chief executive, and there is a normal inclination on the part of the electorate to seek a change. Previous incumbent vice presidents, such as the original George Bush in 1988 and Richard Nixon in 1960, had borne this burden in their own White House campaigns, but Gore's burden was even heavier, because he needed to avoid contact with the ethical stain of Clinton's affair with a White House intern, Monica Lewinsky.

The Perils of Prosperity

The limited impact of economic prosperity is more difficult to explain. Although the public overwhelmingly thought the economy was doing well and saw the nation as on "the right track" economically, Gore received little or no political advantage from this optimism. Only a fraction thought him better qualified than Bush to maintain the good times.

There are at least three possible explanations. First, because prosperity had gone on so long, voters may have come to see it as "natural" and unrelated to the decisions and policies of elected politicians. Second, voters might not know whom to praise and reward for their economic fortunes, since both parties in their platforms claimed credit for the boom. These explanations seem weak, however, because two out of three voters believed Clinton was either "somewhat" or "very" responsible for the nation's rosy conditions.

A third explanation, better supported by the opinion data, finds that Gore did not properly exploit the advantages offered by his administration's economic record. In his campaign appeals, Gore would briefly mention the record of prosperity but then emphasize his plans for the future. The approach was typified by his convention acceptance speech:

> [O]ur progress on the economy is a good chapter in our history. But now we turn the page and write a new chapter.... This election is not an award for past performance. I'm not asking you to vote for me on the basis of the economy we have. Tonight, I ask for your support on the basis of the better, fairer, more prosperous America we can build together.[25]

Rhetorically and politically, Gore conceded the issue of prosperity to Bush. The Texas governor, too, saw both a good present economy and a challenge for future improvement in his convention speech:

> This is a remarkable moment in the life of our nation. Never has the promise of prosperity been so vivid. But times of plenty, like times of crisis, are tests of American character.... Our opportunities are too great, our lives too short, to waste this moment. So tonight we vow to our nation: We will seize this moment of American promise. We will use these good times for great goals.[26]

Gore lost the advantages of the strong economy he inherited when, reviewing the past, he did not tie himself to this record. In the public's evaluation of the present, the vice president won among those who considered the economy "excellent" and their own financial situation improved in the past year. But he did not reap votes from those who considered the economy simply "good," or their own situation unchanged (see table 6.3, p. 142).

Looking to the future, Gore led among those who thought the economy would improve in the next year, and trailed among the smaller number who expected an economic deterioration. The critical group, however, was the majority

Table 6.3 Economic Effects on the Presidential Vote (percentage voting for Gore)

View of National Economy	Change in Personal Financial Situation			
	Better Off (51%)	About Same (38%)	Worse Off (11%)	Total
Excellent (19%)	76	52	58	70
Good (68%)	56	34	31	45
Not so good/poor (13%)	44	29	29	33
Total	61	35	33	

Source: Calculated by the author from VNS exit poll data.

who thought the economy would remain stable — in this group, Gore trailed slightly (by 47 to 49 percent). Gore failed in the election because he failed to convince this swing group that continued prosperity depended on continued Democratic governance.

Gender may also have played a role in undermining Gore's inherited advantage on the economy. Although voters who emphasized this vital factor did favor the vice president (59 to 37 percent), he gained far fewer votes (a 15-percent gain) on the issue than Clinton had four years earlier (34 percent), even though the economy had strengthened during the period. Here, too, as on issues generally, Gore emphasized the "female" side of his policy positions, such as targeting tax cuts toward education or home care of the elderly. He offered little for men who would not benefit from affirmative action in the workplace or who would use money returned from taxes for other purposes. As a result, he gained far less from men (57 percent) than from women (68 percent) who gave priority to economic issues.

In theoretical terms, the vice president turned the election away from an advantageous retrospective evaluation of the past eight years to an uncertain prospective choice based on future expectations.[27] Because the future is always clouded, voters often use past performance to evaluate the prospective programs offered by candidates,[28] but Gore did little to focus voters' attention on the Democratic achievements. As the academic literature might have warned him, even in good times "there is still an opponent who may succeed in stimulating even more favorable future expectations. And he may win."[29]

More generally, Gore neglected to put the election into a broader context — of the administration's record, of party, or of the Republican record in Congress. All of these elements might have been used to bolster his chances, but he, along with Bush, instead made the election a contest between two individuals and their personal programs. In editing his own message so severely, Gore made it less persuasive. If the campaign were to be only a choice of future programs, with their great uncertainties, a Bush program might be as convincing to the voters as a Gore program. If the election were to be only a choice of the manager of a consensual agenda, Bush's individual qualities might well be more attractive.

The Democratic candidate had the advantage of leadership of the party that held a thin plurality of voters' loyalties. His party was historically identified with the popular programs that were predominant in voters' minds — Social Security, Medicare, education, and health care, and the Democrats were still regarded in 2000 as more capable to deal with problems in those areas. Yet Gore eschewed a partisan appeal. In the three television debates, illustratively, he mentioned his party only four times, twice citing his disagreement with other Democrats on the Gulf War, and twice incidentally.[30] Only Bush would ever commend the Democratic Party, claiming a personal ability to deal effectively with his nominal opposition.

Gore neither challenged this argument, nor attacked the Republicans who had controlled Congress for the past six years, although promising targets were available. The vice president might have blamed Republicans for inaction on his priority programs, such as Social Security and the environment. He might have drawn more attention to differences on issues on which his position was supported by public opinion, such as abortion rights or gun control. He could even have revived the impeachment controversy, blaming Republicans for dragging out a controversy that Americans had found wearying and partisan.[31] The public had certainly disapproved of Clinton's personal conduct, but it had also steadily approved of the president's job performance. That distinction could have been the basis for renewed criticism of the Republicans. Yet Gore stayed silent.

Gore's strategy was based on an appeal to the political center and to the undecided voters gathered there. At the party convention and in his acceptance speech, he did try to rouse Democrats by pointing to party differences — and the effort brought him a fleeting lead in opinion polls. From that point on, however, moving in a different direction, he usually attempted to mute those differences, and his lead disappeared. If there were no important differences, then Democratic voters had little reason to support a candidate whose personal traits were less than magnetic. Successful campaigns "temporarily change the basis of political involvement from citizenship to partisanship."[32] By underplaying his party, Gore lost a vital margin of votes, as more Democrats than Republicans defected.

Turnout may have made the difference in the election results. Nationally, there was only a small increase over the last election in voter participation, to 51 percent of all adults, although there were considerable increases in the most contested states, particularly by union household members and African Americans.

Usually, the preferences of nonvoters are not much different from those who actually cast ballots,[33] but the 2000 election may have been an exception to that rule. CBS News polls immediately before and after the balloting suggested that, if every citizen had actually voted, both the popular and electoral votes would have led to an overwhelming Gore victory.[34] The nonvoters, however, had less

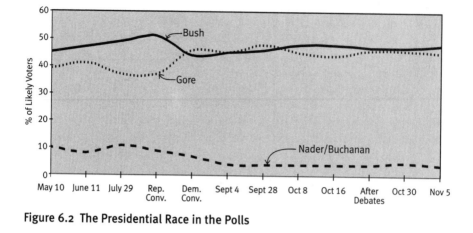

Figure 6.2 The Presidential Race in the Polls

Source: ABC News/*Washington Post* polls.

information about the election and less confidence in the political system, and they were less likely to see a difference between the parties.[35]

A stronger Gore effort to explain these differences and to bring those uncommitted citizens to the polls might have made the election result quite different. A greater emphasis on the economic record of the administration might have been particularly important in spurring turnout among lower-income voters, who voted in considerably lower proportions than in recent elections.[36]

Issues and Character in the Campaign

In 2000 the campaign was sharply contested, but reasonably civil — until the postelection period. Attacks abounded, but they focused on real issue differences between Gore and Bush, as each contestant worried over the public's declared aversion to personal, negative campaigning.

Bush is credited with a skillful campaign, but this judgment may be nothing more than the halo effect of eventually being the winner. Actually, Bush was criticized for his campaign both at its beginning and when he faced defeat during the recount. Moreover, the exit polls indicated that those who made up their minds later in the campaign were more likely to vote for Gore, despite his defective strategy, than for the presumptively better campaigner, Bush. Overall, in fact, the campaign seemed to have had very little effect. Once the nominating conventions concluded, Bush and Gore were tied at the outset of the active campaign on Labor Day, and they remained tied on the day of the balloting—and beyond. The lack of substantial change is seen in the track of the polls, as shown in figure 6.2.

Specific events, such as the television debates, probably changed opinion from day to day, as indicated by the incessant polls, but they are probably given

Table 6.4 Issues in the Campaign of 2000 (Days Emphasizing Designated Issues)

Topic	Bush	Gore
Foreign and defense Policy		
Diplomacy	3	2
Military defense	2	
Domestic Issues		
Education/family policy	8	10
Health coverage	1	2
Social Security	5	3
Medicare, prescription drugs	4	5
Crime, gun control, drugs	1	
Economic management	1	8
Taxes, budget	11	9
Environment/energy	4	5
Social Issues		
Morality, pornography, media	2	3
Campaign finance	1	1
Civil rights		2
Abortion		
Clinton behavior		
Political Focus		
Candidate character	8	4
Debates/preparation	10	8
No public activity	3	2
Total	64	64

Source: Lead issue reported daily in the *New York Times,* 4 September–7 November 2000.

exaggerated importance (see chapters 3 and 4). Bush made some errors in language, and Gore was not a model of etiquette. Gore could have been more vivacious in appearance, and Bush could have been more humble in demeanor. In the overall campaign, however, voters focused on the central decisions — the direction and leadership of their nation in the new century.

No single issue dominated the campaign. Education, health care, Medicare and Social Security, defense, the federal budget, and taxes were among the priority issues for the voters, but none focused the voters' minds in the way that the economy had done in the Clinton elections.

Both Gore and Bush talked about these issues and each gave considerable attention to the same issues, enabling the voters to make a reasoned choice between the two candidates (see table 6.4). Bush apparently won on important elements of the issue debate. A slightly greater proportion found that he shared their general view of government (51 percent compared to 47 percent). More specifically, voters tended to prefer the Republican's plan for across-the-board tax cuts and his proposal to allow individual investment of Social Security taxes.

Table 6.5 Sources of the Presidential Vote

	Percentage Mentioning	Percentage Voting for		Contribution to Vote of	
		Gore	Bush	Gore	Bush
Issue					
Economy/jobs	18	59	37	12	8
Education	15	52	44	9	8
Social Security	14	58	40	9	6
Taxes	14	17	80	3	13
World affairs	12	40	54	5	7
Health care	8	64	33	6	3
Medicare/prescription drugs	7	60	39	5	3
Totals				49	48
Traits					
Honest	24	15	80	4	21
Experienced	15	82	17	13	3
Strong leader	14	34	64	5	10
Deal with complexity	13	75	19	10	3
Good judgment	13	48	50	7	7
Cares about people	12	63	31	8	4
Likeable	2	38	59	1	1
Totals	93			48	48

Source: Calculated by the author from VNS exit poll data.

When voters evaluated the candidates on Election Day, they took two different approaches. On most issues, Gore was preferred. On seven possible issues, Gore won the votes of more voters who emphasized five of them. Bush was seen as better only among those who were primarily concerned with taxes and world affairs, the latter reflecting men's concern with military defense.

When it came to individual character traits, however, Bush was deemed superior on most traits, particularly honesty and strength of leadership. He was also viewed as less likely "to say anything to get elected" and less prone to engage in unfair attacks. These individual characteristics are relevant to the conduct of the presidency, and voters should not be denigrated because they used these standards at the ballot box. On the other hand, voters gave little stress to Bush's greater "likability," a criterion of little relevance to government. Ultimately, his perceived character traits carried the day for the governor (see table 6.5).[37]

The vote showed significant shifts from 1996 (see figure 6.3), working to Bush's advantage. There was more party switching by former Clinton supporters than by former Dole supporters, and previous backers of Perot also moved more heavily toward the Republicans.

The Clinton scandal probably had some effect on these patterns, giving more prominence to character traits and providing more reason for party switching. Although most of the country gave little weight to the Lewinsky affair, a fourth did find it "very important." Majorities of voters continued both to praise Clinton's

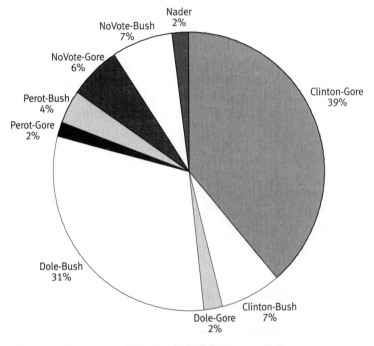

Figure 6.3 Dynamics of the Presidential Vote, 1996–2000

Source: VNS exit poll.

job performance and to disapprove of his personal behavior. A particularly important group was made up of those who combined these two attitudes, a fifth of the electorate. Although these voters strongly supported Gore (by 63 percent to 33 percent for Bush), that was still a smaller vote harvest than Gore might have been reaped in an electoral field unsown with Clinton's wild oats. Among these ambivalent voters, Gore lost 15 percent of former Clinton supporters, not a large number but enough (2 percent of the national total) to be the decisive difference in the electoral standoff.

The election carried implications for the parties beyond the close and confusing results of 2000. Both could read the returns as encouraging portents for the future. The Republicans had won control, however narrow, of all branches of the government. The congressional revolution of 1994, which ended four decades of Democratic control, was maintained into a fourth Republican term. They would hold the White House for four years, and could fill the three likely vacancies on the Supreme Court. The public was more conservative than liberal, and more supportive of the party's call for reduced government. If prosperity held, the ranks of upper-income voters and the entrepreneurial spirit would grow.

Democrats could also find comfort. The taint of Bush's minority victory and the ballot recounts might enfeeble his administration and provide an immediate platform for the Democratic Party's return to power in 2002 and 2004. The population was increasingly diverse ethnically, and the demographic growth among Latinos, African Americans, and Asian Americans was likely to bolster Democratic ranks. The party's modernist cultural values, including gender equality, were increasingly shared throughout the nation.[38] The union movement had revived and had demonstrated skill and unity in mobilizing its members. The nation was divided in 2000, but Democrats could hope to revive and thrive in the future.

THE OUTLOOK FOR AMERICAN POLITICS

The long election of 2000 eventually settled the basic question: the identity of the new president. Yet it raised new issues, even fundamental questions about the effectiveness and legitimacy of American institutions.

The Presidency

President George W. Bush enters the presidency without any mandate, and with half the nation questioning his legitimate title to the White House. He shares power with a Congress essentially evenly divided between the parties, and he will confront the bitterness of disappointed Democrats. The public, now more knowledgeable and more cynical about political maneuvering, provides no clear policy direction for governing a divided nation (see chapter 4).

Still, the government will function. Even though the president had only half the votes, he has all of the executive power. His predecessor, Clinton, also lacked a popular majority yet managed effectively to use the powers of his office — appointments, executive orders, vetoes, budgets, and agenda-setting. The mail will be delivered, the diplomatic corps and the armed forces will be ready to defend American interests abroad, appropriations will eventually be passed.

Perhaps the new president will show unexpected skill in conciliating his opposition and bringing the citizenry together on a moderate agenda. Perhaps he will develop a personal magnetism to inspire public enthusiasm, a quality unseen in either candidate during the campaign. More likely is failure to innovate solutions to national problems and continued deadlock on such issues as health care, Social Security, campaign finance reform, and foreign policy in the post-Cold War world. Most likely is a contentious election in 2004, when the incumbent president will try to defend his questionable title to office.

The result of the election of 2000 will reinforce the recently diminished status of the presidency. With the ending of the Cold War, foreign policy became less of an immediate concern for the nation, and the institutional effect was to decrease the significance of the president, the principal officer of foreign policy. Economic prosperity has had a similar effect. With no apparent need for government intervention to maintain employment and growth, the economic leadership of the president has become less critical. Instead, the vital decisions seem to be those of the unelected Federal Reserve Board, whose chair, Alan Greenspan, is often given the most credit for the long-term boom.

In addition to these general impersonal influences, Clinton weakened the moral standing of the presidency by his personal conduct, and the office was further diminished by the Republican impeachment and its focus on Clinton's salacious affair. The presidency has been a powerful position because it combines the "dignity" of a head of state with the "efficiency" of a head of government.[39] Losing much of the majesty of the office also means a partial loss of its utility.

Because of the Clinton-Lewinsky-impeachment controversy, the personal traits of the next president became an important element in the 2000 election, and this was a principal source of Bush's appeal. The nation now may regain ritualistic "dignity and honor" in the White House, as both candidates pledged. It is less likely, however, to regain the political advantages of a strong presidency — national unity, policy leadership, and inspiration to great goals.

The Electoral College

The election vindicated the genius of the seemingly plodding institutions of the American republic, the Constitution and particularly the electoral college. The Framers had devised the electoral system for an age in which transportation and communication were slow, but it served the country well in a time of jet planes and e-mail. By providing a long interval between the popular vote and the meeting of the electors, the system provided time to count and recount votes, to argue and settle lawsuits, to begin cooling passions, and to allow a degree of routine transition to a new administration.

Those advantages should be kept in mind in the inevitable consideration of changes in the electoral college.[40] If the present system were changed, politics would change, as campaigners altered their techniques and redirected their efforts, and we cannot predict all of the consequences. We can, however, make some estimates of the political impact.

The most obvious change would be to abolish the electoral college altogether and to choose the president by direct popular vote. In 2000 the result would have been a narrow Gore victory. Realistically, this change is unlikely to pass the difficult barriers to constitutional amendment, since the present system works to the advantage of small states, which could prevent such an amendment from passing the Senate or the state legislatures.

If adopted, however, this new system would have its own problems. In a close election such as 2000, recounts would surely be demanded throughout the nation. The clumsy election administration evident in Florida is not unique; defects exist in every state and county. A difference of only a hundred votes per county —

as little as one vote in every other precinct — would have reversed the results in 2000, so partisans would be mining every possible vein of new votes. A national recount would mean that the extended delays already experienced in the one state would be replicated everywhere, making it unlikely that America would have a president clearly accepted in time for the inauguration.

A frequently heard proposal for change within the electoral college is to alter the means of choosing the electors within the individual states, which could be done simply by state legislatures without amending the U.S. Constitution. Imitating the system presently used in Maine and Nebraska, one elector could be awarded to the leading presidential candidate in each congressional district (corresponding to the members of the House), and two (corresponding to the state's senators) could be awarded to the statewide winner. One immediate effect would be to extend the partisanship of congressional redistricting, known as gerrymandering, to the presidential election.

In 2000 the result of this system would probably be a clear Bush victory, despite his minority in the country. Assuming the presidential vote had followed that for the House, Bush would win 222 votes from the individual congressional districts where Republicans won House seats, and he would add 60 votes from the 30 states he captured. This total of 282 electoral votes would be an even greater distortion of the popular vote than the actual results in the election.

Another proposal has been to divide the electoral college vote of each state in proportion to the popular vote in each state, rather than awarding blocs on the winner-take-all system. In 2000, a proportional division would have led to an even closer result, in favor of Bush, than the actual count: Bush would receive 262.6 electoral votes, Gore 261.4, and Nader 13.8.[41] The proportional system would make Bush the president with neither a majority nor a plurality of the popular vote. This result would again evidence the tilt of the electoral college toward the small states, but it would certainly not reflect the total electorate's preferences any better than the present system does.

Any change other than direct popular vote would lack democratic legitimacy, but the direct vote would suffer such great problems in operation that it is unlikely to be adopted. Perhaps the only change that can be easily made is to abolish the actual position of elector — to avoid the possibility of "faithless" electors — and simply award the votes mathematically. A minimum and necessary statutory change would provide a better and uniform system of electoral administration under federal law.

Restoring Legitimacy

Beyond the presidency, the election of 2000 has raised troubling questions about the stability of American government generally. In the heat of the recount controversies, the integrity of the entire electoral process was questioned. Each of the contending camps saw the opposition as preparing a "legal coup d'état." Party competition was denigrated as illegitimate opposition, directly contradicting the basic premise of a healthy democracy.

Democrats saw ballot manipulation in the actions of the Florida secretary of state — who was characterized as a "Soviet commissar" — and in the counting of overseas ballots. Republicans attacked the courts for "legalistic" interpretations of statutes, although courts are precisely designed for such work. Demonstrators attempted, with some apparent success, to disrupt the recount in Miami. A leading conservative intellectual found a "constitutional crisis...preferable to supine yielding to an imperial judiciary."[42] In keeping with this defiant attitude, the Florida legislature considered choosing electors regardless of the ballot count, and congressional Republicans prepared plans to count the electoral vote for Bush and Cheney whatever the reported tallies.

The institutions of American democracy were eventually vindicated, but the threats themselves are very worrisome. Safety came without much help from politicians who might have acted as statesmen. The art of politics, as eloquently stated by James Madison, is to reconcile the competitive "impulse of passion, or of interest, adverse to the right of other citizens" in a way that promotes "the permanent and aggregate interests of the community." This vital task is entrusted to elected representatives, "whose wisdom may best discern the true interest of their country, and whose patriotism and love of justice will be least likely to sacrifice it to temporary or partial considerations."[43] These qualities were not evident among American politicians in 2000. No major official in either party spoke for any interest other than his party's victory.

Safety came instead from the American public, who showed remarkable restraint and calm, even as they avidly followed events. Americans' "willingness to accept a less than perfect outcome reflects both a realism about the way we run elections and a lack of passion about either candidate."[44] Even as media pundits and partisan advocates became increasingly antagonistic, the public held to two goals — completion and accuracy — and reiterated two basic commands: get it done, and get it right.[45]

The concluding words on the presidential election were spoken long ago, by Benjamin Franklin at the conclusion of the Constitutional Convention of 1787. When a spectator outside asked whether the Framers had created a monarchy or a republic, Franklin replied, hopefully, "A republic, madam, if you can keep it."[46] After the tumult, division, and enmity born of the election of 2000, Americans will need to try harder if they still want to keep their republic.

NOTES

1. In 1876, Rutherford B. Hayes defeated Samuel Tilden, 185–184, although Tilden led in the popular vote by 50.9 percent to 47.9 percent. Before the selection of electors by popular vote was universal, the House of Representatives chose John Quincy Adams in 1824, and Thomas Jefferson in 1800. Technically, Gore only received 266 electoral votes in 2000, because one of the District of Columbia electors pledged to him actually returned a blank ballot.

2. John P. Roche, "The Founding Fathers: A Reform Caucus in Action," *American Political Science Review* 55 (December 1961): 799–816. For the definitive account of the early history of the electoral college, see Richard P. McCormick, *The Presidential Game* (New York: Oxford University Press, 1982).

3. In Maine and Nebraska, state law provided that the winning candidate in each congressional district would receive one vote, and the statewide winner would receive two votes. In the actual voting, this variation made no difference — Gore won all of Maine's four votes, and Bush won all of Nebraska's five.

4. The awkward ballot had been devised by the Democratic county elections commissioner, in a well-intentioned effort to aid elderly voters by making space for larger print on a small punchcard.

5. This estimate was made in court testimony by a national expert, Professor Henry Brady of the University of California, posted on his web site, http://ucdata.berkeley.edu

6. "St. Chad: Patron Saint of Elections," http://cbsnewyork.com/main/topstories/story_336105226 (1 December 2000).

7. An amusing report of the recount in Broward County was published on the Internet by Ron Gunzburger, son of Democratic County Commissioner Suzanne Gunzburger, at www.politics1.com (1 December 2000).

8. Palm Beach County needed two more hours to finish its hand recount of 14,000 ballots. Harris refused to accept either a partial or a late canvass, which would have reduced Bush's margin by another 215 votes, to 322 overall. The secretary did accept a net gain of 567 votes for Gore in the other major county conducting a recount, Broward (Ft. Lauderdale), and various additional revisions in the vote, including disputed overseas ballots, which together added 174 votes for Bush.

9. An academic analysis sponsored by the *Miami Herald* concluded that Gore would have gained a plurality of 23,000 in "an election where every ballot is fully filled out and every one of those ballots gets counted." See Anabelle de Gale, Lila Arzua, and Curtis Morgan, "If the Election Were Flawless...," www.miamiherald.com (2 December 2000). Another *Herald* analysis suggested that Bush might win the later, terminated recount; see Andres Viglucci, Peter Whoriskey and Geoff Dougherty, "Bush Could Still Hang On," www.miamiherald.com (9 December 2000).

10. John Allen Paulos, "We're Measuring Bacteria with a Yardstick," *New York Times*, 22 November 2000, A27.

11. *Bush v. Palm Beach County Canvassing Board*, No. 00-836 (4 December 2000).

12. *Orlando Sentinel*, 20 December 2000, A16.

13. *Bush v. Gore*, No. 00-949 (12 December 2000).

14. John Mintz and Dan Keating, "A Racial Gap in Voided Votes," *Washington Post*, 27 December 2000, A1.

15. The standard deviation of the Democratic vote was 9.1 in the 2000 election, compared to 7.0 in 1996 and 6.0 in 1992. Two-thirds of the states fall within this range, above or below the national average.

16. For an incisive analysis of the actual patterns of conflict at the Constitutional Convention, see Calvin Jillson, *Constitution Making* (New York: Agathon Press, 1988).

17. This figure is the simple regression of the Democratic percentage of the two-party vote in 2000 and 1996, excluding the outlying District of Columbia. The correlation with the three-party vote of 1996 is .95. Correlation of the 2000 and 1992 vote is .86 for the two-party vote, .79 for the three-party vote.

18. In the VNS exit poll, approximately half (47 percent) of the Nader voters said they would choose Gore in a two-man race, a fifth (21 percent) would choose Bush, and a third (32 percent) would not vote. Applying these figures to the actual vote, Gore would have achieved a net gain of 26,000 votes in Florida, far more than needed to carry the state easily; increased margins in the other close states; and a net gain of nearly 6,000 in New Hampshire, bringing him to a virtual tie there.

19. See Edward G. Carmines and Geoffrey C. Layman, "Issue Evolution in Postwar American

Politics," in Byron E. Shafer, *Present Discontents* (New York: Chatham House, 1997), 89–134; and William G. Mayer, *The Divided Democrats* (Boulder, Colo.: Westview, 1996).

20. Support for Nader was low in all groups, too low for meaningful analysis, and varied little among social groups. He received 5 percent or more in the national exit poll only among 18–29 year-old white men, non-churchgoers, white liberal Independents, and former Perot voters.

21. This analysis is based on the VNS national exit poll, as published in *New York Times,* 12 November 2000, IV, 4, supplemented by data provided by CBS News.

22. There are approximately 39.4 million white male voters: 100 million persons voted, 82 percent are white, and 48 percent of the whites are males (100 x .82 x .48 = 39.4). There is no net candidate advantage among white women. Applying the 12-point white gender difference to the male vote, the net advantage to Bush is 4.7 million votes (39.4 x .12). Among blacks, there is overwhelming support for Gore among both sexes. The gender gap there results in a female advantage for Gore. There are approximately 5.2 million black female voters: 100 million persons voted, 10 percent are black, and 52 percent of the blacks are females (100 x .10 x .52). Black men voted 85 percent for Gore, black women 94 percent. Applying the 9-point gender difference to the black female vote, the net advantage for Gore is under half a million votes (5.2 x .09). Combining the races, the gender gap resulted in a Bush gain of over 4 million votes. Calculations are based on the VNS national exit poll.

23. Gary Langer, "New Republican, Old Issues," analyzing the ABC News poll, reported at www.abcnews.go.com (2 November 2000).

24. Robert G. Kaiser, "Is This Any Way to Pick A Winner?" *Washington Post,* 26 May 2000, A1. On the day of the election, the political scientists were less confident: David Stout, "Experts, Once Certain, Now Say Gore Is a Maybe," *New York Times,* 7 November 2000, A23.

25. *New York Times,* 18 August 2000, A21.

26. *New York Times,* 4 August 2000, A24.

27. Morris Fiorina, *Retrospective Voting in American National Elections* (New Haven: Yale University Press, 1981).

28. Anthony Downs, *An Economic Theory of Democracy* (New York: Harper, 1957), chap. 3.

29. Fiorina, *Retrospective Voting,* 198.

30. My thanks go to co-author Marjorie Hershey, who provided this information from her computer search of the television debates' text.

31. Molly W. Sonner and Clyde Wilcox, "Forgiving and Forgetting: Public Support for Bill Clinton during the Lewinsky Scandal," *PS* 32 (September 1999): 554–57; John Zaller, "Monica Lewinsky's Contribution to Political Science," *PS* 31 (June 1998): 182–87.

32. Samuel L. Popkin, *The Reasoning Voter* (Chicago: University of Chicago Press, 1991), 8–9.

33. Raymond E. Wolfinger and Steven J. Rosenstone, *Who Votes?* (New Haven: Yale University Press, 1980), 108–14.

34. In the CBS poll released on 5 November, those expected *not* to vote favored Gore by 42 to 28 percent. In the CBS poll released on 13 November, as the electoral count remained undetermined, those who regretted not voting favored Gore by 53 to 33 percent.

35. Reported by the Vanishing Voter Project of Harvard University's John F. Kennedy School of Government, at www.vanishingvoter.org (4 November 2000).

36. A minority of the voters (47 percent) had annual family incomes below $50,000, compared to 61 percent in 1996 and 68 percent in 1992. This change is far greater than the growth in income during these years.

37. The calculation for the last columns is a simple multiplication of the percentage of all responses citing the specific issue or trait by the percentage in that group voting for a particular candidate. Since all respondents did not answer these questions, the resulting figures are then normalized to a base of 100. For example, 18 percent cited the economy and jobs as the most important issue, 59 percent of this group voted for Gore, and all responses summed to 88 percent. The contribution to the Gore vote then = .18 x .59 / .88 = .12. Nader's appeal was spread across many issues and traits, with some particular appeal on the foreign policy issues, probably trade, and his presumed caring quality.

38. Alan Wolfe, *One Nation, After All* (New York: Viking Penguin, 1998).

39. Walter Bagehot, *The English Constitution* [1867] (London: Oxford University Press, 1928), chap. 1.
40. See Judith Best, *The Choice of the People?* (Lanham, Md.: Rowman & Littlefield, 1996) for elaboration of the competing arguments and proposals.
41. Calculated, to three decimal places, from the vote totals in table 6.1. The remaining 0.2 electoral votes would be cast for minor candidates such as Buchanan.
42. William Kristol, "Crowning the Imperial Judiciary," *New York Times*, 28 November 2000, A29.
43. *Federalist* No. 10 [1787] (New York: Modern Library, 1941), 54, 59.
44. Andrew Kohut, "May Either Man Win," *New York Times,* 25 November 2000, A19.
45. See, for example, the CBS News/*New York Times* poll of 20 November and the *Washington Post*/ABC News poll of 4 December 2000.
46. Max Farrand, ed. *The Records of the Federal Convention of 1787* (New Haven: Yale University Press, 1923), 3:85.

CHAPTER 7

The Congressional Elections

Paul S. Herrnson

> *The hum of either army stilly sounds,*
> *That the fixed sentinels almost receive*
> *The secret whispers of each other's watch:*
> *Fire answers fire, and through their paly flames*
> *Each battle sees the other's umbered face:*
> *Steed threatens steed, in high and boastful neighs*
> *Piercing the night's dull ear; and from the tents*
> *The armorers, accomplishing the knights,*
> *With busy hammers closing rivet up,*
> *Give dreadful note of preparation.*
> — Henry V (IV, prologue)

THE PRESIDENTIAL ELECTION clearly occupied center stage in 2000, but the congressional elections were more than just a sideshow. Candidates, political parties, and interest groups participated in an electoral drama that followed a traditional script recognizable to veteran political observers. Control over both chambers of Congress was at stake, so candidates, political parties, and interest groups spent extraordinary sums in a relatively small number of races to influence the election outcomes. Roughly half a dozen races either were subjected to recounts or could not be called until mail ballots were opened. Despite all this activity, when the final curtain came down, very few seats had changed hands: the Democrats enjoyed net gains of three seats in the House and four seats in the Senate.

The election did offer some interesting nuances. A First Lady won a Senate seat, and in a state in which she had been resident for less than a year. A deceased challenger defeated an incumbent senator. An incumbent House member lost his primary largely as a result of the efforts of the opposing political party. The Republicans' losses in the upper chamber led to a 50–50 split that promised an unusually prominent role for the new vice president, who would hold the tie-breaking vote.

THE CONTEXT

The political context for the 2000 congressional elections was defined largely by half a dozen factors. First and foremost was the institutional framework that shapes the contours of congressional elections in general, regardless of the year. The United States has a candidate-centered system, in which officeseekers are largely self-recruited, rather than selected by party leaders; they must first win nomination, and thereafter they bear responsibility for waging their own campaigns. Parties and interest groups directly contribute money, advice, and other forms of campaign assistance to candidates in competitive contests, contacting and mobilizing voters on their behalf. Parties and groups do not dominate congressional campaigns, however, but perceive themselves as playing supporting roles in the campaign process. Only rarely, as in 1994, do parties set a national agenda that dominates the election.

The partisan distribution of seats is another important part of the strategic context of any given election year. It has a major impact on the flow of money and on candidate, party, and interest group strategies. The Republicans held slim majorities in both chambers during the 106th Congress: going into the general election they controlled 222 seats, the Democrats had 209, Independents held 2, and 2 seats were vacant. The GOP had to defend 25 open House seats to the Democrats' 7. The Republicans enjoyed an 8-seat majority in the Senate, but they entered the 2000 campaign needing to defend 19 seats, as opposed to the Democrats' need to defend 15.

National conditions — real and perceived — are a third factor that helps define the political context of an election. The 2000 elections took place in a remarkably positive political environment — one that was clearly advantageous for congressional incumbents. Unemployment and inflation were low, the gross domestic product was steadily rising, and record numbers of individuals were investing in the stock market. Moreover, the nation was at peace and enjoying its post–Cold War status as the world's only remaining superpower. These objective indicators suggested that Americans should have been reasonably satisfied with the state of their nation, and indeed most were. At the end of the summer, 70 percent rated the economy as "good" or "excellent," and 59 percent were satisfied with "the way things are going in the U.S."[1] These figures represent a marked contrast to the 14-percent and 16-percent ratings voiced eight years earlier.[2]

Voters' positive assessments of the government and economy were reflected in their appraisals of political institutions. The public hostility that had been directed against Congress during the 1990s was replaced by feelings of relative equanimity. Congress's approval ratings stood at 49 percent, which contrasts sharply with the 79-percent disapproval rating it had suffered before the 1994 elections.[3] Incumbents of both parties were in a position to benefit from the relative good times, but Democrats found themselves in a better position to do so. Not only were they defending fewer open seats; they also were enjoying a

48-percent approval rating—10 points higher than the approval ratings for congressional Republicans.[4] Regardless of their party affiliation, few members of the House or Senate were at risk during the 2000 elections.

The presidential election was another important aspect of the political context. Presidential campaigns dominate the political agenda and focus citizen attention on certain issues, making it virtually impossible for other candidates to avoid discussing them. Health care, prescription drug reform, education, the economy, the environment, Social Security, and tax cuts were all high on the campaign agenda in the 2000 elections and worked to the advantage of candidates who had strong records on these issues.[5] Presidential campaigns also increase citizen interest in politics, draw large numbers of voters to the polls, and boost turnout in congressional elections and other down-ballot races.

In some cases, presidential candidates can pull congressional candidates into office on the strength of their appeal at the top of the ticket. These so-called coattail effects have declined in importance in recent elections, but they can help a congressional candidate in a close race emerge victorious.[6] The presidential candidates' coattails did not appear to have a major impact on the 2000 congressional elections, although numerous congressional candidates ran on the same issues as did their parties' presidential nominees. Both Al Gore and George W. Bush were too focused on their own hotly contested race to spend a great deal of time campaigning for others, and Bush's desire to project a moderate image led him to divorce his campaign from congressional Republicans and electioneer with GOP governors instead. Moreover, some congressional candidates chose not to campaign with their party's presidential nominee for strategic reasons: a few moderate GOP candidates did not want to campaign with Bush because of his position on tax cuts, while some Democratic congressional candidates who had policy differences with Gore had similar reservations about campaigning with him.

Another factor that was important to the political setting for the 2000 congressional elections was the president. Bill Clinton had cast a large shadow over the political landscape since he emerged as the front-runner in the 1992 Democratic presidential nomination contest, and much of his influence on congressional races was to the detriment of his fellow Democrats. Contrary to the historical pattern whereby a successful presidential candidate's party typically enjoys a gain in congressional seats, the Democrats lost ten House seats and broke even in Senate seats in 1992, and they won only ten House seats and even lost two Senate seats in 1996.

Moreover, the election held in the middle of Clinton's first term resulted in one of the most devastating defeats for a president's party in recent history: the Democrats lost fifty-two seats in the House and eight seats in the Senate, enabling the Republicans to claim control of the House for the first time in four decades and of the Senate for the first time in eight years. Clinton was not entirely to blame for the Democrats' 1994 electoral nightmare, but his early missteps on gays in the military, health care reform, tax cuts, and allegations of ethical improprieties by members of his administration contributed to voter animosity toward Washington. Political scandals involving congressional leaders and the federal government's inability to resolve major policy problems had also angered the electorate. Because Democratic congressional candidates — not the president — were the only federal officeholders on the ballot, they were the ones who suffered the voters' wrath.

Clinton's influence also loomed large in the 1998 elections. On the one hand, the tawdry sex scandal involving White House intern Monica Lewinsky, Kenneth Starr's investigation, and the politics of impeachment made Clinton an unwelcome guest in many conservative districts and some moderate districts that have traditionally elected Democrats — districts where congressional candidates would normally welcome a sitting president with open arms. On the other hand, the Republicans' aggressiveness in trying to oust Clinton from the White House mobilized large numbers of Democrats to make campaign contributions and vote. Despite Clinton's difficulties, the Democrats picked up five seats in 1998, bucking a sixty-year trend in which the president's party lost seats in midterm elections. One can only speculate whether the Democrats would have done better or worse if the politics of impeachment had not occupied center stage.

Clinton also helped set the stage for the 2000 congressional elections, despite the fact he was no longer on the ballot. Polls consistently showed that the public opposed the impeachment and conviction of the president by margins approaching 2 to 1. Roughly nine out of ten Democrats opposed impeachment, whereas roughly 60 percent of all Republicans favored it.[7] The partisan impeachment votes and trial in the Senate set the stage for a highly divisive and extremely unproductive Congress. The 106th Congress opened with the resignations of Speaker Newt Gingrich, after his party lost seats in the 1998 House elections, and Speaker-designate Robert Livingston of Louisiana, who chose to leave the House after the media reported that he, like Clinton, had engaged in an extramarital affair. It was downhill from there. Little was accomplished, and partisan disagreements delayed the passage of six of the thirteen appropriations bills necessary to keep the government from shutting down. Members gave up on the appropriations bills on the Friday immediately before the election, setting a new post–World War II record for the latest adjournment date during an election year. Many were unhappy about staying in Washington when they could have been home campaigning.

Impeachment politics and the taint of scandal in the Clinton White House also influenced some individual House races. These themes were featured prominently in the highly successful fund-raising appeals of most of the House impeachment managers and their opponents. They also may have contributed to the defeat of impeachment managers James Rogan of California and Jay Dickey of Arkansas, and they may have cost GOP Representative Bill McCollum some

Table 7.1 The Number of Nonincumbents Contesting House Primaries, 1990–2000

	1990	1992	1994	1996	1998	2000
Democratic open seats	139	318	226	228	139	100
Democratic challengers	314	509	372	427	327	355
Republican open seats	131	272	215	225	150	149
Republican challengers	377	572	497	414	342	354
Total	961	1,671	1,310	1,294	958	958

Source: Federal Election Commission, "FEC Reports on Congressional Fundraising for 1997–98"; "Congressional Campaign Receipts Reach $653 Million," 26 September 2000.

Note: Figures for 2000 are for 18 months and may be slightly incomplete.

critical votes in his unsuccessful race for the Senate in Florida. Given that 44 percent of all voters said that the president's scandals were "somewhat" or "very" important in determining their votes, it is likely that the Clinton factor had an impact on other close congressional races.[8]

In sum, the political context for the 2000 election had similarities to the setting for the previous two elections. Voters were relatively satisfied with the overall state of the nation, relatively few incumbents had retired, Clinton continued to be a polarizing figure among voters and legislators, and Congress had passed little in the way of legislation that would either please or anger voters. The stage had been set for a typical denationalized election that would allow incumbents to focus on their achievements in office and challengers to criticize their records. The presidential election would dominate the national political agenda, but most congressional elections would be local affairs to be determined by the candidates and their campaigns. As has been the case for decades, relatively few elections promised to be competitive, making it possible for parties and interest groups to pursue strategies designed to focus most of their resources on a relatively small number of very close races.

THE PRIMARIES

The strategic context has a major impact on who runs for Congress. Potential candidates typically consider both the national and local contexts when deliberating whether to run. The greatest numbers and most highly qualified nonincumbent House candidates typically run in the elections immediately following redistricting, when new seats have been created, old seats have been redrawn, and large numbers of incumbents typically retire. Election seasons characterized by voter frustration and hostility toward government also bring out large numbers of candidates. Because the 2000 elections were characterized by none of these conditions, the number of nonincumbents who declared their candidacies was not particularly large: 958 major-party challengers and open-seat candidates participated in the 2000 nomination contests (see table 7.1). This figure is about equal to 1998, substantially down from 1992, 1994, and 1996, and roughly equal to 1990 levels.

Substantially more Republican candidates ran in open seats than did Democrats, reflecting the fact that more Republican-held seats had become vacant as a result of retirements. Almost identical numbers of Democrats and Republicans ran as challengers, no doubt because similar numbers of incumbents of both parties were defending their seats. Fund-raising demands, the amount of time a candidate must spend away from home campaigning, and the loss of privacy — combined with the low odds of knocking off an incumbent — discouraged many potential challengers.[9] The possibility of running for an open seat or against an incumbent whose district might be redrawn undoubtedly encouraged many talented politicians to wait until 2002.

The local context is also very important. Potential candidates recognize that it is difficult to defeat an incumbent, especially in a primary. One hundred sixty Democratic and 155 Republican House incumbents went unchallenged for their parties' nominations. When an incumbent seeking reelection has become infirm, is the subject of a major scandal, or has cast salient votes that are out of step with the views of most district voters, he or she is more likely to face a qualified challenger, but experienced politicians recognize that an open seat presents their best opportunity for victory. They also recognize that first-term members and members running for reelection under the cloud of scandal are more easily defeated than are others.

Open seats and seats held by freshman and incumbents tainted by scandal comprised a substantial portion of the ninety-one House seats that the pundits considered competitive early in the 2000 election season.[10] These races attracted an especially strong group of candidates: 39 percent had previously held elective office; another 22 percent were unelected politicians who had not previously been elected to office but who had experience as political aides, party officials, or political appointees, or in running for Congress; and the final 39 percent were amateurs who had no significant political experience.[11]

As is typically the case, the candidates with the most experience were the most successful.[12] Sixty-three percent of the eventual Democratic nominees in these hotly contested races had prior officeholding experience, and they enjoyed a success rate of 54 percent (see table 7.2). Democratic unelected politicians comprised 23 percent of the winners and had success rates of 45 percent. Democratic political amateurs were considerably less successful. The patterns for Republican primary winners were similar, except that Republican unelected politicians constituted a larger portion of the primary winners than did their Democratic counterparts.

Political parties also are well aware that open seats provide excellent opportunities for highly qualified nonincumbents to get elected to Congress, and party leaders usually double their efforts to recruit strong candidates to run for these

Table 7.2 **Political Experience and Primary Success in Competitive Districts**

	Democrats		Republicans	
	Winners	**Success Rates**	**Winners**	**Success Rates**
Officeholders	63%	54%	54%	53%
Unelected politicians	23	45	28	42
Amateurs	14	17	18	18
(N)	(64)	(64)	(60)	(60)

Source: Compiled from various issues of *CQ Weekly, Who's Who in American Politics, The League of Women Voters,* candidate web sites, and other sources.

Note: Figures are for nonincumbents only and include candidates from 91 competitive districts.

seats. Believing that divisive primaries can siphon off campaign money, tarnish the candidates' images, and harm the eventual nominees' election prospects, party leaders also occasionally try to discourage experienced politicians from battling each other in open-seat contests. Recognizing that control of Congress might be determined by a few open and incumbent-occupied seats, the parties worked to recruit highly qualified candidates to run in 2000. Representative Patrick Kennedy of Rhode Island, chair of the Democratic Congressional Campaign Committee (DCCC), and Representative Tom Davis of Virginia, chair of the National Republican Congressional Committee (NRCC), worked with other party leaders and the committees' professional staffs in these efforts.

Competitive situations sometimes call for extraordinary measures, and the Republicans' slim majority in the House led leaders of both parties to take some unusual steps during the primary stage of the election. Party leaders, including President Clinton and Democratic and Republican leaders in the House and Senate, broke with tradition and became heavily involved in substantial numbers of contested primaries, providing candidates with money and endorsements. The DCCC took the unprecedented step of giving preprimary endorsements to four candidates. Two — California Assemblyman Mike Honda and Kentucky State Representative Eleanor Jordan — won their nominations, but two others — Pennsylvania District Attorney Matthew Mangino and Union City, New Jersey, City Manager Mike LaPolla — were defeated, putting the DCCC in the situation of needing to quickly patch things up with the winners and their supporters.[13] The DCCC also endorsed Arkansas State Senator Mike Ross in his successful run-off against television reporter Dewayne Graham.[14]

The most unusual and perhaps controversial party activity occurred in the Democratic primary in New York's first congressional district. Republicans, angry over Representative Michael Forbes's decision to quit the GOP to join the Democrats, got their revenge. The Republican Party and the Republican Majority Issues Conference, which is associated with Republican Majority Whip Tom DeLay, spent approximately $80,000 and $50,000, respectively, to attack Forbes in direct mail that was sent to Democratic primary voters. Forbes was particularly vulnerable to such attacks because of his difficulties in cementing relations with local Democrats, who had opposed him in his previous three congressional races. The Republicans' activities contributed to Forbes's 44-vote defeat in the Democratic primary.[15]

Once the dust had settled, few members of Congress had been defeated in the primaries, as is usually the case. Merrill Cook (R-Utah), who reportedly had been exhibiting bizarre behavior; Matthew Martinez (D-Calif.), whose strong pro-life stance, support for the National Rifle Association, and failure to support legislation favored by organized labor put him at odds with Democratic voters participating in California's open primary; and the party-switcher Forbes were the only House members to lose their nominations. No Senate incumbents lost their party's nominations, and the vast majority of nonincumbent winners had significant political experience.

There were, however, some unusual races. Multimillionaire Jon Corzine, for example, who had no political experience and virtually no visibility when he began campaigning, defeated former Governor James Florio in New Jersey's Democratic primary. Corzine's primary victory was controversial because the candidate spent roughly $33 million of his own money, about eleven times more than Florio's total expenditures. Indeed, some supporters of Corzine's rivals, both in the primary and later in the general election, showed up at public events holding signs urging "Make Him Spend It All," referring to Corzine's estimated $400 million fortune. Corzine was not the first candidate to finance his own House or Senate campaign, but the level of expenditure he undertook to get elected is unlikely to be matched for years to come.

Once the primaries were over, party officials, interest group leaders, and numerous pundits quickly surmised that control of the House would depend on the outcomes of a relatively small number of competitive elections. They revised their lists of close races considerably to reflect changes in the prospects of different candidates. During the last few weeks of the campaign season, most pundits narrowed their focus to about forty House races, although some speculated that as many as sixty would be closely contested.[16] Political scientists, using a variety of models, predicted that the Democrats would pick up between three and eight seats in the House.[17] The initial outlook for the Senate elections was that sixteen races would be competitive.

THE GENERAL ELECTION CAMPAIGN

The contestants in the 2000 general elections were fairly typical. A total of 805 major-party candidates and 74 minor-party and Independent House candidates made it onto general election ballots. Sixty-three incumbents and one open-seat candidate faced no major-party opposition, all but guaranteeing their election.

This meant they would not have to campaign actively and would not be held accountable for their issue positions or previous performance in office.

Only one Senate candidate—incumbent Jon Kyl (R-Ariz.) began the general election season without an opponent. A few weeks before Election Day, however, Missouri Governor Melvin Carnahan, who was challenging Republican Senator John Ashcroft in a hotly contested race, died in an airplane crash. Election officials in the Show Me State ruled that it was too late to take Carnahan's name off the ballot, leaving Ashcroft in the awkward position of running against a deceased opponent. Ashcroft's situation became even more uncomfortable when Missouri's new governor announced that he would appoint Carnahan's widow to the seat in the event that the late governor received more ballots than did Ashcroft. Carnahan's wife let voters know she was ready to serve in the Senate if called, and the Missouri Democratic Party endeavored to keep their party's Senate hopes alive by sending out 750,000 letters urging voters to cast their ballots for the governor and distributing buttons proclaiming "I'm still with Mel."[18] History was made when the deceased Senate challenger outpolled a living incumbent.

Another unusual Senate race occurred in New York, where First Lady Hillary Rodham Clinton first competed against Republican New York City Mayor Rudolph Giuliani and later against Republican Congressman Rick Lazio. Clinton established residency for the purpose of running for the Senate, and she engaged in a street brawl of a campaign with Giuliani, until health problems and allegations about an extramarital relationship forced him to withdraw from the campaign. Then Lazio jumped into the fray, waging a campaign that was every bit as spirited as the earlier matchup.

Beyond the First Lady's race and the confusion that Carnahan's sudden death caused in Missouri, the general election followed the usual script. Candidates for Congress waged two fairly distinct, but overlapping campaigns: one, a campaign for money and other resources, and the other for votes.[19] As is usually the case, candidates began the campaign for resources early and focused their efforts in Washington, D.C., New York City, Hollywood, and the nation's other major financial centers as well as in their own districts. The campaign for votes, which historically begins on Labor Day, commenced earlier in some cases, as candidates in marginal districts sought to set a campaign agenda that worked to their advantage.

Congressional aspirants raised record sums in the 2000 elections. Candidates for the House and Senate collected $533.6 million and $366.77 million in contributions, respectively—roughly 28 percent and 51 percent more than had been raised in 1998.[20] The close competition for control of Congress was largely responsible for the surge in congressional fund-raising, as endangered incumbents collected large sums to protect their seats, and many not so endangered incumbents ran scared, raising and spending large amounts of money to preserve their peace of mind. Other members of Congress also raised large sums, and then used some of their funds to help elect other party members. A small but important group of nonincumbents — mainly open-seat candidates and challengers running in marginal seats — also raised impressive amounts.

As is the case in virtually every aspect of congressional elections, incumbents possess significant advantages over challengers in the campaign for resources. Their high expectation of victory — more than 90 percent of all House incumbents and more than 80 percent of all Senate incumbents win in most election years — is both a cause and an effect of incumbents' fund-raising advantage. Incumbents' high reelection rates benefit them in raising money from donors who seek to influence the policymaking process and from those who wish to interact personally with officeholders and other influential supporters. Additional advantages stem from incumbents' head start in the fund-raising process, their hiring professional consultants to help them collect money, and their lists of previous donors and the solicitation appeals to which they have responded.[21]

House incumbents raised a record $353 million in the 2000 elections, topping incumbent receipts for the last election season by 22 percent. House members raised an average of $811,494, and eighteen of them had collected $2 million, surpassing the 1998 record by a factor of 8. At the top of the list was Representative James Rogan, who had raised more than $6.8 million.[22] Both Rogan's financial need and his fund-raising prowess stemmed from his role in Clinton's impeachment trial, which gave the congressman national visibility, earning him celebrity status among Republicans and the enmity of Democrats. Money from both parties and numerous interest groups poured in to help or harm his general election prospects.

Fund-raising by House challengers is the mirror image of incumbent fundraising. Virtually every advantage possessed by the typical House incumbent qualifies as a disadvantage for the typical challenger. Access-oriented donors and those who give because they like attending fund-raising events are less motivated to contribute to challengers because so few of them win. Many challengers lack the resources needed to employ professional fund-raising consultants, and few have donor lists that are as extensive or well-documented as those of incumbents. As a result, most challengers have to prospect for new donors. In most election years, major-party House challengers raise about one-third of the money raised by incumbents, although a few challengers raise extremely large amounts.[23] The 2000 elections were no exception: challengers raised an average of $315,288, and only nine had raised more than $2 million. Democrat Adam Schiff collected the most money — $4.3 million — which he used to defeat Rogan in what became the most expensive House race in history.[24]

Candidates for open House seats have neither the advantages of incumbents nor the disadvantages of challengers. They typically build war chests that are at least as substantial as those built by incumbents, and 2000 was no exception. The typical major-party open-seat candidate had raised about $1.2 million.[25]

Senators running for reelection in the 2000 general elections posted a fund-raising record that was just as impressive as that set by their colleagues in the House. It is difficult to draw comparisons with earlier election cycles, however, because different groups of senators are up for election every two years. Preliminary figures show that Senate incumbents raised $128.3 million, and nine raised more than $5 million. Spencer Abraham (R-Mich.), emerged as the Senate's No. 1 fund-raiser, collecting $11.8 million in an unsuccessful attempt to defend his seat against former House member Debbie Stabenow.[26]

Senate challengers typically raise less money than do their opponents, but differences in incumbent-challenger spending are not as stark for Senate candidates as they are for House candidates. Senate challengers usually have more political experience, are better known, possess identifiable supporters from previous bids for office, and assemble more professional campaign teams than do their House counterparts. The higher visibility of their races, the greater power wielded by an individual senator, and Senate challengers' relatively better odds of success make them more attractive than House candidates to some donors. Of course, these fund-raising advantages are to some degree offset by the fact that Senate candidates usually need to raise daunting sums of money: according to preliminary figures, five Senate challengers each managed to collect more than $5 million.[27]

Open-seat Senate candidates set fund-raising records during the 2000 elections. Six candidates each raised $5 million or more, and three of these each raised in excess of $29 million. Corzine, who won in New Jersey, accounted for almost $63.1 million, or 39 percent of the total raised by all open-seat candidates. Corzine's fund-raising set yet another record: as of three weeks before the election the candidate himself had provided $60.1 million for his campaign (95 percent of its receipts). Corzine's opponent, Republican Representative Bob Franks, by contrast, raised less than $6.4 million. The next highest-spending race was more evenly matched: in New York, Rick Lazio raised almost $38.9 million in his unsuccessful race against Hillary Clinton, who collected approximately $29.9 million.[28]

The campaign for votes involves setting a campaign agenda, targeting voters, developing a message, communicating that message, and mobilizing voters. Public concerns and the presidential election had a major influence on the campaign agendas of most House and Senate campaigns. Most polls showed that education, health care, Social Security, and Medicare were the top issues on the minds of voters, with taxes often ranked next. The economy, which had been a major issue from the 1970s through the mid-1990s, had receded in importance in 2000.[29] The Democratic Party has traditionally been favorably associated with the top three issues, and its candidates have benefited when voters have focused on them. The Republicans have benefited when elections have centered on taxes, national defense, crime and drug prevention, and moral issues.[30]

The 2000 elections were unusual in that the two major-party presidential candidates blurred traditional party lines. Bush took traditional GOP stances on tax cuts and the military, but he went on the offensive on education and Social Security, proposing vouchers for parents who send their children to private schools and advocating privatizing part of the Social Security system. Gore campaigned on education, Social Security, health care reform, and Medicare, but he also proposed a tax cut and articulated a plan to rebuild the military. The agenda-setting efforts of the presidential candidates encouraged some congressional candidates to discuss campaign issues they often seek to downplay.

There were limits to the extent to which congressional candidates embraced their standard-bearers' issue positions, however. Seven-term Republican Representative Constance Morella of Maryland, who represents a primarily Democratic district, is one of a small group of House members who often take issue positions that are in direct opposition to those of other members of their parties. Morella, for example, opposed Bush's proposal to privatize part of the Social Security system and disagreed with most Republicans' anti–gun control stances. Her positions on the environment were closer to those of Al Gore and the Democrats than to those of the leaders of her own party. Moreover, Morella, like many other members of Congress from the Washington area, is a champion of federal employees, which put her at odds with most Republicans' preferences for downsizing the federal government.[31] Conservative Democrats, such as "Blue Dog" Representative Gene Green of Texas, took more conservative positions on gun control, juvenile crime, and the environment than did the rest of the Democratic Party.[32]

One of the basic rules of campaigning is to target party members and sufficient numbers of persuadable voters to build an electoral majority. Another basic rule is to focus most campaign communications, particularly mail, telemarketing calls, and other forms of direct contact on habitual voters.[33] Members of the political consulting industry have developed these rules of thumb because they are cost-efficient and effective. The major shortfall of these guidelines is that some groups of voters (the elderly, middle-class, and wealthy) are bombarded with campaign communications, while others (youths and the poor) are virtually ignored.

The available evidence suggests that in 2000 most candidates followed the general rules of voter targeting. As a result, a substantial portion of the electorate, particularly young voters and those with lower incomes, never became fully engaged in the election. Indeed, 18-to-34 year olds, who make up 31 percent of the population, comprised only 14 percent of the viewing audience for television ads aired in connection with the presidential campaign and probably comprised an equally minor portion of the viewers for congressional campaign ads.[34] Youthful voters were undoubtedly among the least likely to be exposed to the direct mail or telemarketing calls that campaigns use to mobilize voters.[35]

PARTY CAMPAIGN EFFORTS

Political parties give candidates contributions, make coordinated expenditures on their behalf, provide them with campaign services, disseminate campaign communications to voters, and mobilize voters. Most of these activities are targeted on behalf of candidates contesting competitive seats.[36] In 2000 the potential for turnover of control of the House and the Senate encouraged the parties to raise and spend record funds to help their candidates. Democratic Party organizations contributed more than $1 million in campaign contributions and coordinated expenditures to House general election candidates in 2000, as opposed to the nearly $1.8 million distributed by their Republican counterparts. Senate candidates also were the beneficiaries of significant largesse, as the Democratic and Republican Party organizations distributed $426,000 and $530,000 to their respective candidates.[37]

Party committees also spent record sums of soft money (funds raised outside the federal regulatory system) on voter registration, get-out-the-vote drives, and issue advocacy ads (which resemble regular campaign ads in most ways, except that they stop short of calling for an individual candidate's election or defeat and generally are more negative than candidate ads).[38] The DCCC and DSCC raised $56.6 million and $63.1 million for these purposes, $6 million and $19.6 million more than their Republican counterparts. The Democratic and Republican National Committees, which focused primarily on the presidential contest but also sought to influence congressional races, raised $136.6 million and $158.9 million in soft money, respectively.[39]

Party leaders made unprecedented efforts to support the work of formal party organizations during the 2000 elections. House Democrats donated $12.6 million in dues and contributions to the DCCC's "Majority Makers" fund; House Republicans contributed more than $18 million for the NRCC's "Battleground 2000."[40] Republican leadership PACs donated roughly $9.6 million to federal candidates, and their Democratic counterparts contributed about $5.1 million. Leading among the donors were Republican Majority Leader Tom DeLay of Texas, whose Americans for a Republican Majority PAC contributed more than $920,000, and California Democratic Representative Nancy Pelosi, whose PAC to the Future donated about $732,000. Thirty-four Republican congressional candidates and one Democrat — Representative Joseph Hoeffel of Pennsylvania — received $100,000 or more in leadership PAC contributions.[41]

Party leaders helped congressional candidates in other ways. Senator John McCain of Arizona, the most popular member of the Republican Party in 2000, logged approximately 61,000 miles by plane, train, bus, and automobile to appear at 220 campaign events for at least sixty-five House candidates.[42] During the August recess House Speaker Dennis Hastert raised $690,000 for seventeen GOP candidates, and House Minority Leader Richard Gephardt raised about

$180,000 for nine candidates.[43] Both traveled thousands of miles in order to make appearances on behalf of competitive House contestants.

INTEREST GROUP CAMPAIGN EFFORTS

Interest groups become involved in elections because they want to influence public policy. Ideological (or election-oriented) groups believe that the best way for them to influence the policymaking process is by electing candidates to Congress who share their views. Many become heavily involved in candidate recruitment and make substantial campaign contributions and expenditures to help their campaigns. They focus most of their efforts in marginal seats, including the primaries leading up to the general election. Access-oriented groups believe that they are best served by maintaining close relations with incumbents who are in a position to influence a group's policy priorities. They give donations to party leaders, committee members, and policy entrepreneurs to ensure that these powerful members of Congress will meet with the group's lobbyists. A third group of organizations, mainly labor unions, use both strategies. Labor directs most of its contributions to Democratic candidates, but it divides its support between Democrats in close races and powerful incumbents who are virtually assured of reelection.[44]

All three types of interest groups geared up for the 2000 elections. Interest group political action committees (PACs) contributed record funds to congressional candidates. Business-oriented PACs contributed the most. PACs sponsored by corporations donated $66.2 million to House and $22.5 million to Senate candidates. Those sponsored by trade associations donated $53.6 million and $12.7 million to contestants for the lower and upper chambers.[45] Both sets of PAC contributions favored the Republicans, reflecting that party's control of Congress. Labor PACs ranked third in terms of contributions, and their donations overwhelmingly favored Democrats.[46]

Interest groups also provide candidates with endorsements and campaign services, carrying out internal communications, independent expenditures, and issue advocacy advertisements on their behalf. The 1996 elections are perhaps best remembered for the air wars funded by interest groups. The unions spent approximately $30 million to air 27,000 television commercials to advance the candidacies of forty Democratic House candidates.[47] A coalition of interest groups, led by the National Federation of Independent Businesses, spent about $5 million on TV advertising to help thirty-seven Republican House candidates. Other groups also spent significant sums on issue ads. The 1998 elections were noteworthy for the ground war, as the U.S. Chamber of Commerce, the Christian Coalition, and numerous other groups employed direct mail, telephone calls, door-to-door campaigning, and other fieldwork activities to mobilize voters. Labor was especially effective in using its members to register other union workers and get them to the polls.[48]

The 2000 elections featured substantial air- and ground-war offensives. Labor unions, led by the American Federation of Labor–Congress of Industrial Organizations, spent $4.5 million on television ads to help Democrats in forty-three competitive House races.[49] The unions deployed 1,000 full-time workers and another 100,000 volunteers to carry their pro-Democratic message via weekend door-knocking campaigns and nightly telephone calls to union workers and their families. The AFL-CIO also sent every member of its affiliated unions at least two pieces of direct mail and called them at least twice.[50] This worker-to-worker get-out-the-vote drive had a significant effect in turning out union voters and played a key role in elections held in California, Michigan, Missouri, and New York.

Numerous business, environmental, pro-choice, pro-life, and other groups also spent millions of dollars on ground- and air-war efforts in 2000. Citizens for Better Medicare aired almost $6 million worth of ads to help Republicans in forty-three of the most closely fought House contests.[51] The National Rifle Association spent between $15 million and $20 million, laying the groundwork for its efforts by airing half-hour infomercials as early as 1999.[52] Some groups became the source of significant controversy when it was revealed they had been bankrolled by only two or three people who had created the groups so that they could spend hundreds of thousands — and in some cases millions — of dollars in order to influence federal elections without publicly disclosing their contributions or the groups' finances. Congress passed legislation in July 2000 to require such groups to disclose both their lists of contributors and their expenditures.

THE ELECTION OUTCOME

Numerous factors influence the outcomes of congressional elections. Foremost is incumbency. More than nine of ten House and eight of ten Senate candidates routinely win reelection in a given election year. The 2000 elections were no different. Three hundred and ninety-four House incumbents were victorious, while only nine lost; and only six of twenty-nine members of the Senate seeking reelection were defeated (see table 7.3, p. 170).

Money is also important, especially for congressional challengers and open-seat candidates, who are generally less well-known than are incumbents. Nonincumbents need to spend money to improve their name recognition, to familiarize voters with their images and issue stances, and to appear viable in order to attract media coverage. Nevertheless, it is not essential for these candidates, or for incumbents, to outspend their opponents in order to win. For example, in races for the House, the Democratic challenger Schiff defeated Rogan in California despite being outspent more than $6.8 million to $4.3 million, and Republican Shelley Moore Capito defeated James Humphreys in an open-seat contest in West Virginia although Humphreys spent $7 million to her $1.3 million.[53] In elections for the Senate, Clinton defeated Lazio in New York even though Lazio outspent

Table 7.3 Winners and Losers in the 2000 Congressional Elections

	House		Senate	
	Democrats	**Republicans**	**Democrats**	**Republicans**
Incumbents				
Reelected	200	192	10	13
Defeated in primaries	2	1	0	0
Defeated in general elections	2	4	1	5
Open Seats				
Successfully defended seat	3	20	3	0
Gained seat held by opposing party	4	5	1	1
Seats held in 107th Congress	212	221	50	50

Note: Two seats were held by Independents.

her by more than 25 percent. Once a candidate reaches a spending threshold, the rest may be overkill.[54] Corzine probably could have won without spending $63.1 million, which was roughly ten times more than Franks spent—and about $4.30 per New Jersey voter.[55]

Other factors matter besides incumbency and money. The partisan leanings of the district play a significant role in determining election outcomes. Challengers who have had to defeat an opponent in the primary derive benefits in the general election, presumably from the exposure received from their primary campaign efforts and media coverage. Challengers who face House freshmen or incumbents tainted by scandal also do better in the polls than do others. A host of campaign-related variables also are relevant. Strategic decisions about voter targeting and the issue focus of the campaign are particularly important in helping House challengers garner votes. The same is true of the communications methods that candidates use: direct mail and radio advertising, which can be targeted to specific population groups, are particularly effective. Newspaper coverage and endorsements also contribute significantly to challengers', incumbents', and open-seat contestants' vote shares.[56]

Finally, party and interest group spending in the form of televised issue advocacy ads, direct mail, and other communications can be extremely important, although their effects can help or hurt the intended beneficiaries. Outside spending can help a candidate attract attention and voter support, but it also can move the campaign agenda to issues that a candidate would prefer not to discuss, sometimes overshadowing the candidate's preferred message and preventing the campaign from persuading or mobilizing a key constituency. Outside spending can neutralize the effects of a candidate's strategic decisions and communications expenditures.[57] Even worse, it can backfire: Republican Senate candidates Abraham of Michigan and George Allen of Virginia saw their poll numbers decline after the NRA spent $600,000 on their behalf.[58]

Table 7.4 Candidate, Party, and Interest Group Television Advertising in Closely Contested Congressional Elections (in millions of dollars)

	House		Senate	
	Democrats	**Republicans**	**Democrats**	**Republicans**
Candidates	12.2	11.7	18.1	24.6
Political parties	10.2	7.6	10.6	6.2
Interest groups	6.4	8.4	2.0	1.2
Total	28.8	27.7	30.6	32.1

Source: Brennan Center for Justice, press release, 30 October 2000.

Note: Figures include spending on television advertising in forty-three of the most competitive House districts and three of the most competitive Senate districts (Michigan, New York, and Virginia) that occurred between 1 June and 24 October 2000. Some columns do not add up due to rounding.

Political parties' and interest groups' outside campaign efforts probably had a considerable impact on numerous 2000 House and Senate races. Parties and groups spent roughly $32.6 million on election-related television advertising to influence forty-three of the closest House contests (see table 7.4). This spending exceeded the candidates' own television expenditures by $8.7 million. Parties and groups also were very active in the Senate races in Michigan, New York, and Virginia, which were among the year's most competitive contests. They spent $20 million on television advertising in these races—almost half as much as the candidates' expenditures. Had it not been for an agreement between the candidates in New York to discourage their supporters from airing issue advocacy ads, parties and groups probably would have spent even more in these contests.

PROSPECTS FOR THE 107TH CONGRESS

The 2000 elections produced a mixed message for members of Congress: We support you enough to reelect most of you, but we do not agree on what we want you to do. The election was an overwhelming endorsement of House incumbents: 98 percent of those who sought reelection were successful. It also signaled strong general support for incumbents in the Senate, where almost 80 percent held on to their seats. The Republicans' already slim margin in the House grew even slimmer, and the GOP lost its majority in the Senate. Neither party won a policy mandate. This fact, coupled with the close struggle over control of the White House, suggested that it would be extremely difficult for the new Congress to get much done.

The fierce partisan conflict that marked the waning days of the 106th Congress also would pose challenges to the new Congress. Party leaders in the House, including Hastert and Gephardt, had not spoken to each other for months prior to the elections. Senate Republican leader Trent Lott of Mississippi and Democratic leader Tom Daschle of South Dakota were not on good terms either. Neither party's members were enthused about returning to battle over the appropriations bills they had not completed during the regular session. Party members in both chambers approached the upcoming session with an eye toward ensuring their own reelection and increasing their party's seats in 2002. If the last few legislative sessions were to serve as a guide, the paper-thin margins that divided the majority and minority parties would encourage party leaders to focus on gaining the upper hand in the polls rather than on passing legislation.

The tensions that normally exist at the start of a new session of Congress were exacerbated in the Senate. After the 107th Congress was sworn in on 3 January, members of the House and Senate voted on the organizing rules for their respective chambers. Because the Senate was divided 50–50 and Gore was then vice president, he cast the tie-breaking vote, giving the Democrats control of the upper chamber. Recognizing their control would be fleeting — lasting only until 20 January, when Vice President-elect Dick Cheney would be sworn into office and thereafter be in a position to cast the tie-breaking vote — the Democrats took control of the committee chairmanships but opted not to force the Republicans to give up their numerical advantage on most committees. Instead, the Democrats worked with their Republican colleagues to schedule confirmation hearings for President Bush's cabinet nominees and negotiated with Republican leader Trent Lott for an even distribution of committee slots and staff for the period following 20 January. The deportment of both sides during the negotiations helped set the stage for the degree of bipartisanship that followed.[59]

The vote for Speaker and for the rules organizing the House did not set the stage for much bipartisanship in the lower chamber, where the Republicans did little to adjust the committee ratios in response to the Democrats' net gain of three seats. They gave the Democrats one additional seat on each of four exclusive committees — Appropriations, Commerce, Ways and Means, and Select Intelligence — which they then offset by also adding a GOP member to each committee. This infuriated the Democrats, many of whom agreed with the assessment of Representative Joe Moakley (D-Mass.), ranking member of the Rules Committee, that the election's "mandate for cooperation [was] not reflected in [the GOP's] rules package," and that the Republicans were "acting as if they had won in a landslide."[60]

In addition to tensions between the parties, the organizing process created some tensions within them, especially in the House. The term limits for committee chairs that House Republicans had enacted during the 104th Congress had set off an unprecedented jockeying for advantage among senior Republican legislators prior to the 2000 elections, and that continued once the election was over. House Democrats also had engaged in some competition over leadership posts prior to the election, but their failure to win the majority narrowed their postelection struggles to the DCCC chairmanship (open as a result of Patrick

Kennedy's resignation) and a small number of committee assignments. Power struggles in the Senate centered around the more than half a dozen openings on the chamber's Finance Committee. With the exception of the contests for House committee chairs, such competitions are normal, but the majority's tiny margins seemed certain to magnify the impact of any grudges that might result from them. There was also the possibility that some members disgruntled about the outcomes of that process might retire early or switch parties.

Still, there were some prospects for a modestly productive session. Should the new president pursue a centrist agenda and reach out to moderates in both parties, he might be able to mobilize enough representatives and senators to pass some bipartisan legislation. The irony of the 107th Congress was to be that, following a fiercely fought partisan battle for control of the federal government, it would probably require extraordinary bipartisanship to succeed.

CONCLUSION

The 2000 congressional elections can be described as ordinary for modern-day congressional races. They were fought in a candidate-centered environment and focused heavily on local issues. Incumbents were overwhelmingly reelected to the House, and neither party's seat totals changed by much. The Senate witnessed somewhat more incumbent turnover and partisan change, but even those effects were modest. A few elections could not be called in a timely manner because absentee ballots had to be opened or because they were subjected to recounts. Candidates, parties, and interest groups raised and spent record sums on the elections, most of it to reach selected blocs of voters in a small group of closely contested races. Neither party won a policy mandate. These statements apply equally well to most recent congressional elections.

Still, many aspects of the 2000 elections were unique. The victories of First Lady Hillary Clinton and the deceased Governor Mel Carnahan were the most visible of them. The Republican Party's role in defeating incumbent Michael Forbes in a Democratic primary also was unusual. Some political observers might comment that the high levels of party and interest group soft-money spending were unusual, but these are a continuation of a trend associated with the demise of federal campaign finance law.

Students of politics might argue over whether the 2000 congressional elections were ordinary or unusual, but few would disagree over their importance. Congress, closely divided when the campaign season began, had been relatively unproductive. The elections offered the potential to give either party a mandate to break the gridlock. Instead, the slim margins of control in the House and Senate became even slimmer, and this result promised only continued partisanship and stalemate in the national legislature.

NOTES

I wish to thank the Pew Charitable Trusts for funding this research, Peter Roybal for providing some of the candidate background information, Robert Biersack for furnishing some of the campaign finance data, and David Clifford, Peter Francia, Gregory Jennings, Hellmut Lotz, and Scott Swenson for their research assistance. The views expressed in this chapter are mine and do not reflect the views of the Pew Charitable Trusts.

1. The economic evaluations are from a Gallup poll taken in August 2000, and the figures for the state of the nation are from a Gallup poll taken September 2000, www.gallup.com

2. The 1992 figures are from a Gallup poll taken June 1992.

3. The 2000 poll figures are from a CBS News/*New York Times* poll taken in 27 September 2000, www.pollingreport.com/congjob.htm; the figures for 1994 are from Gary C. Jacobson, "The 1994 House Elections in Perspective," in *Midterm: The Elections of 1994 in Context,* ed. Philip A. Klinkner (Boulder, Colo.: Westview, 1996), 3.

4. The figures are from a Harris poll taken 8–17 September 2000, www.pollingreport.com/congjob.htm

5. According to a poll taken by Garin-Hart Strategic Research Group, the percentages of voters who identified each of these issues as the most important issue in determining their votes were almost even. Geoff Garin, presentation at Election 2000 Conference, Washington, D.C., 9 November 2000.

6. On coattails effects, see, for example, Richard Born, "Reassessing the Decline of Presidential Coattails: U.S. House Elections, 1952–1980," *Journal of Politics* 46 (1980): 60–79; James E. Campbell, "Predicting Seat Gains from Presidential Coattails," *American Journal of Political Science* 30 (1986): 397–418; and Gary C. Jacobson, *Electoral Origins of Divided Government, 1946–1988* (Boulder, Colo.: Westview, 1990), 80–81.

7. See Gary C. Jacobson, *The Politics of Congressional Elections* (New York: Addison-Wesley Longman, 2000), 270, n. 31.

8. Peter Baker, "The Clinton Effect: Vindication Was Not on the Ticket," *Washington Post,* 12 November 2000.

9. L. Sandy Maisel, Walter J. Stone, and Cherie Maestas, "Quality Challengers to Congressional Incumbents: Can Better Candidates Be Found?" in *Playing Hardball: Campaigning for the U.S. Congress,* ed. Paul S. Herrnson (Upper Saddle River, N.J.: Prentice Hall, 2000), 12–40.

10. "At the Races," *Roll Call,* 27 April 2000.

11. On candidate quality and strategic decision making, see Gary C. Jacobson and Samuel Kernell, *Strategy and Choice in Congressional Elections* (New Haven: Yale University Press, 1983), chap. 3; William T. Bianco, "Strategic Decisions on Candidacy in U.S. Congressional Districts," *Legislative Studies Quarterly* 9 (1984): 360–62; David T. Canon, *Actors, Athletes, and Astronauts: Political Amateurs in the United States* (Chicago: University of Chicago Press, 1990), 26–32, 76–79, 106–8; L. Sandy Maisel, Linda L. Fowler, Ruth S. Jones, and Walter J. Stone, "The Naming of Candidates: Recruitment or Emergence?" in *The Parties Respond: Changes in the American Party System,* ed. L. Sandy Maisel (Boulder, Colo.: Westview, 1990); Linda L. Fowler and Robert D. McClure, *Political Ambition: Who Decides to Run for Congress?* (New Haven: Yale University Press, 1989), 231. For more information about the classification of candidates, see Paul S. Herrnson, *Congressional Elections: Campaigning at Home and in Washington* (Washington, D.C.: CQ Press, 2000), 42–43.

12. Herrnson, *Congressional Elections,* 42–43.

13. Ibid.

14. Ibid.

15. Juliet Eilperin, "With Stealth, the GOP Turns Tables on the Turncoat Rep. Forbes," *Washington Post,* 14 September 2000; Lizette Alverez, "Republican Group Uses Gingrich Ad to Attack Party Switcher, *New York Times,* 14 September 2000.

16. See for example, Bob Benenson, "Neither Party Likely to Win Clear-Cut Control of Agenda," *CQ Weekly,* 21 October 2000; Rhodes Cook, "It Hinges on Primes, Misfits and Fickles," *Washington Post,* 29 October 2000.

17. An approach that Ken Goldstein and I used, which attached various probabilities to races

categorized as toss-ups, leaning toward one party, or having a small chance of switching hands, predicted a Democratic net gain of three seats. The other estimates are based on an aggregate model and were provided by Gary Jacobson, e-mail correspondence, 25 October 2000. See Edward R. Tufte, "Determinants of the Outcomes of Midterm Congressional Elections," *American Political Science Review* 69 (1975): 812–26; and Jacobson, *Politics of Congressional Elections,* 143–46.

18. The deceased candidate led Ashcroft by 47.2 percent to 45.4 percent, a statistically insignificant amount. William Claiborne, "Widow Says She'd Accept Senate Seat," *Washington Post,* 31 October 2000.
19. Herrnson, *Congressional Elections.*
20. These are preliminary figures and include funds raised between 1 January 1999 and 27 November 2000. Federal Election Commission, "Congressional Activity Soars for 2000," press release, 9 January 2001.
21. Herrnson, *Congressional Elections,* 156–58.
22. See note 20.
23. Herrnson, *Congressional Elections,* 155–56, 164–65.
24. See note 20.
25. Ibid.
26. Ibid.
27. Ibid.
28. Ibid.
29. PollingReport.com, "Problems and Priorities: Priorities for Government," 24 September 2000, www.pollingreport.com/prioriti.htm
30. Herrnson, *Congressional Elections,* 234.
31. Congresswoman Morella on the Major Issues, www.morella.com/
32. Proudly Serving the 29th Congressional District of Texas Congressman Gene Green, www.house.gov/green/
33. Michael T. Hannahan, "Campaign Strategy and Direct Voter Contact," in Herrnson, *Playing Hardball,* 108–26.
34. Dale Russakoff, "Young Voters See Little in It for Them," *Washington Post,* 2 November 2000.
35. Hannahan, "Campaign Strategy and Direct Voter Contact," 116–19.
36. Paul S. Herrnson, *Party Campaigning in the 1980s* (Cambridge, Mass.: Harvard University Press, 1988), 56–111.
37. These are preliminary figures for contributions and coordinated expenditures raised between 1 January 1999 and 27 November 2000. (Source: Federal Election Commission).
38. Paul S. Herrnson and Diana Dwyre, "Party Issue Advocacy in Congressional Elections," in *The State of the Parties,* 3d ed., ed. John C. Green and Daniel M. Shea (Lanham, Md.: University Press of America, 1999), 86–104; Herrnson, *Congressional Elections,* 113–14. See the essays in David B. Magleby, *Outside Money: Soft Money and Issue Advocacy in the 1998 Congressional Elections* (Lanham, Md.: Rowman & Littlefield, 2000).
39. These are preliminary figures that include funds raised between 1 January 1999 and 27 November 2000. Federal Election Commission, "Party Fundraising Escalates," press release, 12 January 2001.
40. Juliet Eilperin, "Democrats Shatter Goal for House Fund," *Washington Post,* 30 October 2000. (These calculations are based on preliminary figures.)
41. Derek Willis, "Colleagues Come to the Rescue of Cash-Needy Candidates," *CQ Guide to the New Congress,* 9 November 2000. (These calculations are based on preliminary figures.)
42. Juliet Eilperin, "McCain Hits the Road to Ensure GOP House Candidates," *Washington Post,* 4 November 2000.
43. Alexander Bolton, "Speaker Hastert Wins August Fundraising Battle," *The Hill,* 6 September 2000.
44. See, for example, Janet M. Grenzke, "PACs and the Congressional Supermarket: The Currency Is Complex," *American Journal of Political Science* 33 (February 1989): 1–24; John Wright, "Contributions, Lobbying, and Committee Voting in the U.S. House of Representatives,"

American Political Science Review 84 (1990): 417–38; Thomas Romer and James M. Snyder Jr., "An Empirical Investigation of the Dynamics of PAC Contributions," *American Journal of Political Science* 38 (1994): 745–69; and Herrnson, *Congressional Elections,* 126–37.

45. See note 37.
46. For a full breakdown of PAC contributions, see table 7A at www.chathamhouse.com/pomper2000
47. On the role of labor unions in recent congressional elections, see Robin Gerber, "Building to Win, Building to Last: The AFL-CIO COPE Takes on the Republican Congress," in *After the Revolution,* ed. Robert Biersack, Paul S. Herrnson, and Clyde Wilcox (Boston: Allyn and Bacon, 1991), 77–93; and Gary C. Jacobson, "The Effect of the AFL-CIO's Voter Education Campaigns on the 1996 House Elections," *Journal of Politics* 61 (1999): 185–94.
48. Herrnson, *Congressional Elections,* 140–46; Peter L. Francia, *Awakening the Sleeping Giant: The Renaissance of Organized Labor in American Politics* (University of Maryland, College Park, Ph.D. dissertation, 2000), 53–56; David B. Magleby, "Outside Money and the Ground War in 1998," in Magleby, *Outside Money,* 63–76.
49. Figures include spending between 1 June and 24 October 2000. Brennan Center for Justice, press release, 30 October 2000, www.brennancenter.org/cmagpdf/cmag2000.10.30.table.pdf
50. Thomas B. Edsall, "Unions in High-Tech Fight for their Fortune," *Washington Post,* 31 October 2000.
51. Juliet Eilperin, "A Pivotal Election Finds NRA's Wallet Open," *Washington Post,* 1 November 2000.
52. Ibid.
53. See note 20; and Center for Responsive Politics, "West Virginia District 2: Total Raised," www.opensecrets.org/2000elect/dist_total/wv02.htm
54. Gary C. Jacobson, *Money in Congressional Elections* (New Haven: Yale University Press, 1980), 152–55, but see Donald P. Green and Jonathon S. Krasno, "Salvation for the Spendthrift Incumbent: Reestimating the Effects of Campaign Spending in House Elections," *American Journal of Political Science* 32 (1988): 844–907.
55. Ben White, "Politics," *Washington Post,* 10 December 2000.
56. Herrnson, *Congressional Elections,* 226–39.
57. Ibid.
58. Eilperin, "Pivotal Election."
59. Mark Preston, "Frustrated Senators Threaten Bush Plans," *Roll Call,* 4 January 2001; and Helen Dewar and Juliet Eilperin, "Divided Congress Takes Oath with Promises of Unity," *Washington Post,* 4 January 2001.
60. Damon Chappie and John Bresnahan, "Panel Ratios Spark Battle," *Roll Call,* 4 January 2001.

CHAPTER 8

The Meaning of the Election

Wilson Carey McWilliams

> *Things are in the saddle,*
> *And ride mankind.*
> *There are two laws discreet,*
> *Not reconciled,*
> *Law for man, and law for thing,*
> *The last builds town and fleet*
> *But it runs wild,*
> *And doth the man unking.*
> —Ralph Waldo Emerson,
> "Ode to W.H. Channing"

THE ELECTION OF 2000 was memorable, even bizarre, but well short of millennial — in retrospect rather like the Y2K scare, a season of hype followed by the prospect of business as usual. For much of the year, despite what was evidently a close race, the electorate seemed pressed to stifle a yawn. And if there was excitement election night and some days thereafter over the down-to-the-wire contest for the biggest prize in politics, relatively few Americans cared passionately about the outcome: it felt something like watching a Super Bowl in which your own team isn't playing.[1] Unlike the contests in 1800 or 1876, it didn't have the makings of a public crisis. "There will be no mobs gathering to shout 'Gore or blood' or 'Bush or blood,'" Adam Clymer wrote. "Nobody cares that much." Where 82 percent of eligible Americans voted in 1876, in 2000 only 51 percent of us even made it to the polls.[2] For a while, in any case, Americans were talking politics over lunch counters and around watercoolers, feeling (whatever the statistical realities) like citizens whose votes mattered and even learning a little about the intricacies of our electoral institutions. Then, very quickly, the election turned into politics by other means. The lawyers took over, along with a language of "evasions and platitudes."[3] Neither side, for example, admitted that the desire to win had any effect on their devotion to high principle. Bush's advocates were a little more offensive in their self-righteousness than Gore's, but not much, and Bush's "presidential" sententiousness was matched by Al Gore's claim that he felt no anxiety or anger. The rhetoric of the Florida contest was off-putting, not only because it lacked candor—Americans, after all, are used to that—but because it lacked *art,* something that, over the Clinton years, we have come to expect. Politics and public life looked to be only so much graceless fakery, and the postelection moment of civic interest dissolved into impatience if not disgust.

The spins and maneuvers, the recounts ordered and aborted were bound to result in a tainted victory and a presidency of suspect legitimacy.[4] Republican campaigners in Florida went to such extremes in their desire to win that they succeeded in uniting Democrats, otherwise tepid, behind Gore's challenge. But both parties, looking ahead, had reason for ambivalence about winning, especially with an economic downturn rumbling in the wings.[5]

Bush, trying to win broader confidence, will have to rely on his much-proclaimed talent as "a uniter, not a divider," governing by conciliation and compromise.[6] In Washington, however, things may be more difficult than they were in Austin: Clinton, after all, aspired to be a "great national unifier," and at the start of his second term, two-thirds of Americans foresaw harmony and cooperation between the branches of government.[7] In any case, one of the casualties of the campaign was Bush's early-expressed hope for a stronger, less encumbered presidency.[8]

All our institutions were hurt, and they had already been severely wounded: postimpeachment in 1999, the Center on Policy Attitudes reported that only 19 percent of Americans trusted government to do what is right "always" or "most of the time."[9]

The electoral college was bound to be a target, since — for the first time since 1888 — it ended by choosing a candidate who had received fewer popular votes than his opponent, giving new force to the chronic impulse for abolition or reform.[10] Yet paradoxically, the college (in practice, probably invulnerable to serious change) came through fairly well. The other virtues of the electoral college aside—it promotes attention to smaller and less metropolitan states, and the custom of awarding all a state's electors to the candidate who "carries" it adds to the power of minorities—this election made clear that a *national* recount would be a nightmare.[11]

By contrast, the Supreme Court shook the pillars of its own temple. Twice, by predictable 5–4 votes, a majority devoted to federalism in principle overruled a state's highest court on the interpretation of state electoral law.[12] Terrance Sandalow, a conservative legal scholar, called the Court's stay of the Florida recount "unmistakably partisan" and "incomprehensible."[13] And one need not take Justice Stevens's side to agree with his judgment that the real loser before the Court was "the nation's confidence in the judge as an impartial guardian of the rule of law."[14]

It wasn't just governmental institutions that suffered. The election was a disaster for the media, notably in its bumbling over-eagerness to "call" Florida on election night. By early December, the Gallup Poll found record levels of distrust, with 65 percent of Americans saying that news organizations can't be trusted to "get the facts straight."[15]

So in the end, American citizens, taken as a whole, seem to have settled even further back into the relatively comfortable corners of private life, distrustful of politics and public life, but hopeful about future well-being.[16]

In popular culture, however, there were signs of deeper worries, apocalyptic shadows on the new millennium, a sense that technology may be out of control and that economic and social change is "speeding semi-blindly" into areas that will change "what it means to be human."[17] On stage and screen, Americans had recently been fascinated by the story of the *Titanic,* riven by inequality, its technological marvels entrusted to imperfect humans, safety sacrificed to speed and profit, rushing to meet its nemesis. In that old tragedy, contemporary audiences were almost certainly seeing the mirror of their fears. Even Bill Joy, a titan of the "Information Age," was moved to write that "there is a limit to our material needs, and . . . certain knowledge is too dangerous and is best foregone," arguing that we are rapidly approaching "the last chance to assert control" of a technology that threatens to make humanity superfluous.[18]

These changes, of course, still resemble a slide more than an apocalypse: part of the genius of American institutions, Edward Tanner notes, is the ability to "convert catastrophic problems into chronic ones," an argument that is accurate but imperfectly consoling.[19] The voters' anxiety about the moral direction of the country was more than "Clinton fatigue," though that was real enough. It also reflected a desire to move beyond the old conflicts and played-out debates, the hope of finding some way "to do more than just hang on."[20] The real, if largely silent, argument in the election of 2000 was not the quarrel between the candidates and the parties, but the possibility of self-government.[21] And with the winners finally decided, the answer to that larger question remains uncertain.

ARGUING AT THE MARGINS, RACING TO THE CENTER

The campaign certainly didn't set off any skyrockets.

Neither candidate aroused much enthusiasm, let alone suggested greatness, nor was either the object of much antipathy.[22] Slightly more voters professed to be scared by the prospect of a Bush victory (26 percent, as opposed to 23 percent who feared a Gore presidency), but here any numerical edge was more than balanced by the ferocious Republican desire to be rid of Clinton and all his works.[23] The electorate's reaction to the candidates was typified by a television commercial for the candy bar "Snickers," which featured animated figures representing the Republican elephant and the Democratic donkey, each caricaturing the foibles of their parties' respective candidates ("My dad and I wear the same pants," the elephant declares, to which the donkey responds, "I invented pants.") Advertising research, in other words, established that it was safe to treat both candidates as jokes. The true popular choice on 7 November, Frank Rich wrote, was "None of the above."[24] The only president the country really wanted was Josiah Bartlet, the incumbent on *West Wing*.[25]

Al Gore, of course, was already a familiar figure, undeniably brainy and knowledgeable about policy, but too visibly eager for office, alternately wooden or overly aggressive in his public appearances and famously inclined to exaggeration. Despite his reputation as a debater, soon to be shaken in his encounters with Bush, his speaking style was a caricature of rhetoric: scripted, stagy, and humorless, vacillating between a patronizing moralism — Steven Pinker called it "motherese" — and stupefying attention to technical detail.[26] "Inspirational?" David Broder asked, responding to Gore's acceptance speech, "No. Informational, yes. If you want a wonk, Al Gore is best."[27] And where Clinton was convincing even in his untruths, Al Gore's sentiments sounded false even when they were genuine.

Still, despite his shortcomings, the economy should have won it for Gore and his party. Unemployment and inflation were both low, wages had been rising faster than inflation since 1996, and most Americans were enjoying at least a modest well-being. And in early September, Gore led in the polls, just about where economic models predicted he should be.[28] But Gore, aware of the strength of Clinton fatigue, and hoping to lessen his association with the seamier side of the administration, largely "airbrushed" both the president and the immediate past in favor of an emphasis on "the future."[29] Retrospection — remembered experience — offered Gore the advantage of comparing present prosperity to the economic troubles of the last Bush family presidency, as in the celebrated question, "Are you better off now than you were eight years ago?" Neglecting memory instead encouraged voters to take good times as something close to given, an equal starting point for both candidates.[30] In addition, it permitted voters to devote their attention to other issues, like foreign policy or the moral direction of the country, where Bush's position was stronger. Sometimes, putting distance between himself and Clinton helped Gore, as choosing Senator Lieberman for a running-mate probably did.[31] But it also made him look disloyal, somewhat weakening the moral credentials Gore hoped to strengthen. And it denied him full use of the president's undeniable skills as a campaigner.

It was also futile. Gore was inseparably linked to Clinton in the minds of the voters and in his own. His effort to "reinvent" himself required the pretense that this artifact, the "new" Al Gore, was real (in its several variations), and Gore was not a good enough actor to carry it off. He lacked the character either to be candid or grandly false, and in the end, too many voters found themselves suffering from a measure of nostalgia for Clinton and a larger dose of "Gore fatigue."[32]

In a sense, Gore was fortunate in his opponent. Almost from the beginning, most voters saw George W. Bush as amiable, though smirky, reportedly no worka-holic and indifferently informed about national politics. His speeches were often incoherent, given to elision and reflecting something close to innumeracy, ele-vated only by sonorous but very abstract appeals to values and to faith. In George Will's devastating assessment, Bush was surrounded by an "atmosphere of ado-lescence, a lack of gravitas — a carelessness, even a recklessness, perhaps born of having gone a bit too easily so far."[33]

Yet most of the public also saw positive qualities of character in Bush. They forgave the "irresponsibilities" of his younger years, and even admired him for surmounting them, and they credited him with trustworthiness — a perception at least somewhat damaged by the late-campaign revelation that Bush had concealed a drunk-driving conviction from the 1970s.[34] More substantively, voters on the right saw in Bush a cultural anti-Clinton, a man who had passed through the '60s without rebellion, and an appropriate leader for their crusade against the legacy of that decade.[35] But few if any Americans saw in Bush even the slightest promise of great statecraft.

His strongest claim to leadership, in fact, was the promise to "bring people together," a candid pragmatism and an eagerness to please that seemed part of his character (rather than, as in Gore's case, a pose driven by ambition). Significantly, in this soft ingratiation, Bush was stylistically closer than Gore to Bill Clinton.

In fact, Bush or his handlers implicitly recognized — perhaps better than Gore — the force of Bill Clinton's legacy. Bush ran against Clinton and his era, of course, but when he attacked the "if it feels good, do it" ethics of "the last *few decades*" (my emphasis), he also put distance between himself and negative mem-ories of the years when Reagan and his own father occupied the White House. And if George W. Bush promised to make government smaller, he also pledged to "get it done," to make government effective, active within bounds, pursuing "great goals" and rejecting the "destructive" idea of a government with "no no-bler purpose than to leave us alone" — a Republican Clinton uniting rectitude with results.[36] With Bush, however, such poetic moments quickly turned back to prose.

Just as the candidates did not scintillate, the campaign was not defined by any great debate or grand vision. The parties seemed "brain dead," in Theodore Lowi's phrase: both walked a political tightrope, trying to conciliate warring factions while addressing a fragmenting public, playing it safe, offering only variations on old ideas, arguing at the margins and racing to the center, hop-ing to appeal to a fairly narrow spectrum of moderate voters.[37] The result, inevitably, was what Robert Kuttner called a "stunted" debate in which many crucial issues — and virtually all deeper ones — went ignored.[38]

Republicans found their internal conflicts softened by the desire for power and, especially, for revenge. After 1994 the party had been frustrated and out-generaled; the setback in the election of 1998 was bad enough, but impeachment was a humiliation.[39] Conservatives, anguished and prodded to recognize their own political marginality, were more willing to swallow affronts in the interest of victory, and GOP leaders — whether they inclined toward Main Street or Wall Street, social conservatism or libertarianism — felt a need to reshape the Republican image.[40]

They were drawn, consequently, to the depiction of George W. Bush as a candidate who could attract Hispanics, suburbanites, and Independents without alienating conservatives (largely, as it turned out, by a reliance on code words aimed to persuade the right that Bush's departures were matters of *style* more than substance.)[41] Bush, in Karl Rove's vision, would be "the McKinley of the new century," building a new, right-center majority.[42]

The great majority of Republican leaders embraced Bush's candidacy, and — in the interest of avoiding a prolonged battle for the nomination — helped him raise a war chest so full as to drive many potential rivals out of the race. In the end, the plan succeeded, although John McCain raised a brief scare. In so many ways a more attractive candidate than Bush — articulate, a war hero, with a serious cause in campaign finance reform — McCain's candidacy was an artifact of open primaries, attracting support from Independents, Perot voters, even disaffected Democrats. Bush never lost his significant lead among Republicans, and most important, in order to turn back McCain, he ran as the candidate of the religious right, an identification rightists never forgot, even when it faded from the headlines and from many memories.[43]

That bond gave Bush more room to pursue his "compassionate conservatism," the endorsement of modest governmental activism and a certain moderation on social issues. Adam Nagourney called it "confusion by design," a doctrine intended more to blur old lines than to redraw them.[44] "Inclusiveness," the grand theme of the Republican Convention, was evidently largely cosmetic, and it signally failed to move African-American voters. But in the most fundamental sense, the appeal to inclusion was aimed not at minority voters, but at moderate whites, in the effort to relieve the GOP of the stigma of exclusion, a political taboo in an America where "tolerance" has become a reigning tenet of civil religion.[45] (In the same way, Bush's position on abortion was calibrated to be relaxed just enough to attract Independents — increasingly reticent about abortion, but still committed to some "choice" — without offending conservatives.)[46]

Similarly, Bush sought to put distance between himself and the rule-or-ruin extremism of congressional Republicans, faulting his fellow partisans, among other things, for being overly concerned with the interests of the wealthy. (Characteristically, he quickly — but in a softer voice — backed away from this position when he came under attack from conservatives.)[47] In fact, he sought to associate Gore and the administration *with* Congress as part of an undifferentiated set of failures in Washington: "They've had eight years, and they couldn't get it done." And Al Gore's reluctance to address the past let this go relatively uncontroverted, offering Bush aid and comfort in his effort to redecorate the Republicans' shrine of party.

The Democrats' house had its own disarray, less visible than the Republicans', but at least as serious, with "Old" Democrats ranged against "New," organized labor opposing the Democratic Leadership Council, about the policies and future direction appropriate for the party.

Clinton and his New Democratic allies — including Al Gore — had furnished plenty of proof that they cared about the well-being of working and middle-class America. Clinton and his administration did in fact "feel your pain," so that, without too much strain, his policy could be called "compassionate liberalism." Neither Clinton nor Gore, however, showed any particular concern about inequality, especially given their zeal for the new economy and its new fortunes. Everett Carll Ladd, writing in *The New Democrat,* called traditional egalitarianism "the politics of envy," while Richard Reeves, for the other side, observed that New Democrats sound like "the folks we used to call 'liberal Republicans.' "[48] Moreover, for all of Clinton's skill as a campaigner, his style of governing turned on bureaucratic expertise: at times, the president seemed purblind to the claims of self-government.[49]

The Democrats' internal division was sharp enough that, in 1998, before the Lewinsky affair erupted into impeachment, Clinton was actively courting labor activists and pursuing a fairly high-level search for partisan common ground.[50] The impeachment crisis itself — particularly the loathsome quality of Clinton's enemies — worked to unify the party behind the president.[51] But plenty of observers thought that in 2000, the party would face bitter and divisive conflict. After all, this was the unstated premise of Karl Rove's Republican strategy: the new Republican coalition in 1896 was not made possible by any positive qualities of McKinley's, but by the Democratic schism resulting from the nomination of William Jennings Bryan, and Everett Carll Ladd saw enough similarity to counsel Democrats against going that way again.[52]

The crisis never materialized. Like Bush, Gore was able to deter most challengers by a combination of money and endorsements (and by Richard Gephardt's decision to try for the Speakership instead). His only serious opponent, Bill Bradley, had some advantages: thoughtful and free of any associations with the administration, as a former athlete he was something of a "guy candidate," which Gore decidedly was not. But Bradley was a speaker even more tedious than Gore, and he had little taste for political combat. Most important, his views were not that much different from Gore's. Bradley's political hopes depended on attracting the Democratic left, but he himself was a moderate liberal, like Gore devoted to free trade and globalization. "When did he become more liberal?" Mario Cuomo asked. "As a candidate." Bradley created a stir for a while, and his championship of a "new politics" — support for campaign finance reform and disdain for political fakery — won him considerable support among younger Democrats. He lacked, however, any galvanizing issue, and Gore fairly easily brushed him aside.[53]

Discontent among Old Democrats was not so easy to disperse. By the time of the conventions, it was clear that Democrats lagged behind Republicans in enthusiasm for their candidate, and many were voicing sympathy for Ralph Nader's protest. Gore's adoption of the cause of "working families," calculated to shore up his base of support, partly followed the argument of Ruy Teixeira and Joel Rogers, who pointed to the working class as America's "forgotten majority."[54] That theme, decisive in Gore's most effective period, contributed to his postconvention surge in the polls.

At bottom, however, Gore's advocacy had only limited credibility. He wasn't talking "class war," George W. Bush to the contrary; he was, as Frank Rich observed, a New Democrat attacking "a few focus-group chosen industries."[55] Certainly, the political necessity that required Gore to pursue a deluge of money from corporations and large donors undercut his claim to be an opponent of "special interests." And in fact, Gore soon retreated to the center: "working families" became "middle-class families" in his speeches, just as social programs tended to give ground to fiscal responsibility.[56]

In general, Gore appeared to be overly aware of the conflicts within the coalition he hoped to assemble. Hypercautious, he regularly shielded himself by retreating to carefully qualified technicalities, rarely venturing beyond the assurances of the latest poll. And since Gore was evidently competent and aggressive, it *showed,* especially in the debates; Bush's muddlings seemed more genuine, and probably were.

Yet despite the half-truths and half-measures, voters professed to care about the issues, and they had little trouble discerning a difference between the parties.[57] (It wasn't a good year for third parties: Nader drew enough votes to defeat Gore, but not many, and Pat Buchanan's candidacy virtually destroyed the Reform Party.) Most had at least some sense that Bush would take greater chances with Social Security, and that his tax plan offered something for everyone but more for the rich. It wasn't hard to see differences on the environment or gun control; not many doubted which candidate had more sympathy for abortion rights, and so on.

But, as Peter Applebome wrote, the specific issues seem to have mattered less than "a cultural divide in American life."[58] Both parties attempted to reach beyond their traditional bases, and both pretty much failed. Identification with political parties and local party organizations are weaker, but party *voting* is remarkably consistent, paralleling the elections of the 1880s, the heyday of the party state.[59] Bush made some gains among Catholics — who were split down the middle — and among Hispanics, but his voters were almost monochromatic, drawn overwhelmingly from white men and married white women.[60] Gore's support came from minorities — African Americans, Jews, about two-thirds of

Hispanics, and a majority of Asians (who had voted for Bush Sr. in 1992 and, more narrowly, for Dole in 1996) — from union members and from unmarried women. The electoral map suggested something close to two nations: Republicans all but everywhere victorious in the South and the Prairie and Mountain West, Democrats in the great cities, the Northeast and the West Coast, the party of metropolitan and industrial America, with a few islands of strength like the southern Black Belt or Hispanic New Mexico.[61] (Anyone over-impressed with the niceties of campaign tactics should notice that Canadian election returns produced an electoral map — periphery vs. metropole — strikingly parallel to that in the United States.)[62]

Where the candidates and the parties only supplied an election narrative that was muddled or encrypted, voters broke the codes or supplied their own. The great majority seemed to recognize that Bush's mantra, "I trust the people," signaled a broad distrust of government, a disposition — not radical but incremental — to scale back government wherever possible, at least most of the time.[63] Bush spoke, consequently, to and for Americans — especially those socially distant from the centers of power — who, whether from confidence or a sense of vulnerability, want little from government except to be left alone.[64]

In Gore's "I'll fight for you," voters heard the voice of Democrats as the defenders of "the little guy," willing to *use* government to check and limit corporate and private power: almost every poll registered a Democratic advantage as protectors of the interests of "people like you." But despite the media, Gore was no Populist: he portrayed himself, not as *one* of us, but as our *champion.* Unlike Bryan — and unlike Clinton, a wonk with the common touch — Gore could never be called a "Great Commoner." He offered himself as a leader in the Progressive mold, an expert, able to battle for us in the corridors of power, like Fox Mulder of *The X-Files,* but without that character's vulnerable charm. And Gore's message was tailored to those areas and constituencies where antigovernment sentiment is not strong enough to override the need for public authority or the hope of turning it to one's cause. As one Gore supporter in Oregon put it, "What can one person do? That's why we turn to government, and that's why we want someone who shares our values."[65]

There were, in other words, great issues behind the petty contest. In every republic, Machiavelli discerned two "humors," that of the great or princely, who desire to command, and that of the people, who — exposed and fearful — have no wish to rule, but hope only to be left alone.[66] Gore, in his maladroit way, clearly typified the first; Bush appealed to, and to some extent reflected, the second. But many of Gore's supporters (and more Americans, for that matter) do not fit Machiavelli's categories easily: they hint at, and sometimes voice, a desire for self-government, an itch for citizenship that indicates, as Aristotle taught, the political animal in our souls.[67] In this election, however, that yearning was heard only in rumbles offstage.

OPERATING ON THE EDGE

Americans had reason to be uneasy, despite the good times. For one thing, prosperity is terribly uneven. Inequality, already at startling levels, is still rising; in 1999 Bill Gates's net worth was greater than that of the lowest 45 percent of his countrymen, and in objective terms, the Clinton years were "far less egalitarian than the... Reagan 'era of greed.' "[68] The poor are better off, in some respects, but "the middle class of political exhortation and national myth" is being squeezed: incomes are not high — in 1997 John Schwartz found 16 million more households than adequately paying jobs — with the tendency toward a "two-tier society" evident in advertising strategies, as well as the job market and the gulf created by the "digital divide."[69]

It doesn't help that, with communities and neighborhoods also less stable and more anonymous, people are more apt to measure their standing and their aspirations in the primarily upper-income scale of the media. As Louis Uchitelle writes, "being solidly middle class is no longer good enough."[70] Americans are chronically apt to overspend and to borrow, an impulse that fuels the economy but leaves households out in the wind of change, scratching to hang on.[71]

It was also hard not to notice that the American — and the global — economy, intricate and operating at high speed, was multiply vulnerable to disruption. Many of the details of this exposure, like our dependence on the willingness of foreign investors to fund the trade deficit, went undetected on the public's radar screen.[72] But there was a broad suspicion that the stock market was overexuberant — "pure bubble," Robert Kuttner said — and a sense that the American economy, like so many Americans, might be operating on the edge.[73]

Even those who are doing well, moreover, are likely to feel their position is precarious. Talk of a "new economy" that operates in radically new ways, the spectacle of new fortunes made as if by magic: these can be exciting, but they are certainly not reassuring. The economy is littered with unknowns and unfamiliarities, as in the old prophecy of Marx and Engels, "All that is solid melts into air...."[74] The new vocabulary of the workplace is marked by terms — *downsizing, outsourcing, free agency* — that point to a new insecurity that reaches a good way up the class ladder.[75] The workplace is less reliable and more competitive, "leaner, but definitely meaner," in Kirstin Downey Grimsley's phrase, and it's hard not to suspect that in resenting political "bickering," voters are also thinking of incivilities closer to home.[76]

Almost of necessity, economic anxieties prompt a greater devotion to self-interest, just as greater social distance — inherent in a larger scale, less egalitarian, more specialized way of life — reduces the strength of any impulse to help others. Our sense of commonality, already thin, threatens to become anorexic: even Alan Greenspan saw the tendency toward a divided, two-tier society as a potential opening for demagogues and a "major threat to our security." A rising percentage of Americans — 45 percent as against 25 percent during the Great Depression —

see a fundamental conflict of interest between employers and employees, but this perception lacks a sense of class outrage: with surprising frequency, employers are regarded as doing no more than obeying an imperial economic necessity.[77]

Everyone, in that understanding, is caught up in the dynamics of globalization in which international markets — radically more pervasive and powerful — increasingly call the tune. But they do not call the same tune for all players: capital finds it easier to move, to adapt its organization and to suit itself to the new environment; labor is relatively immobile, its organization more tied to the nation-state, its power constrained by the threat of low-wage competition, from immigrants or overseas, an immediate or prospective "race to the bottom." The practical rule of globalization, G.M. Tamás writes, is "Deregulation for capital, stringent regulation for labor."[78]

Notably, those responsible for enforcing antitrust laws have approved a good many "mega-mergers" in terms of the necessities of competition in international markets. But their discussions appear to focus narrowly on the effect of such mergers on price competition: they ignore or slight the ways in which these combinations add to the inequality of political power, not merely by permitting larger contributions, but in the capacity to evade or minimize regulation.[79] And in the same way, pursuing profits and low-cost goods, policymakers have been willing to ignore the authoritarian excesses of a "trading partner" like China.[80] Democratic considerations, in other words, more often seem to be subordinated to the hope of economic gain, marking a tilt toward oligarchy in American politics.

Globalization is increasingly presented in public discourse as a set of inevitabilities. Government, by contrast, is treated as ancillary, increasingly irrelevant, able only to help its people adapt to the new order of things. In some ways, the language and practice of this Second Global Economy is similar to the first, the great era of international markets that was brought to an end by World War I.[81] Yet despite these likenesses, the organizational interconnections of contemporary globalization are much more pervasive; corporations are far less national; international communication is easier and involves multitudes.

Yet if the political foundations of the Second Global Economy are stronger than those of the first, they may not be strong enough. The new order is "tolerated but not loved," and resentment shadows appreciation.[82] The triumphal days of market ideology have passed: there have been enough crises and near-disasters to create a fairly strong mood that the "excesses of global capitalism" need to be curbed. But even international regulation in the interest of "humane social values" would not satisfy the widely heard complaint that international bureaucracies are at best distantly paternal and always beyond the reach of ordinary citizens.[83]

The demonstrations in Seattle during the WTO meetings in December 1999 were a straw in the wind. The protesters were a complicated, even contradictory coalition: many (most visibly, the anarchists, ironically the best organized contingent) were eager for the elimination of the WTO and international bureaucracy generally; others (notably organized labor and environmental groups) arguing for stronger, more political international bodies capable of enforcing rules on recalcitrants like China. In one way or another, however, they were united in defending the claims of democratic self-government.[84]

Beyond disrupting the WTO meetings, nothing much came of the protests. Adroit as always, President Clinton switched front, making himself the spokesman for the "new voices" demanding to be heard, identifying far enough to tell the delegates that "We won't be silent any more."[85] It defused what could have been a difficult situation for Al Gore and, in the end, it may even have helped the president get approval for normalizing trade with China. Still, having shattered the serenity of latte-land, the demonstrations were a portent, and Alan Greenspan was right to warn of the possibility of a more serious backlash, should the economy falter.[86]

There were other stirrings, less theatrical but possibly more important. Organized labor showed some signs of reversing its long decline, demonstrating muscle in politics (where unions continued their turn away from the media in favor of "infantry politics," personal contact with the rank and file) but also in collective bargaining. Unions had some striking success among professionals: engineers at Boeing won a strike, and by 1999 the number of unionized dentists and physicians had grown to something like 40,000, almost twice what it was in 1997. (The American Medical Association even voted to help salaried doctors unionize.)[87] A majority of younger workers, moreover, say they favor union membership. New economy ideologues celebrate the "free agent," the worker who, hired for projects, is liberated from ongoing commitments and traditional workplaces, but experience may be teaching Americans that, to the contrary, free agents are mostly more exploited than glamorous; the rule, as Max Frankel observes, is that in modern society, a worker without collective or organized force is "an underprivileged citizen."[88]

The search for a greater measure of control over the condition and direction of their lives prods Americans toward public life, albeit in a way that is subtle, disorganized, half-willing and half-articulate, imperceptible to most campaign polls. Robert Reich expressed the hope that the election would eventually provide an opening for ideas "about something truly important," giving that impulse words and form, although he knew the odds were all the other way.[89]

That's about the way it went. Pat Buchanan talked protectionism and Ralph Nader went his own quixotic way, but the major candidates stuck close to the orthodoxies of economic globalization. In fact, Bush and Gore addressed none of the issues specifically relevant to the new economy, avoiding it, David Sanger said, "like a bad neighborhood."[90]

Globalization, however, did sidle into the election through the discussion of foreign policy. At peace, facing no serious challenge to its hegemony, America also felt no moral calling, no great crusade drawing it into international affairs. Foreign policy, when not simply a matter of interest, was a reminder of the ways in which the interdependences of global society impinge on and, especially in the case of terrorism, threaten domestic life, a story of "meaningless disorder" that offers only a disincentive to involvement.[91]

Al Gore tried to offer an alternative account, stressing — as he did in the second presidential debate — that the United States is committed to American "values," to democracy and human rights, as well as to its interests in a narrower sense.[92] Pragmatic considerations, however, undercut the moral basis of Gore's thesis: the United States embraced China, with a bad human rights record that was growing worse, but maintained an embargo against Cuba, a regime hardly more objectionable.

Encouraged by media coverage, American imagery of foreign involvement framed a parade of terrorist attacks, petty wars, and ethnic genocides, where an ambivalent success like the Gulf War is balanced by memories of failed missions and lost lives. The Vietnam Syndrome endures in an indisposition to intervene that rises above the old distinctions of right and left: Bush, the sometime Air National Guardsman, and Cheney, with his personal "priorities," spoke for and to generations that take minimizing one's commitments as normal, if not admirable.

In Kosovo, by June 1999 President Clinton's air war had forced a Yugoslav withdrawal without the use of ground troops and without American casualties. But throughout that campaign, the president's support and standing fell, as Americans worried about combat losses that might occur and inclined to favor negotiations. Sensing political blood, House Republicans voted a ban on the use of ground troops and even defeated a resolution supporting air strikes. In May, Trent Lott could be found saying "Give peace a chance," standing on the same side of the question as an old antiwar radical like Tom Hayden. (Another old SDSer, Todd Gitlin, supported the president, finding himself aligned with the conservative editor Bill Kristol.)[93]

When the president's strategy ultimately succeeded, one might have expected his critics to suffer politically. But the victory was flawed: it led to the commitment of American troops to Kosovo (in addition to those already in Bosnia), and the Albanians, whose cause we had taken up, proved to be as savage and oppressive as their Serbian enemies. It left Americans suspecting a quagmire.[94] When, in October 2000, Yugoslavia's President Milosevic eventually decided to yield power, accepting the result of his country's election, any benefit to the administration and to Al Gore was balanced by the terrorist attack, less than a week later, on the USS *Cole*, and by the renewed fighting between Palestinians and Israelis.

Bush, on the whole, was the beneficiary of these continuing crises. He was, of course, no great shakes at the details of foreign policy or the names of foreign leaders. In the debate about international politics, however, Bush managed to capture most of the middle ground. Always more or less an internationalist—he endorsed American intervention in Kosovo, for example—his campaign emphasized scaling back American military involvements, eschewing "nation building" and always providing an "exit strategy." (In the same way, although nominally committed to nuclear nonproliferation, he opposed the proposed test ban treaty as "flawed," failing to provide America with adequate securities.)[95] And he recognized that, given public worries about vulnerability, an emphasis on strengthening and remoralizing the military—even the Strategic Defense Initiative—would resonate with much of the public and would not greatly offend any but his most implacable opponents.

But characteristically, Bush seemed to be seeking to provide Americans with an element of immunity to globalization by limiting government's activities, while leaving economic and social dynamics more or less unchecked. There is little prospect, in that sort of leadership, of greater real scope for self-government.[96]

DRIFTING APART, REACHING FOR REFORM

Bush relied heavily on civil society — families, churches, localities and associations — to provide the bases of moral and public life. So did Gore, in softer accents. Neither, however, did much to acknowledge its developing disorder. Talk about civil society, E.J. Dionne observed, tends to be a "cheap grace" that lets liberals express support for family and neighborhood and conservatives parade compassion without having to confront, let alone pay, the price of their devotion.[97] Technology and the market, after all, relentlessly are breaking down barriers and boundaries, shaking or shattering communities and relationships, making old forms and institutions seem outdated and draining them of their authority.[98] A 1998 Isuzu commercial shows a world filled with obstacles in which a formally dressed older man pursues but fails to catch a speeding Rodeo, finally falling on his face; the voice-over then offers explicit advice about rules and authorities: "Ignore them."

Married couples with children, 45 percent of all households in 1972, had fallen to 26 percent by the late '90s; more children were living with single parents; more families took new and often complex forms.[99] Local communities, less able to be repressive, were also more likely to be shallow, transient, and virtually interchangeable, encouraging a perception of people as interchangeable, too. And face-to-face associations, which give their members voices and make claims on their senses, are declining in favor of "tertiary" groups whose members never meet or speak, linked only by the private and relatively passive donation of money. "Volunteerism," much trumpeted as a mark of community involvement, does show decent sentiments, but is also unreliable, episodic (and often one-shot), and moved by private, self-oriented impulse and convenience.[100]

With institutions — and official creeds — increasingly "decertified," more and more Americans are turning, from choice or necessity, to an inner basis for morality and obligation, deciding "which God bests suits their temperament, which family structure works for them, and whether the country's government is worthy of trust."[101]

Americans, in fact, mostly adhere to fairly traditional values, and they think that, morally, the country may be on the "wrong track." Significant majorities say things were better when people didn't move around so much, or that true love has become harder to find; they believe crime to be increasing, statistics to the contrary.[102] But they also are inclined to think that "imposing" your beliefs on others is wrong; some 70 percent, the *Washington Post* reported, agreed that we should be "more tolerant of people who choose to live according to their own standards, even if we think they are wrong."[103] Beliefs, in this view, are personal choices, not much more than preferences — so many "particularities," James Davison Hunter writes, joined by a "thin fabric of therapeutic, consumer oriented individualism."[104]

Of course, that culture of deauthorization and tolerance is most advanced among elites and in the metropolitan centers, a difference visible in the election returns. Yet everywhere, Americans are appealing to the language of faith or psychology, to inner morality or goodness as opposed to righteous or civic conduct.[105]

Despite expressions of alarm, there is nothing new in the political invocation of religion, so much in evidence in the election of 2000: Bryan likened the gold standard to the Crucifixion, Teddy Roosevelt saw Armageddon in the election of 1912, and in 1936, Franklin Roosevelt saw in "Divine justice" an endorsement for the New Deal. These earlier invocations, however, tried to enlist religion in support of policies or programs. *Faith,* by contrast, was kept largely off the public stage.

In 2000, on the other hand, candidates paraded personal faith. Al Gore referred to himself as a born-again Christian, and belief was often a theme of Joe Lieberman's speeches, but George W. Bush's appeals were almost his stock in trade.[106] And notably, when asked to elaborate what it meant to say that Jesus was his "favorite political philosopher," Bush could only answer that it was "hard to explain" to nonbelievers. He did, however, indicate that he was able to stop drinking when Jesus "touched my heart." Religion, in these terms, may affect personal conduct, but it is fundamentally inward and ineffable, a way of being rather than a way of acting. (In this respect, George W. Bush differed from his father, who made conservative Christians uneasy by insisting that right conduct was more decisive than the particularities of faith.)[107]

The religious right's willingness to adopt Bush as a candidate despite his leanings toward the moral center was partly a pragmatic adjustment. Having learned the hard lesson of its marginality during the Clinton years, the right was prepared to trust Bush's personal journey of faith and the fact that he could "talk the talk."[108]

This, however, is also part of a broader pattern, one that affects American life in general. As public life grows more pluralistic, its unities thinner, moral commitment becomes more personal and particular. At the beginning of the late century, John Dewey and James Tufts described a movement "from code to conscience," a dynamic soon to be expanded into the dogma of a separation of facts from values.[109] And today, on the intellectual left, the prevailing school sees values as only so many private perspectives, set against a public world reduced to a competition for power.[110]

As the public sphere expands, Tocqueville argued, the circle of private life contracts, to small coteries if not, ultimately, to the prison of the self.[111] Just so: the language of public life is increasingly confined to the idiom of interest. The contemporary culture of tolerance — like George W. Bush's compassion — has no desire to harm others and may even wish them well, but it feels no great imperative to help them, either. We live, as Todd Gitlin contends, in a "twilight of common dreams," with every need to rebuild the linkages between private and public life.[112]

Evidently, the fragmentation of civil society makes the electronic media more important to that task, but the media themselves are a major part of the problem.

Certainly, television builds no adequate bridges between citizens and public life. Lacking any organic relation to its audience, facing growing competition from other channels and the Internet, television news is desperately anxious to hold an audience, fearful of seeming partisan or giving offense, as in Jim Lehrer's notoriously harmless moderation of the presidential debates.[113] (The networks have reason for their worries: the Pew Research Council reports that 75 percent of viewers under thirty, and 54 percent of those over fifty, watch the news with remote in hand.)[114]

Moreover, television speaks to us, for the most part, in private settings where private values tend to prevail. During the Lewinsky scandal, the public consistently told pollsters that it wanted less coverage, judging — in a civic-minded way — that it hurt our institutions. The networks knew, however, that as private individuals, Americans would find it hard to resist the salacious details. They played the story to our least civic selves, with the result that most of us had expected.

In fact, fearing that it will be boring, networks have been inclined to shrink their coverage of politics, and they are certainly less inclined to let candidates speak for themselves. That, in turn, forces campaigns to rely more heavily on commercials, contributing to the escalating demand for money as the precondition of effective politics.[115] (To be fair, the media are not the whole story: given the decline of party organizations, even an effective use of face-to-face campaigning, like Jon Corzine's in New Jersey, is likely to require considerable sums.)

The centrality of money is the most visible sign of the oligarchic tendency in our politics, narrowing as it must the field of entrants and influence, perhaps most problematic because it deepens the distrust of government among ordinary citizens. George W. Bush, so signal a beneficiary of the current system of campaign finance, has no reason to want it changed. In fact, Bush vetoed a proposal from the Republican National Committee that sought to limit the defining power of money in nominations, and to keep the contest open, by moving the big state primaries to the end of the season.[116]

But while Gore also gained by overawing potential rivals financially, Democrats do have reason to think seriously about campaign reform. With less natural connection to great wealth, Democrats can't afford to be too choosy about donors and they are tempted to cut corners (as in Gore's appearance in a Buddhist temple in 1996, or the question of fund-raising from White House telephones). This year, just when Democrats — aided by the Lieberman nomination — were having some success as moral critics of the media, Gore and his running-mate felt it necessary to reassure their Hollywood donors, attending a fund-raiser featuring luminaries from the sex-and-violence crowd.[117] With an interest in shedding the mantle of sleaziness, Democrats have reason to look favorably on changing the rules of the game. But the Democrats, of course, are out of power.

In any case, the obstacles to reform are formidable, beginning with the Supreme Court's 1976 decision that donating money is speech and entitled to constitutional protection. Every effort at reform since 1996, moreover, has been blocked by the inability to end debate in the Senate. And public pressure is limited by the widespread belief, despairing but shrewd, that reform legislation will not make that much difference, given the protean power of money. Nevertheless, more and more Americans are convinced that the United States, as Warren Buffett says, is "on the way" to "a government of the moneyed, by the moneyed and for the moneyed."[118] And both the government and the citizenry have every reason to find that conclusion unacceptable.

Many observers — including some very shrewd ones — hope that a new civil society will be created by the Internet and other new media.[119] So far, however, the evidence in support of these hopes is pretty limited. The new technologies tend to drown us in information, putting a premium on the ability to relate to that information — and the relationships that go with it — quickly and superficially. The great scarcity in human life, after all, is not information, but time. And of course, the new media offer only very limited appeal to the body, the senses and the erotic dimension of our souls. It is not surprising, then, that two studies find among frequent Internet users only a "lonelier crowd," and Norman Nie discerns a new wave of social isolation.[120]

The new media do allow for political communication that is quicker and cheaper, but making use of that information presumes interest in politics; the media themselves do not create it. So far, the connection between mainstream politics and the Internet is very limited.[121] The Internet does make it easier for marginal groups to find one another, but while that sometimes affords encouragement to our better angels, as or more often it allows some fairly monstrous people to form networks of support.

In general, as Nie suggests, the Internet privatizes or encourages privatization, but it is a means of intrusion, utterly destructive of privacy.[122] The last private citadels, long under siege by the media, are now falling, and so that genuinely private life will increasingly depend on the protection afforded by public authority.

America's civil fabric is frayed and fraying, and we need, urgently, to use the respite afforded by good times to reweave it in a way adequate to the strain of crises to come. And there is no strategy of reconstruction that does not point to democratic political life.

YEARNING FOR SELF-GOVERNMENT

Government, to contemporary Americans, is bound to seem distant and a little forbidding, one of the great forces transforming our lives. It is massive, baffling, often arcane, and, in relation to individuals, overwhelming, so that public life tends to make us feel impotent and inadequate, if not stupid.[123] Most of us recognize that this must be so — to be at all capable of dealing with the titanic forces reshaping the world, government must arm itself with their skills and powers. But that necessity does not make it less formidable, especially because, with the weakening of the parties and associations that once linked us to government, we are apt to feel only thin and formal connections to it.[124]

Failures and disappointments — lovingly exposed by the media — have made us aware that government is often blundering, and we suspect that it is often irrelevant, unable to do more than adapt to the tides of economic and technological change.[125] And, all too aware of our powerlessness, we harbor at least some fear that government may be malign: in 1999, a poll by Research/Strategy/ Management reported that only 7 percent of respondents believed the government is genuinely responsive to public opinion, seeing it as the creature of great interests.[126] Americans, Lance Bennett observes, have come to worry that government is "at worst responsible for the economic conditions that dominate their private lives, and at best, of little use for remedying them."[127]

Still, Americans know that government is more accountable than economic power or technological change. Imperfect and suspect, it is all we have in dealing with the terrors of the world — just as, in *The X-Files,* while government is half obtuse and honeycombed with conspirators, our champions are *also* government agents, who could not fight for us without the resources of the state.[128] Americans cannot afford to take government's benignity for granted, but neither can they afford to dispense with it — or even "downsize" it overmuch — at a time when private institutions are becoming more gigantic and capable of domination.[129]

In reality, active government is an everyday feature of our lives; many of the old lines of division are played out, although they enjoy a kind of posthumous existence in our politics.[130] Here and there, conservatives are acknowledging that the market is the greatest agent of relativism: "unbridled capitalism," William J. Bennett observes, "is a problem...for the whole dimension of things we call the realm of values and human relationships."[131] Here and there, on the left, there is recognition that a "politics of difference" undercuts the claims of equality.[132] And across the spectrum, people are hesitantly looking to government for help in rebuilding civil society.[133] For all of his campaign's vacuity, George W. Bush ran as a candidate who could make advances toward that goal.

But above everything else, Americans are eager for a sense of greater control over their lives. In a crisis, many might be attracted by a leader who promised to "take charge," but what was striking at century's end was the vitality of the yearning for self-government.

All summer, American audiences, especially younger viewers, were mesmerized by *Survivor,* a show that was only infrequently concerned with survival: its drama was politics, maneuvers and alliances and persuasions, all on a small scale in which every character had a say and every vote mattered, each episode ending with a vote that sent one participant into exile. And in true democratic fashion, the winner of the two finalists was selected by the losers. (By contrast, *Big Brother,* a similar show with a less exotic location, left decisions to an anonymous, call-in audience, rather like mass politics. It enjoyed a considerable vogue overseas, but here, it gave *Survivor* no serious competition.) Watching *Survivor,* Americans felt a kind of vicarious citizenship, a version of the excitement Gail Collins found among voters during primary season in New Hampshire.[134]

Approximations of that sort of citizenship are all Americans can hope for, but we need to think of democracy as a *goal,* one that calls for extending the possibilities of democratic self-rule and the nurturing of democratic souls.[135] Democratic citizens need the capacity for "strong reciprocity," the willingness to sacrifice interests to uphold common norms and ideas of justice. Given the scale and complexity of modern life, civil society cannot guarantee that such sacrifice will not be exploited by free riders: democratic citizenship needs the support of institutions and forms and laws.[136] It needs the parties and associations that give citizenship some human force in a mass state.

In contemporary America, oligarchy — the belief that wealth provides the most deserving contribution to public life — is leveling a strong challenge to the democratic conviction that a freely given life, a love of equal citizenship, is the greatest political gift.[137] And with that contest undecided, Richard Rorty is right that our country is waiting to be "achieved," looking to the new millennium.

NOTES

1. The metaphor is especially appropriate because some research suggests that sports loyalties — affiliations in a pure sense, without *anything* at stake other than vicarious dignity and a kind of civic pride, are displacing political and religious partisanship. (James C. McKinley Jr., "It Isn't Just a Game," *New York Times,* 11 August 2000, A1.) This year, ABC would not preempt

even *preseason* Monday Night Football in order to cover the opening nights of the Republican and Democratic conventions, offering a half-time report instead. (Peter Marks, "On ABC, Coverage of Football Tops Politics," *New York Times,* 21 June 2000, A19). NBC offered its affiliates the option of covering the first presidential debate or a game in the baseball playoffs (*New York Times,* 30 September 2000, A9). It was an event, years ago, when Babe Ruth earned more than President Hoover — "I had a better year than he did," the Babe explained, accurately enough. This year, in order to persuade Manny Ramirez to move to Boston, the Red Sox offered him an annual salary (about $20 million) almost one and one-half times that of the entire U.S. Senate.

2. Adam Clymer, "Now What? This Time Cries for 'Blood' Seem Unthinkable," *New York Times,* 12 November 2000, WK5.

3. Joyce Purnick, "Imagine a Day When Candor Rules Politics," *New York Times,* 11 December 2000, B1.

4. R.W. Apple ("Recipe for a Stalemate," *New York Times,* 9 November 2000, A1) was already referring to a "profoundly serious question of legitimacy." And things might get worse, once Florida's Sunshine Law allowed the tabulation of those uncounted votes.

5. Matthew Vila and Cecil Connolly, "They're Rooting for the Other Side," *Washington Post National Weekly,* 20 November 2000, 12; on the possibilities of a recession, see Louis Uchitelle, "Unfortunate Timing, No Matter Who Wins," *New York Times,* 3 December 2000, BU4.

6. Bush will be especially dependent on Democrats, as Frank Rich observed, given the unrepentant and "ballistic" extremism dominant among congressional Republicans. "Happy Birthday, Mr. Presidents," *New York Times,* 2 December 2000, A19.

7. John Harris, "What Clinton's Problems Have Cost Us," *Washington Post National Weekly,* 10 August 1998, 21; Richard L. Berke, "America Foresees Harmony in Capital," *New York Times,* 20 January 1997, A1.

8. Sebastian Mallaby, "Pumping Up the Presidency," *Washington Post National Weekly,* 19 June 2000, 27.

9. David Broder and Dan Balz, "Who Wins?" *Washington Post National Weekly,* 15 February 1999, 6–7; see also Richard Morin and David Broder, "Worried About Morals But Reluctant to Judge," *Washington Post National Weekly,* 21 September 1998, 10–11; and Alan Wolfe, "America Flunks Civics," *New York Times,* 25 December 1998, A33.

10. For one of the shrewder criticisms, see Akhil Reed Amar, "The Electoral College: Unfair from Day One," *New York Times,* 9 November 2000, A23.

11. See the *New York Times* editorial endorsement of the college: "The Case for the Electoral College," 19 December 2000, A34.

12. The majority, Justice Ginsburg wryly commented, "were not as mindful as they usually are of our system of dual sovereignty." *New York Times,* 13 December 2000, A24.

13. Linda Greenhouse, "Collision with Politics Risks Court's Legal Credibility," *New York Times,* 11 December 2000, A1. Of course, the court can be called "partisan" only in a special sense, since two of the dissenters — Stevens and Souter — are Republican appointees.

14. *New York Times,* 13 December 2000, A1.

15. *New York Times,* 11 December 2000, C8.

16. According to a VNS survey, 48% of voters expect the next generation to have a "better life." Only 20% said that things would be worse. *New York Times,* 8 November 2000, B3.

17. Bob Herbert, "Miracles at Warp Speed," *New York Times,* 31 December 1999, A21.

18. Bill Joy, "Why the Future Doesn't Need Us," *Wired,* April 2000, 256, 258.

19. Edward Tanner, "Dents in the Software," *New York Times,* 4 January 2000, A19.

20. The quotation is from Herbert, "Miracles at Warp Speed"; for the broader argument, see Alan Ehrenhalt, "The Political Era That's Over," *New York Times,* 5 November 2000, WK15.

21. As Jean Elshtain argues in a broader context, democracy was "on trial." *Democracy on Trial* (New York: Basic Books, 1995); see also Michael Sandel, *Democracy's Discontents* (Cambridge, Mass.: Harvard University Press, 1996).

22. James MacGregor Burns, "It's the Vision Thing Again," *Washington Post National Weekly,* 22 May 2000, 22.

23. Andrew Kohut, "May Either Man Win," *New York Times,* 25 November 2000, A19; in the Pew Research Council poll reported by Kohut, 21% of respondents claimed to be excited by the possibility of a Bush victory, as against 17% for Gore.

24. Rich, "Happy Anniversary, Mr. Presidents."

25. Michael Wolff, "Our Remote Control President," *New York,* 4 December 2000, 42–47.

26. Steven Pinker, "Decoding the Candidate," *New York Times,* 31 October 2000, A27. On Gore's debate performance, see Caryn James, "Debates Leave Instant Analysts Hedging Their Bets," *New York Times,* 19 October 2000, A29.

27. David Broder, "The Wonk-in-Chief Candidate," *Washington Post National Weekly,* 28 August 2000, 4.

28. For example, see Robert Erikson, Michael MacKuen, and James Stimson, "What Moves Macropartisanship?" *American Political Science Review* 92 (1998): 901–12; Robert Kaiser, "Deeply Divided We Stand — And That's No Surprise," *Washington Post National Weekly,* 20 November 2000, 22.

29. Richard Cohen, "The Airbrushing of Bill Clinton," *Washington Post National Weekly,* 6 December 1999, 27.

30. The campaign, Senator Robert Torricelli (D-N.J.) observed, "should have been an attempt to make this a third Clinton administration rather than a new beginning." Richard L. Berke, "Missteps Have Kept Presidential Contest Tight," *New York Times,* 5 November 2000, 43. Some of Gore's most effective speeches were essentially retrospective departures from his strategy. For example, see James Dao, "Gore Fires Back, Hoping to Dampen Convention Spirit," *New York Times,* 5 August 2000, A1. On retrospective voting, see Morris P. Fiorina, *Retrospective Voting in American National Elections* (New Haven: Yale University Press, 1979).

31. Alan Mittleman, "Belief and the Ballot Box," *Religion and Values in Public Life,* 2 August 2000, 1–2.

32. Caryn James, "Gore and Bradley as Performers on Political Stage," *New York Times,* 20 December 1999, A33; Frank Rich, "Al Gore's Chicken Soup," *New York Times,* 12 August 2000, A15.

33. Will is cited in Richard L. Berke, "Bush the Man: The Issue Is What He's Made Of," *New York Times,* 22 August 1999, 5. See also Terry Neal and Lois Romano, "Is What You See Really What You Get?" *Washington Post National Weekly,* 10 April 2000, 13.

34. Richard Morin, "What Americans Think," *Washington Post National Weekly,* 30 August 1999, 34. Anna Kornblut correctly emphasizes that the greatest damage in the DUI arrest story was done by the deception rather than the offense itself. "Arrest Story Has Bush Scrambling," *Boston Globe,* 4 November 2000, A1. California Republicans claim that the story hurt Bush badly in that state. *California Journal,* December 2000, 12.

35. Nicholas Kristof, "Ally of an Older Generation Amid the Tumult of the '60s," *New York Times,* 19 June 2000, A1; Hanna Rosin, "The Seeds of a Life's Philosophy," *Washington Post National Weekly,* 28 August 2000, 10.

36. William J. Bennett, "George Bush, the Bold Leader," *New York Times,* 7 October 1999, A31; Edward H. Crane, "The Clintonesque George Bush," *New York Times,* 4 August 1999, A19; Dan Balz, "A Page from the Opposition's Playbook," *Washington Post National Weekly,* 19 June 2000, 10.

37. Theodore J. Lowi, "Toward a Responsible Three-Party System," in *A Republic of Parties,* ed. Theodore Lowi and Joseph Romance (Lanham, Md.: Rowman & Littlefield, 1998), 3; Frank Bruni, "Make Way for the Donkephant," *New York Times,* 8 October 2000, WK1; Alan Wolfe, "The Tyranny of the Undecided Voter," *New York Times,* 22 October 2000, WK15.

38. Robert Kuttner, "Taking It With You," *American Prospect,* 31 July 2000, 4.

39. After 1998, Rush Limbaugh referred to a "general panic" among Republicans. Howard Fineman and Matthew Cooper, "Newt Hits the Showers," *Newsweek,* 16 November 1998, 32.

40. Keith Bradsher, "At Town Meeting, Republicans Begin to Reshape Image," *New York Times,* 16 February 1999, A1. Efforts in this direction by GOP congressional leaders were not notably successful: mid-1999, Richard Cohen could describe Republicans as "dumb as a post," still

identified with militant social conservatism and mindless opposition to Bill Clinton. "The '50s Are Back," *Washington Post National Weekly,* 28 June 1999, 27.

41. Marshall Wittman of the Heritage Foundation described Bush as packaging conservative positions in a "new covering." Alison Mitchell, "Bowing to the Middle, Keeping to the Right," *New York Times,* 5 August 2000, A11. In the same way, Bush's choice of Richard Cheney reflected — in addition to personal regard — a desire to avoid offending any Republican faction more than an effort to add some new constituency. David von Drehle, "Bush's Selection Follows the 'First, Do No Harm' Rule," *Washington Post National Weekly,* 31 July-7 August 2000, 9.

42. Alison Mitchell, "Trying to Escape the Purgatory of Parity," *New York Times,* 26 November 2000, WK3.

43. Richard L. Berke, "Why Certain Political Symbols Stick," *New York Times,* 27 February 2000, WK1; Dan Balz, "Leaving the Primaries Behind," *Washington Post National Weekly,* 1 May 2000, 10.

44. Adam Nagourney, "Republicans Stalk a Slogan, Hunting for Themselves," *New York Times,* June 20, 1999, WK1.

45. Terry M. Neal, "The G.O.P. Credibility Gap," *Washington Post National Weekly,* 19 June 2000, 11; Frank Rich referred to the Republicans as engaged in what amounted to a "lockstep exercise in political correctness." "The G.O.P.'s Age of Aquarius," *New York Times,* 5 August 2000, A15. On devotion to tolerance in contemporary America, see Alan Wolfe, *One Nation, After All* (New York: Viking, 1998).

46. John Judis, "The New Politics of Abortion," *American Prospect,* 31 July 2000, 12–13; Sheryl Gay Stolberg, "Shifting Certainties in the Abortion War," *New York Times,* 11 January 2000, WK3.

47. David Broder, "Governor Bush to G.O.P. Leaders: Step Aside," *Washington Post,* 28 April 2000, A31; Frank Bruni, "Bush Says G.O.P. Stresses Wealth at the Expense of Tackling Social Ills," *New York Times,* 6 October 1999, A1; Frank Bruni, "Bush Softens His View of G.O.P. After Outcry By Conservatives," *New York Times,* 7 October 1999, A28.

48. Everett Carll Ladd, "Nobody's Buying," *The New Democrat,* January/February 1998, 10–11. Richard Reeves, "Optimism from Gore Democrats," *Newark Star-Ledger,* 4 November 1998, 23.

49. Responding to the defeat of "fast-track" legislation in 1997, the president and his aides — John Broder and Lizette Alvarez reported — "seemed genuinely surprised that Democratic lawmakers would be driven by the worries of people who live in their districts." "Demos Sound Like a Couple in Need of Therapy," *New York Times,* 15 November 1997, YNE A11.

50. Richard L. Berke, "Clinton Seeks to Repair Rifts for Democrats," *New York Times,* 19 July 1998, 1.

51. On the importance of Clinton's enemies to Democratic unity, see Andrew Kohut, "A Clear Case of Clinton Fatigue," *New York Times,* 15 August 1999, A23.

52. Ladd, "Nobody's Buying," 12.

53. Richard L. Berke, "Republicans Express a Joint Fear: Of Bradley, Not Gore," *New York Times,* 19 September 1999, 32; James Dao, "Gore-Bradley Race Places Left at Front and Center Among Demos," *New York Times,* 27 October 1999, A22; John M. Broder, "The Faithful," *New York Times,* 11 March 2000, A11.

54. Ruy Teixeira and Joel Rogers, *America's Forgotten Majority: Why the Working Class Still Matters* (New York: Basic Books, 2000).

55. Frank Rich, "Survival of the Fakest," *New York Times,* 26 August 2000, A13.

56. Jeff Madrick, "Economic Scene," *New York Times,* 26 October 2000, C2; Paul Krugman, "Gore's Tax Problem," *New York Times,* 10 September 2000, WK17.

57. Thomas B. Edsall, "Politics Unusual," *Washington Post National Weekly,* 13 November 2000, 12.

58. Peter Applebome, "Divided We Stand," *New York Times,* 26 November 2000, WK3. Thomas Patterson found, in fact, that on twelve key issues, even in the campaign's last days, most voters could not identify the candidates' positions. "Point of Agreement: We're Glad It's Over," *New York Times,* 8 November 2000, A27.

59. Kaiser, "Deeply Divided We Stand…," citing Larry Bartels and James Campbell.

60. E.J. Dionne Jr., noting that Catholic voters are caught between the Church's conservative social morality and its reformist doctrine of solidarity, correctly predicted that a tie would "not be good enough for Gore to win." "Courting the Catholic Vote," *Washington Post National Weekly*, 26 June 2000, 22.

61. Christopher Caldwell, "The Southern Captivity of the G.O.P.," *Atlantic Monthly*, June 1998, 60.

62. James Brooke, "After Election Risk, Premier of Canada Reaps Big Rewards," *New York Times*, 29 November 2000, A1.

63. America's strength, Bush declared, "lies not in the halls of government" but "in the hearts and souls of our citizens." James Dao, "In Michigan, a Swing State, Bush Picks Words Carefully," *New York Times*, 28 October 2000, 11.

64. Reagan's recipe for success, Grover Norquist argues, lay in "the Leave Us Alone coalition." Caldwell, "Southern Captivity," 62.

65. David von Drehle, "A Question of Values," *Washington Post National Weekly*, 9 October 2000, 13. See also Caldwell, "Southern Captivity," 62; John Judis, "The Populist Al Gore," *New York Times*, 20 August 2000, WK15.

66. Niccolò Machiavelli, *Discourses on Livy*, trans. Harvey C. Mansfield and Nathan Tarcov (Chicago: University of Chicago Press, 1996), bk. I, ch. 4, 16.

67. Aristotle, *Politics*, 1252b28–1253a40.

68. George Hager, "While the Rich Get Richer," *Washington Post National Weekly*, 13 September 1999, 19; Robert Reich, "Making Room on the Up Elevator," *Washington Post National Weekly*, 24 May 1999, 23. The quotation is from Joel Kotkin and David Friedman, "Don't Pop the Champagne Yet," *Washington Post National Weekly*, 1 June 1998, 17.

69. Louis Uchitelle, "The Sounds of Silence," *New York Times*, 19 December 1999, WK4; William Finnegan, "Prosperous Times, Except for the Young," *New York Times*, 12 June 1998, A21; David Sanger, "Global Economy Dances to Political Tune," *New York Times*, 20 December 1999, C21.

70. Louis Uchitelle, "Keeping Up With the Gateses?" *New York Times*, 3 May 1998, BU12; Monique Yazigi, "When You Got It, Flaunt It," *New York Times*, 26 December 1999, WK1.

71. Juliet Schor, *The Overspent American* (New York: Basic Books, 1998); Paul Krugman, "Money Can't Buy Happiness, Can It?" *New York Times*, 1 June 1999, A23.

72. Paul Krugman, "Deficit Attention Disorder," *New York Times*, 26 March 2000, WK17.

73. Robert Kuttner, "Giddy About Stocks," *Washington Post National Weekly*, 13 September 1999, 26; Robert J. Shiller, "The Bubble Won't Burst, but It's Deflating," *Washington Post National Weekly*, 22 May 2000, 21.

74. *The Communist Manifesto* (London: Penguin, 1985), 83.

75. Louis Uchitelle, "The American Middle, Just Getting By," *New York Times*, 1 August 1999, BU1; Tom Juravich, "The New Face of Organized Labor," *Washington Post National Weekly*, 11 September 2000, 23.

76. Kirstin Downey Grimsley, "Leaner — And Definitely Meaner," *Washington Post National Weekly*, 20–27 July 1998, 21.

77. W. Lance Bennett, "The Uncivil Culture: Communication, Identity and the Rise of Lifestyle Politics," *PS* 31 (1998): 751; Samuel Bowles and Herbert Gintis, "Is Equality Passé?" *Boston Review*, December/January 1998–1999, 8; Reich, "Making Room on the Up Elevator"; Kotkin and Friedman, "Don't Pop the Champagne Yet."

78. G.M. Tamás, "On Post-Fascism," *Boston Review*, Summer 2000, 46; Theodore Lowi, "Think Globally, Lose Locally," *Boston Review*, April/May 1998, 4–10.

79. Jeffrey Garten, "Mega-Mergers, Mega-Influence," *New York Times*, 26 October 1999, A27.

80. By contrast, the Chinese appear to have opted for Linux rather than Microsoft on the basis of considerations of dependence and power. Craig Smith, "Fearing Control by Microsoft, China Backs the Linux System," *New York Times*, 8 July 2000, A1.

81. John Gray, *False Dawn: The Delusions of Global Capitalism*, New York: New Press, 1999.

82. Paul Krugman, "Once and Again," *New York Times*, 2 January 2000, WK9; Benjamin R. Barber, *Jihad vs. McWorld* (New York: Ballantine, 1996).

83. Steven Pearlstein, "The New Politics of Globalization," *Washington Post National Weekly,* 9 October 2000, 18; William Greider, "Who's Progressive?" *Boston Review,* December/January 1997–1998, 4–8; Floyd Norris, "Economic Thinking Finds a Free Market," *New York Times,* 1 January 2000, E4.

84. For example, see the manifesto of the Turning Point Project, *New York Times,* 29 November 1999, A15.

85. David Sanger, "President Chides World Trade Body in Stormy Seattle," *New York Times,* 2 December 1999, A1; Joseph Kahn, "Clinton Shift on Trade: 'Wake Up Call,'" *New York Times,* 31 January 2000, A6.

86. Richard W. Stevenson, "Trade Support Dwindling, Fed Chief Says," *New York Times,* 26 August 2000, C1.

87. Tom Juravich, "The New Face of Organized Labor," *Washington Post National Weekly,* 11 September 2000, 23; "A Doctors' Union?" *Washington Post National Weekly,* 5 July 1999, 25.

88. Max Frankel, "Free Agents, Unite!" *New York Times Magazine,* 5 March 2000, 36–40; Nina Munk, "The Price of Freedom," *New York Times Magazine,* 5 March 2000, 51–54.

89. Reich, "Making Room on the Up Escalator."

90. David Sanger, "Whistling Past the New Economy," *New York Times,* 16 January 2000, WK1.

91. Michael Ignatieff, "The Big Story," *Religion and Values in Public Life,* Winter/Spring 1999, 3.

92. In a parallel argument, Michael Ignatieff writes that "values trump interests." "The Next President's Duty to Intervene," *New York Times,* 13 February 2000, WK17.

93. Richard Morin, "Wearying of War?" *Washington Post National Weekly,* 24 May 1999, 34; Steven Pearlstein, "The Little Engine That Would Not Stop," *Washington Post National Weekly,* 11 May 1999, 18.

94. Serge Schmemann, "Kosovo Problems Just Beginning," *New York Times,* 4 June 1999, A23.

95. Richard Berke and Katharine Seelye, "Treaty Ricochets into Presidential Race," *New York Times,* 15 October 1999, A11.

96. Nicholas Kristof, "It's a Bad Time for Weak Leadership," *New York Times,* 16 February 1999, A1.

97. E.J. Dionne Jr.,"The New Bleeding Hearts of American Politics," *Washington Post National Weekly,* 24 February 1997, 22.

98. Richard Morin, "The Way We Are — and Were," *Washington Post National Weekly,* 12 June 2000, 34.

99. See the findings of the National Opinion Research Center, reported in the *New York Times,* 2 November 1999, A31.

100. Robert Putnam, *Bowling Alone: The Collapse and Revival of American Community* (New York: Simon and Schuster, 2000).

101. Alan Wolfe, "The Pursuit of Autonomy," *New York Times Magazine,* 7 May 2000, 54.

102. Wolfe, *One Nation, After All; New York Times Magazine,* 7 May 2000, 66, 76; Richard Morin, "Not a Clue," *Washington Post National Weekly,* 14 June 1999, 34.

103. Morin and Broder, "Worried About Morals, but Reluctant to Judge."

104. James Davison Hunter, "Bowling with the Social Scientists," *Weekly Standard,* 28 August– 4 September 2000, 31.

105. Peter Steinfels, "Beliefs," *New York Times,* 5 September 1998, YNE A11; Richard Morin, "Can We Believe in Polls about God?" *Washington Post National Weekly,* 1 June 1998, 30.

106. Gustav Niebuhr, "God and Man and the Presidency," *New York Times,* 19 December 1999, WK7.

107. Hanna Rosin, "Personal Faith and Public Policy," *Washington Post National Weekly,* 11 September 2000, 10.

108. Gustav Niebuhr, "Evangelicals Found a Believer in Bush," *New York Times,* 21 February 2000, A13; it helped, of course, that unlike John McCain — who eventually was driven to attack the "evil influence" of leaders like Pat Robertson — Bush did not threaten the right's ability to use soft money as a tool of political influence. Jill Abramson, "The Religious Right vs. McCain," *New York Times,* 5 March 2000, WK5.

109. John Dewey and James Tufts, *Ethics* (New York: Henry Holt, 1908), 419, 422.

110. Russell Jacoby, "From Utopia to Myopia," *Boston Review,* April/May 1999, 26–28.
111. Tocqueville, *Democracy in America,* 2:98–99, 215–16.
112. Todd Gitlin, *The Twilight of Common Dreams* (New York: Metropolitan, 1995).
113. Richard L. Berke, "Critics Accuse Moderator of Letting Debates Wander," *New York Times,* 17 October 2000, A27.
114. Richard Morin, "It's No Longer All the News That Fits," *Washington Post National Weekly,* 19 June 2000, 34.
115. Peter Marks, "Commercials Dominating Politics on TV, Study Finds," *New York Times,* 13 June 2000, A20; Thomas Patterson, *Out of Order* (New York: Knopf, 1993).
116. Kevin Phillips, "The Venal Center," *Los Angeles Times,* 23 February 1997, M1; Adam Clymer, "A G.O.P. Overhaul of Primary Season Is Killed by Bush," *New York Times,* 29 July 2000, A1.
117. Thomas B. Edsall, "Gore May Be Picking Up a Double-Edged Sword," *Washington Post National Weekly,* 28 August 2000, 14.
118. Warren Buffett, "The Billionaire's Buyout Plan," *New York Times,* 10 September 2000, WK 17.
119. See the comments of Amitai Etzioni in John Markoff, "A Newer, Lonelier Crowd Emerges in Internet Study," *New York Times,* 16 February 2000, A1.
120. Kirstin Downey Grimsley, "Beep Her to Get the Fax about the Voice Mail on her E-Mail," *Washington Post National Weekly,* 1 June 1998, 30; Markoff, "Newer, Lonelier Crowd"; Amy Harmon, "Sad, Lonely World Discovered in Cyberspace," *New York Times,* 30 August 1998, 1.
121. Claudia Buck, "Coming of Age on the Web," *California Journal,* September 2000, 10–16; Leslie Wayne, "Online Coverage Falls Short of Hype," *New York Times,* 19 August 2000, A12.
122. Richard Powers, "Losing Our Souls, Bit by Bit," *New York Times,* 15 July 1998, A19; Jeffrey Rosen, *The Unwanted Gaze: The Destruction of Privacy in America* (New York: Random House, 2000).
123. Hunter, "Bowling with the Social Scientists," 31; Michael Paul Rogin, "JFK: The Movie," *American Historical Review* 97 (1992): 503–5.
124. In a Council for Excellence in Government survey in 1999, some 64% described themselves as "distant and disconnected." Bob Herbert, "A Nation Loosening its Bonds," *New York Times,* 26 August 1999, A17.
125. Adam Clymer, "The Body Politic," *New York Times,* 2 January 2000, 1. See also Ronald Inglehart, *Modernization and Postmodernization* (Princeton: Princeton University Press, 1997).
126. Richard Morin, "Have the People Lost Their Voice?" *Washington Post National Weekly,* 28 June 1999, 34.
127. Bennett, "Uncivil Culture," 758.
128. See Colin Harrison's comments in Harper's Forum, "The Searchable Soul," *Harper's,* January 2000, 59.
129. Benjamin R. Barber, "Big = Bad, Unless It Doesn't," *New York Times,* 16 April 1998, A23.
130. Alan Ehrenhalt, "Political Era That's Over"; Louis Uchitelle, "The Economics of Intervention," *New York Times,* 31 May 1998, BU1; Peter Drucker, *Post-Capitalist Society* (Oxford: Butterworth Heinemann, 1993).
131. Cited in Dionne, "Courting the Catholic Vote."
132. Rogers Smith, *Civic Ideals* (New Haven: Yale University Press, 1997); Richard Rorty, *Achieving Our Country* (Cambridge, Mass.: Harvard University Press, 1998).
133. E.J. Dionne Jr., *They Only Look Dead* (New York: Simon and Schuster, 1996).
134. Gail Collins, "Savor the Moment," *New York Times,* 1 February 2000, A21.
135. Amartya Sen, *Development as Freedom* (New York: Knopf, 1999).
136. Samuel Bowles and Herbert Gintis, *Recasting Egalitarianism: New Rules for Markets, States and Communities* (London: Verso, 1999).
137. Aristotle, *Politics,* 1279a11–1281a11.

President George Walker Bush: The Inaugural Address 20 January 2001

CHIEF JUSTICE REHNQUIST, President Carter, President Bush, President Clinton, distinguished guests and my fellow citizens,

The peaceful transfer of authority is rare in history, yet common in our country. With a simple oath, we affirm old traditions and make new beginnings.

As I begin, I thank President Clinton for his service to our nation. And I thank Vice President Gore for a contest conducted with spirit and ended with grace.

I am honored and humbled to stand here, where so many of America's leaders have come before me, and so many will follow.

We have a place, all of us, in a long story — a story we continue, but whose end we will not see. It is the story of a new world that became a friend and liberator of the old, a story of a slave-holding society that became a servant of freedom, the story of a power that went into the world to protect but not possess, to defend but not to conquer. It is the American story — a story of flawed and fallible people, united across the generations by grand and enduring ideals.

The grandest of these ideals is an unfolding American promise that everyone belongs, that everyone deserves a chance, that no insignificant person was ever born. Americans are called to enact this promise in our lives and in our laws. And though our nation has sometimes halted, and sometimes delayed, we must follow no other course.

Through much of the last century, America's faith in freedom and democracy was a rock in a raging sea. Now it is a seed upon the wind, taking root in many nations. Our democratic faith is more than the creed of our country, it is the inborn hope of our humanity, an ideal we carry but do not own, a trust we bear and pass along. And even after nearly 225 years, we have a long way yet to travel.

While many of our citizens prosper, others doubt the promise, even the justice, of our own country. The ambitions of some Americans are limited by failing schools and hidden prejudice and the circumstances of their birth. And sometimes our differences run so deep, it seems we share a continent, but not a country.

We do not accept this, and we will not allow it. Our unity, our union, is the serious work of leaders and citizens in every generation. And this is my solemn pledge: I will work to build a single nation of justice and opportunity. I know this is in our reach because we are guided by a power larger than ourselves who creates us equal in His image. And we are confident in principles that unite and lead us onward.

America has never been united by blood or birth or soil. We are bound by ideals that move us beyond our backgrounds, lift us above our interests and teach us what it means to be citizens. Every child must be taught these principles. Every citizen must uphold them. And every immigrant, by embracing these ideals, makes our country more, not less, American.

Today, we affirm a new commitment to live out our nation's promise through civility, courage, compassion, and character.

America, at its best, matches a commitment to principle with a concern for civility. A civil society demands from each of us good will and respect, fair dealing and forgiveness.

Some seem to believe that our politics can afford to be petty because, in a time of peace, the stakes of our debates appear small. But the stakes for America are never small. If our country does not lead the cause of freedom, it will not be led. If we do not turn the hearts of children toward knowledge and character, we will lose their gifts and undermine their idealism. If we permit our economy to drift and decline, the vulnerable will suffer most.

We must live up to the calling we share. Civility is not a tactic or a sentiment. It is the determined choice of trust over cynicism, of community over chaos. And this commitment, if we keep it, is a way to shared accomplishment.

America, at its best, is also courageous. Our national courage has been clear in times of depression and war, when defending common dangers defined our common good. Now we must choose if the example of our fathers and mothers will inspire us or condemn us. We must show courage in a time of blessing by confronting problems instead of passing them on to future generations.

Together, we will reclaim America's schools, before ignorance and apathy claim more young lives. We will reform Social Security and Medicare, sparing our children from struggles we have the power to prevent. And we will reduce taxes, to recover the momentum of our economy and reward the effort and enterprise of working Americans. We will build our defenses beyond challenge, lest weakness invite challenge. We will confront weapons of mass destruction, so that a new century is spared new horrors.

The enemies of liberty and our country should make no mistake: America remains engaged in the world by history and by choice, shaping a balance of power that favors freedom. We will defend our allies and our interests. We will show purpose without arrogance. We will meet aggression and bad faith with resolve and strength. And to all nations, we will speak for the values that gave our nation birth.

America, at its best, is compassionate. In the quiet of American conscience, we know that deep, persistent poverty is unworthy of our nation's promise. And whatever our views of its cause, we can agree that children at risk are not at fault. Abandonment and abuse are not acts of God, they are failures of love. And the proliferation of prisons, however necessary, is no substitute for hope and order in our souls.

Where there is suffering, there is duty. Americans in need are not strangers, they are citizens, not problems, but priorities. And all of us are diminished when any are hopeless.

Government has great responsibilities for public safety and public health, for civil rights and common schools. Yet compassion is the work of a nation, not just a government. And some needs and hurts are so deep they will only respond to a mentor's touch or a pastor's prayer. Church and charity, synagogue and mosque lend our communities their humanity, and they will have an honored place in our plans and in our laws.

Many in our country do not know the pain of poverty, but we can listen to those who do. And I can pledge our nation to a goal: When we see that wounded traveler on the road to Jericho, we will not pass to the other side.

America, at its best, is a place where personal responsibility is valued and expected. Encouraging responsibility is not a search for scapegoats, it is a call to conscience. And though it requires sacrifice, it brings a deeper fulfillment. We find the fullness of life not only in options, but in commitments. And we find that children and community are the commitments that set us free.

Our public interest depends on private character, on civic duty and family bonds and basic fairness, on uncounted, unhonored acts of decency which give direction to our freedom.

Sometimes in life we are called to do great things. But as a saint of our times has said, every day we are called to do small things with great love. The most important tasks of a democracy are done by everyone.

I will live and lead by these principles: to advance my convictions with civility, to pursue the public interest with courage, to speak for greater justice and compassion, to call for responsibility and try to live it as well. In all these ways, I will bring the values of our history to the care of our times.

What you do is as important as anything government does. I ask you to seek a common good beyond your comfort; to defend needed reforms against easy attacks; to serve your nation, beginning with your neighbor. I ask you to be citizens: citizens, not spectators; citizens, not subjects; responsible citizens, building communities of service and a nation of character.

Americans are generous and strong and decent, not because we believe in ourselves, but because we hold beliefs beyond ourselves. When this spirit of citizenship is missing, no government program can replace it. When this spirit is present, no wrong can stand against it.

After the Declaration of Independence was signed, Virginia statesman John Page wrote to Thomas Jefferson: "We know the race is not to the swift nor the battle to the strong. Do you not think an angel rides in the whirlwind and directs this storm?"

Much time has passed since Jefferson arrived for his inauguration. The years and changes accumulate. But the themes of this day he would know: our nation's grand story of courage and its simple dream of dignity. We are not this story's author, who fills time and eternity with his purpose. Yet his purpose is achieved in our duty, and our duty is fulfilled in service to one another.

Never tiring, never yielding, never finishing, we renew that purpose today, to make our country more just and generous, to affirm the dignity of our lives and every life.

This work continues. This story goes on. And an angel still rides in the whirlwind and directs this storm.

God bless you all, and God bless America.

The Bush Administration

Position / Name	Age	Residence	Occupation	Political Experience	Education
President **George W. Bush**	54	Texas	Business	Governor of Texas	B.A., Yale Univ.; M.B.A., Harvard Univ.
Vice-President **Richard B. Cheney**	60	Wyoming	Business	U.S. Representative; White House Chief of Staff; U.S. Secretary of Defense	B.A., Univ. of Wyoming; M.A. Univ. of Wyoming
Secretary of State **Colin L. Powell**	63	Virginia	U.S. Armed Forces	National Security Adviser; Chairman, Joint Chiefs of Staff	B.S., City Univ. of New York; M.B.A., George Washington Univ.
Secretary of the Treasury **Paul H. O'Neill**	65	Pennsylvania	Business	Deputy Director, Office of Management and Budget	B.A., Fresno State College; M.P.A., Indiana Univ.
Secretary of Defense **Donald H. Rumsfeld**	68	Illinois	Business	U.S. Representative; White House Chief of Staff; U.S. Secretary of Defense	B.A., Princeton Univ.
Attorney-General **John D. Ashcroft**	58	Missouri	Law	Missouri Attorney General; Governor of Missouri; U.S. Senator	B.A., Yale Univ.; J.D., Univ. of Chicago
Secretary of the Interior **Gale A. Norton**	46	Colorado	Law	Associate Solicitor, U.S. Department of the Interior; Attorney General, Colorado	B.A., Univ. of Denver; J.D., Univ. of Denver

Position/Name	Age	Residence	Occupation	Political Experience	Education
Secretary of Agriculture **Ann M. Veneman**	51	California	Law	Deputy Secretary, U.S. Department of Agriculture; Secretary, California Department of Food and Agriculture	B.A., Univ. of California, Davis; M.A., Univ. of California, Berkeley; J.D., Hastings College of Law, San Francisco
Secretary of Commerce **Donald L. Evans**	54	Texas	Business	Chairman, Bush gubernatorial campaigns; Chairman, Bush-Cheney 2000	B.S. Univ. of Texas; M.B.A., Univ. of Texas
Secretary of Labor **Elaine Lan Chao**	47	Kentucky	Business	Deputy Secretary, U.S. Department of Transportation; Director, Peace Corps	B.A., Mount Holyoke College; M.B.A., Harvard Univ.
Secretary of Health and Human Services **Tommy G. Thompson**	59	Wisconsin	Law	Governor of Wisconsin	B.A., Univ. of Wisconsin; J.D., Univ. of Wisconsin
Secretary of Housing and Urban Development **Melquiades R. Martinez**	54	Florida	Law	Chairman, Orlando Public Utilities Commission; Chairman, Orange County, Florida	B.A., Florida State Univ.; J.D., Florida State Univ.
Secretary of Transportation **Norman Y. Mineta**	69	Virginia	Business	U.S. Representative; U.S. Secretary of Commerce	B.S., Univ. of California
Secretary of Education **Roderick R. Paige**	67	Texas	Education	Dean, Texas Southern Univ. School of Education; Superintendent of Schools, Houston	B.S. Jackson State Univ.; M.S., Indiana Univ.; D.P.Ed., Indiana Univ.
Secretary of Energy **E. Spencer Abraham**	48	Michigan	Law	U.S. Senator	B.A., Michigan State Univ.; J.D., Harvard Univ.
Secretary of Veterans Affairs **Anthony J. Principi**	56	California	Law	Deputy Secretary of Veterans Affairs	B.S., U.S. Naval Academy; J.D., Seton Hall Univ.

Position/Name	Age	Residence	Occupation	Political Experience	Education
Administrator, Environmental Protection Agency **Christine Todd Whitman**	55	New Jersey	Public Administration	N.J. Public Utilities Commission; Governor of New Jersey	B.A., Wheaton College
White House Chief of Staff **Andrew H. Card Jr.**	53	Virginia	Business	White House Deputy Chief of Staff; U.S. Secretary of Transportation	B.S., Univ. of South Carolina
Director of the Office of Management and Budget **Mitchell E. Daniels Jr.**	51	Indiana	Law	White House Political Director; Director, Hudson Institute	B.A., Princeton Univ.; J.D., Georgetown Univ.
National Security Adviser **Condoleezza Rice**	46	California	Education	Director of Soviet and East European Affairs, National Security Council; Provost, Stanford Univ.	B.A., Univ. of Denver; M.A., Univ. of Notre Dame; Ph.D., Univ. of Denver
Director of Central Intelligence Agency **George J. Tenet**	48	Maryland	Political Science	Director of Intelligence Programs, National Security Council; incumbent CIA director	B.A., Georgetown Univ.; M.A., Columbia Univ.
Ambassador to the United Nations					
United States Trade Representative **Robert Bruce Zoellick**	47	Illinois	Law	Undersecretary of State; White House Deputy Chief of Staff; Executive Vice President, Fannie Mae	B.A., Swarthmore College; M.P.P., Harvard Univ.; J.D., Harvard Univ.
Assistant to the President for Economic Policy **Lawrence B. Lindsey**	46	Virginia	Economics	Professor of Economics, Harvard Univ.; Governor, Federal Reserve Bank	B.A., Bowdoin College; M.A., Harvard Univ.; Ph.D., Harvard Univ.

*Presidential selections as of Inauguration Day 2001.

Index